Also by Larry Mogelonsky:

Are You an Ostrich or a Llama?
Llama Rules
Hotel Llama

The Llama Is Inn

Essays in Hotel Marketing and Management

Larry Mogelonsky
Edited by Adam Mogelonsky

authorHOUSE®

AuthorHouse™
1663 Liberty Drive
Bloomington, IN 47403
www.authorhouse.com
Phone: 1 (800) 839-8640

Published by AuthorHouse   03/13/2017

ISBN: 978-1-5246-7488-5 (sc)
ISBN: 978-1-5246-7489-2 (hc)
ISBN: 978-1-5246-7487-8 (e)

Print information available on the last page.

Any people depicted in stock imagery provided by Thinkstock are models,
and such images are being used for illustrative purposes only.
Certain stock imagery © Thinkstock.

This book is printed on acid-free paper.

Because of the dynamic nature of the Internet, any web addresses or
links contained in this book may have changed since publication and
may no longer be valid. The views expressed in this work are solely those
of the author and do not necessarily reflect the views of the publisher,
and the publisher hereby disclaims any responsibility for them.

This book is dedicated to the team at Four Seasons Hotels and Resorts that gave me my first opportunity to learn about this industry: Janis Clapoff, Kuno Fasel, Jack Moore, Klaus Tenter and the late Linda Jalbert.

TABLE OF CONTENTS

Foreword

Guest Service

Branding

Traditional Marketing

Operations

Food & Beverage

Technology

Internet Marketing

Examples of Excellence

Conclusion

FOREWORD

This remote 22-room property makes the full-day journey to Fogo Island Inn completely worthwhile with exceptional services and incredible attention to detail.

Photos copyright of the hotel and cannot be reproduced without its permission.

An Article a Day Keeps Ignorance Away

To be a smart hotelier, you must read the news and op-ed pieces. You should stay abreast with the latest developments, keep up with what thought leaders are saying about the hot issues and familiarize yourself with trending industry jargon. Looking beyond industry publications, you must expand your comfort zone and seek out some variety by extending your horizons to related fields like real estate, technology, cuisine, wellness and entertainment. This prevents tunnel vision and allows for the cross-pollination of ideas to occur.

However lackadaisical reading may be when compared to the doldrums of your quotidian tasks, it still takes up time – 15 minutes to half an hour – that could be allocated to productive work or to dedicated leisure activities once you've punched your ticket for the day. As such, daily education is constantly getting pushed aside.

But routine is good, and the quicker the better. Moreover, it's better to read one article for each of the seven days of the week versus seven articles in a single sitting because you are giving your brain added time to digest the material. Hence, the catchy title of this article, and my wish for you for the coming year.

On a final note, there's the question of where to fit this routine into your daily schedule. Some people may prefer a light read whilst quietly sipping their morning tea whereas others may use it as a tactic to hurdle past the mid-afternoon lethargy. This requires some trial and error as well as knowing what sort of learner you are.

In other words, commit to this one-article-per-day regimen no matter what. Keep a journal, too. In this logbook, record what articles you read, when you opened them, what their messages were and how you felt about each one. Then at the end of each month, review your notes, looking for what you remembered and whether there is a correlation with the time of day. You may even notice a trend in the types of material you gravitate towards. Who knows; it may change your career path and help you discover hidden passions you never knew existed.

Business Four Ways: Re-thinking the Classic Approach to Hotel Finances

There are many ways to assess and categorize the strengths and weaknesses of a hospitality business. The following presents a slightly different and holistic way of organizing how you approach the daunting task of where to allocate funds for the next cycle.

For one, we tend to drill down to the minutia of a venture. Most GMs know the intimate details of the variable cost of each amenity, the labor costs at the front desk or even the number of yards of drapery fabric required per room for an upcoming renovation. After all, it's our business to know such detailed metrics, and we pride ourselves in this depth of expertise.

But a hotel is a complex piece of machinery – in fact, much more complex than we often appreciate. With so many different challenges at hand, this is a revised way of categorizing these issues from a financial standpoint and of simplifying our analyses. The issues are broken down into four somewhat-overlapping sections. As a hotel typically faces a challenge in one or more of these categories, priorities should be established accordingly.

Costs

When was the last time you conducted an independent audit of your entire cost structure? Hoteliers are experts in this category, ensuring that the purchasing manager is delivering the best combination of price, quality and availability. Costs go well beyond the domain of the purchasing manager, though, and must reflect the needs of every department.

Cost analysis includes other components such as staffing, finances, marketing, sales, amenities and maintenance. Each department's expense requires careful analysis. Could suppliers be consolidated? Are newer technologies available that minimize labor, or offer the same services at even better costs? One hotel I've worked with reviewed a long-standing contract for internet-related services and was able both to enhance guest service while at the same time reducing their costs – a win-win!

Revenue

This pertains to building the top line gross operating revenue, and a thorough examination in this regard ensures that you don't leave money on the table. Caution is required, of course, as all pricing decisions need to reflect the value that you provide to guests within a competitive context.

Do your revenue management models test ways to heighten revenue, reviewing not just STR reports, but spreads on rooms and suites? How do you take advantage of local economics and seasonality? How do you transfer business from higher to lower commission segments? Should you consider a resort or hotel fee? Have you examined packages to ensure that revenue is maximized, while still delivering value to the guests? How do your F&B charges stack up relative to your competitive set? These are just a sample of what's in store on this front.

Margins

One might think that by fixing costs and revenues the margins do not need to be identified separately. This is not always the case. Sometimes the issue is itself the margins.

For example, in looking at a menu item, it may not be a cost issue (the product is well-sourced) or a revenue issue (the number of orders matches what's required), but the margin might be insufficient to subsidize other necessary operating expenses. In this case, you might want to assess whether a simple price increase will fix the issue without deterring consumption, or if you would be better off replacing this menu item entirely.

Capital

Have you ever seen a hotel starved for capital? Revenue is solid while costs and margin are all effectively managed, but, for instance, the carpets are threadbare and the guestrooms look outdated. In this sense, the soft and hard goods are well past their 'best before' date and there doesn't seem to be enough cash in reserve to gain momentum on any revitalization in the near future.

Capital challenges manifest themselves in many ways such as delays in replacement normally associated with wear and tear, failure to upgrade internet and technology systems to conform with today's consumer requirements, HVAC systems that no longer effectively handle workloads or failure to adopt LEED standards.

Owners who fail to invest adequate capital in their product will feel the result through lower guest satisfaction scores and, when carried to the extreme, de-flagging. There's no easy solution to issues involving capital and, ultimately, they rest with the owners and corporate managers who will determine whether a large monetary stimulus will not only ensure greater property longevity but also an increase in asset value.

Visit a Hotel School and Reinvigorate Your Passion for Hospitality

Attending the biennial Cornell Hospitality Research Summit and listening to a plethora of hotel 'intelligentsia' speak on various topics is a very inspirational experience. As a think tank on the industry at large, I'd recommend the conference to anyone looking for a worthwhile networking event or to catch up on some of the latest research hitting the hospitality airwaves. However, the fact that it was held at a hotel school had an unintended effect. It put me face to face with many young, bright minds who will soon enter the workforce, most likely in the hospitality field.

Meeting students is always a positive experience, especially when they are enthusiastically volunteering to help orchestrate a symposium of this nature or willingly serving you at a restaurant. These encounters are opportunities for you to invigorate the next generation of hoteliers with your passion and wisdom, but they are also chances for you to rekindle your youthful (and perhaps naïve) excitement to start your career.

I took the time to talk with several Cornell Hotel School undergrads, both while attending the summit and in the adjoining Statler Hotel that employs student interns for the front desk, reception duties and in the restaurants. Universally, the hotel students I met showed an unfailing commitment to hospitality. They were eager to embrace the fundamentals of guest service and recognized these values that we hold so precious.

Unbridled by the need to deliver a RevPAR target or meet some unseen corporate head office revenue commitment, they have yet to be ground down by the P&L gremlins. They were consummate learners, eager to discuss all manners of hotel management or travel with gusto and not a hint of fatigue.

Remember back to the start of your career in hospitality. What was it that drove you to this profession in the first place? I will bet that the lion's share of your day-to-day job was part of that train of thought. By chatting with the young minds of hospitality, you are in essence absorbing their aura. Yes, the conversation may be rather one-sided as said students prod you with never-ending questions, but this unto itself should 'show you the light' in terms of what outlook you must have for consummate success.

So, what can you do to reinvigorate this youthful passion? Simple: go back to school! For most of us, there should be a hotel school relatively close by. If not, then no doubt one is only a short flight away.

I am confident that they would welcome your involvement. And there are many ways to shoehorn your way in, among them: give a lecture, request a tour with a senior manager, have students visit your property, present your company as a vendor at a job fair, reach out to the alumni association or participate in student internship programs. The students will benefit immensely from your experience, and so will you.

Four Horsemen of the Hotel Apocalypse

We survived Y2K. We outlived the end of the Mayan calendar. But are you ready for the total annihilation of everything your property holds sacred?

These four ever-present issues are what I see as the four largest problems that we hoteliers will need to confront within the next decade. As I present the hypothetical 'Four Horsemen of the Hotel Apocalypse', let's keep in mind that not only has the idea of the biblical four horsemen changed over time, but so too will the four main detractors to our industry's current practices.

PLAGUE (Red Horse) – The OTAs

This one is like beating a dead horse. Nothing better represents a constant pestilence on the state of affairs in our industry as the damage that the OTAs have done by warping consumer behavior. Much like a virus or airborne pathogen that weakens its host, by allowing these high commission platforms to thrive by giving them inventory, the OTAs have reduced our margins and cash flow, rendering us, in essence, sick. Furthermore, as the OTAs aggregate properties primarily according to price, and taken together with their standardized formats that reduce the perception of product differentiation, it is one more step towards commoditization.

WAR (White Horse) – Airbnb and the Sharing Economy

Sometimes called the horseman of conquest, this represents something that serves to not simply alter what channels travelers use, but where they will eventually stay. Airbnb allows anyone to become a hotel operator, and indeed millions have already taken the site up on the offer. Each apartment, mansion or even treehouse that's posted on the website represents a new product offering in direct competition with preexisting members of the hospitality industry. It's been argued that Airbnb has opened the door to a wholly new set of travelers who would never have otherwise utilized hotel accommodations, but this can only be partially true and ultimately hotel customers are being stolen.

FAMINE (Black Horse) – Too Many Brands

It seems like every week there is an announcement of sorts of a new branded hotel concept into an already crowded marketplace. According to the psychology theory of the 'Paradox of Choice', when you give people too many options to choose from, it makes the decision-making process increasingly difficult, which can reduce satisfaction with the final selection or even prevent a verdict from being made. It's like spreading butter over too much bread; too many brands means that it is harder for any single brand to create a lasting impression from marketing or advertising efforts alone.

DEATH (Pale Horse) – Lack of Entrepreneurship

In other words, your property will die if you are lazy or only do what's required. Entrepreneurship means having a passion about your line of work as well as the motivation to put in those grueling long hours to see tasks through to fruition. It's all too easy to become a punch card employee, doing only the bare minimum to stay afloat. What's needed for any semblance of success is initiative – for instance, the desire to spend an extra hour every day reading the trades so you are in touch with the latest service advancements or putting into action those projects that your team has only talked about but can't seem to find the time to get underway. It means doing more than just pay-per-click or transactional marketing which, in effect, buys business rather than generating lasting loyalty or branded 'reasons to purchase and keep on purchasing'.

Four Horsemen of the Hotel Post-Apocalypse

While it is one thing to identify and explain four critical issues facing the hospitality industry, it is another thing altogether to offer clear and present solutions. Thus, here are the most salient and actionable steps towards mitigating each potential problem.

The OTAs

While they can dilute your brand and drive customers away from booking direct, the OTAs do have a few pronounced advantages. Particularly for independent or small-chain properties, they allow hotels to gain exposure in territories and languages beyond the capacities of a typical marketing budget. My solution is to embrace the fact that the OTAs exist, and then find out how to best leverage them for added revenues. Know their limits and understand their disadvantages. If you need help, the leading OTAs all have knowledgeable reps who can clue you in to missed opportunities. And note, there are changes afoot regarding contractual agreement restrictions that often frustrate hoteliers, so you can reduce your inventory allotment while you wait for the current parity laws to be fixed.

Airbnb and the Sharing Economy

Yes, it's a big threat to every property from big corporate monoliths to boutique B&Bs, but there's still hope! If you aren't already, petition your local and regional tourism agencies to appeal for proper, equal taxation enforcement and regulatory measures – even if we can't make it go away, at least Airbnb can play fair. In other words, level the playing field!

Next, ask yourself why this new hospitality giant has grown so quickly. You could argue in favor of the flexibility of the sharing economy or the inherent demand for interesting lodgings, but at its core Airbnb grew because a sizeable number of hotel guests didn't feel as though they were getting their money's worth out of their guestrooms. Knowing that this is the fundamental issue, you can remedy it by promoting features of your hotel that no freelanced

Airbnb accommodation can ever match. It's your amenities, your F&B, your property security team, your concierge service and every other brand standard guarantee that will sell your hotel to this new breed of traveler.

Too Many Brands

This is the trickiest one to solve as effective rebranding takes years to accomplish and you have to weigh the owners' needs against those of the brand as well as the management company. Any sort of brand consolidation or new venture must be undertaken with the utmost prudence. The world is changing rapidly and so too are its consumers. New niches are presenting themselves every year and only the most observant and nimble brands will be able to design product that successfully targets these segments. Keep your ear to the street to stay in touch with the latest trends, and when the time is right for a change you'll have the wherewithal to know which direction is best.

Lack of Entrepreneurship

While rebranding is a company-wide affair, developing your intrapreneurship is something that any manager can shepherd. Start by finding those employees who value hospitality as a career and not just as a job. Next, empower these individuals by giving them the space and freedom to operate projects autonomously. The key word here is mentorship. If you motivate and promote those team members who have a passion for the industry, they will not only take some of the food off your plate to make your job easier, but they will also identify areas in need of improvement and act to fix them before they become recurring issues.

GUEST SERVICE

Now a Marriott Autography property, the Algonquin Resort in New Brunswick, Canada has experienced a remarkable renovation and is once again a premier destination resort.

Larry Mogelonsky

Glanceability and Your Hotel

Yes, that's a made-up word in the title, but with any luck this neologism will soon be a mainstay in every hotelier's vocabulary. As it relates to hospitality, 'glanceability' is how noticeable or different a property is with respect to the average guest's preconceived notions. When consumers research hotels online – whether for business or leisure – statistics indicate that they typically browse over 20 different sites. Glancing through so many properties, what makes yours pop?

It's interesting to note how this harks back to the neuroscience concept of 'preemptive processing' whereby most stimuli to reach our brains (let's only consider visuals for now) are rapidly processed as unimportant and will not imprint onto our memories. On the flip side, the one or two entities that are truly different from all others will not necessarily engrave themselves automatically into our consciousness, but they will force our brains to at least give them a moment's pause. In other words, an extraordinary object or person won't be instantly dismissed as insignificant, and therefore has a fighting chance at being remembered.

There's a lot of psychological jargon in that last paragraph, so let's rephrase glanceability through some examples. Start with your drive to work this morning. How many of the other cars on the road do you still remember? Probably close to zero, unless, of course, a hotrod red Ferrari zoomed past you in the fast lane or you were nearly sideswiped by a rusty old cube van. Next consider your eating habits. Do you remember what you ate for lunch every day last week? Maybe, but probably not in much detail, though. But I bet that you remember what you (and possibly others at your table) ordered when you last visited an exceptional restaurant.

Getting back to the field of hospitality, to elicit quality glanceability, your hotel must be significantly different within under one second of attracting consumers' eyeballs. Whether it be through your brand.com, a third-party website, a social network or (especially) onsite, you only have one moment to jog a consumer's mind. Rarely will you be given a second chance.

Along these same lines comes the idea of 'micro-glanceability' — that is, a certain dish at your restaurant that is both remarkable in flavor and presentation, so much so that any patron would be hard-pressed not to remember it. Or maybe there is a bold piece of artwork showcased in the lobby that is near-impossible for visitors to overlook. These small points of differentiation will contribute to a better overall guest experience because they will help to proactively engage consumers' minds.

Outside of drastic revamps or other capital expenditures, one of the best strategies to make a property more glanceable is to cut to the chase. By that I mean that you must present the key benefits of choosing your hotel in a clear and concise manner. Nowadays, there are simply too many internet-born distractions to be successful otherwise.

As a cross-example, consider the proliferation of 'top ten' list articles. Be honest with yourself: how often have you opened one such list-styled op-ed and only read the numbered subheadings while completely skipping over the body of text? I know I'm guilty of this, and not because I don't want to peruse all that's written, but because I am rushed for time. I imagine many of you are in a similar circumstance.

To prevent any such cognitive skimming, do yourself a favor and keep your information presentation simple. It's been documented that people can only hold 3-7 pieces of information in their short-term memories at any single time. Therefore, why would you present to them a list of property features which numbers in the dozens? Why lead with any photo of your hotel that isn't the most iconic and captivating image that you own?

So, ask yourself: is your hotel 'glanceable'? Do you have any true operational standouts that aren't currently being given enough of the spotlight? And if nothing comes to mind, what can you do to generate a little bit more glanceability?

Guest Service Perfection Through Team Actualization

Perfecting your guest service delivery is a perpetual task. As consumer behaviors change and expectations rise, so too must we adapt to the times. Thus, improving guest service should be a foremost thought every day.

This area of operations – which I deem paramount to customer satisfaction and, directly related to this, long-term success on the balance sheet – involves many inanimate elements such as inscribed protocols, available resources and technological enablers. However, your effectiveness inevitably comes down to your personnel and each associate's intrinsic motivations to perform at the best of his or her abilities – primarily, in this case, making guests feel satisfied with their hotel selection.

Hospitality is about people interacting with people. No new features, nuanced details or technological innovations will change this core precept. If a staff member isn't motivated to help guests to his or her fullest, then everything else unravels. As seasoned hoteliers, we all understand this ideology in one version or another. But knowledge is different than action. As such, when it comes to the integral relationship between staff motivations and guest service delivery, there is nevertheless a vast expanse of room for improvement.

Chiefly, when we talk about how guests feel, we are insinuating our collective aspiration for consumers to attach a positive emotion to our properties and brands. To achieve this, we need to go above and beyond expectations in any way, shape or form, lest we fail to break through the contemporary guests' hardened shell of apathy. While mishaps can result in negative press and exceeding expectations will earn you praise and loyalty, the middle zone of mediocrity – of apathy – gives you nothing.

We all need not high but remarkable levels of customer satisfaction to ensure return visits, build a healthy brand reputation, increase our social media presence, encourage word of mouth, accrue proper feedback and everything that's in-between. Yes, you can pluck a guest's emotional harpsichord with new features, updated amenities and lavish gifts, but those can cost a pretty penny. Instead, motivating your staff to want with all their hearts to make a hotel's guests feel a full range of positive sentiments is a far stronger and longer lasting option.

Many purport that new technology products like wearable devices, hyper-advanced touchscreens or service system integration tools will act as contemporary guest service panaceas. While many of these investments will undoubtedly augment your service delivery, human beings will remain at the center of any hotel-customer interaction – at least in our lifetimes!

Suppose your guests want to watch Netflix in their rooms, and to cater to this demand you've installed the appropriate software and hardware so they can stream through the shiny new 55" OLED monitors mounted on the walls. The problem is that the system has glitches and guests are complaining. When that happens, it is up to your team to quell their frustrations with calming words, attentiveness and proactive solutions. If your staff members do their job right, they'll easily be able to turn this adversity into a positive guest experience. They likely won't be able to resolve the issue with Netflix as this falls under the IT department's purview, but they can get creative with their compensatory tactics. Yes, you can have situational protocols in place, but ultimately this on-the-spot ingenuity harnesses each staffer's internal drive to give guests the best possible experience despite any hiccups.

If you want your employees to pass along the utmost concern to others, that is what you must give to them. Take care of your staff and they will take care of your guests. Simple enough, right? With plenty of new studies in the field of organizational behavior illuminating key employment drivers, it's time for us to reevaluate how we develop a fundamental desire for consummate success in our team members.

The Key Word is Actualization

There are many factors that contribute to one's desire for perfection in the workplace, but one stands above the rest. Actualization – a word as ethereal as they come – is not actually a new concept, and indeed this is not the first time it has sat on top. Look back to the 1950s and Abraham Maslow's Hierarchy of Needs, where even in this budding period of psychology, we nonetheless recognized one's self-actualization as the apex of personal growth and development.

In a nutshell, this self-actualization describes the point at which people reach their full potential insofar as career milestones or personal achievements. As it pertains to you, your leadership and your management of a team, this developmental peak shifts into the 'actualization of others'. What can you do, as a leader, to help each individual member of your team to better reach his or her own life goals?

Part of any good interview or screening process should lead into a question of this sort. After all, if a person's life goals are directionless or don't overlap with any prerequisite hotel-minded traits – such as the intrinsic desire to help others, meet new people or gain novel experiences via new cultures, places, languages or foods – then such a candidate is clearly unfit for a career in hospitality.

Obvious characteristics to look for are enthusiasm, attentiveness and curiosity. This last attribute is one I am especially keen towards as it indicates a person with a natural eagerness for self-directed learning which in turn reveals a strong intrinsic drive for perfecting one's skills and advancing the efficacy of work processes.

Reviewing the First Four in the Hierarchy

Sadly, nurturing team actualization isn't as easy as asking poignant interview questions or pulling each employee aside for a heart to heart. That's indeed part of it – and an important part – but it's still overlooking the foundation needed to reach this point. Namely, you must first fulfill the four preceding levels of the Hierarchy of Needs pyramid.

Satisfying an employee's physiological needs is as straightforward as they come. Give your team enough salaried income so they can put a roof over their heads, eat to their heart's content and afford to buy some decent apparel. A fully stocked cafeteria or team lunches on the company's dime are nice touches here, as is a well-filtered water cooler.

The second level – safety – has quite a few overlaps with its antecedent – financial security through fair wages as well as personal security via a high enough salary to meet the expense of rent or mortgage payments in a reasonable and relatively close neighborhood. Two other emerging factors that managers have some control over pertain to health and job security. What coverage does your organization provide for adequate family medical and dental benefits? What physical or verbal assurances can you offer employees so they feel secure in their lines of work? These are crucial conversations to have in tandem with any talks about one's higher aspirations. Making someone fear for his or her job is never a good motivation tactic; it might work in the short run but it will eventually come back to bite you.

Third is interpersonal belonging – that is, good people and a good team. While you cannot account for anyone's actual family or romantic relationships, you should do your best to make every team member feel like they are a part of your organization's family. The key question to ask here is how do you make for a comfortable and friendly office atmosphere? As mentioned above, regular team lunches are great facilitators of this. Ditto for group outings, collaborative meetings and social gatherings. Also, be aware of how you organize teams to deepen collegial relationships and to dissuade the formation of cliques as well as how you spatially arrange office spaces to encourage such familial bonds.

Fourth and last is esteem. Essential words for this phase are recognition, respect, confidence and independence. How do you demonstrate that you value the work of others? Do you publicly praise team members, and then save the not-so-pleasant feedback or reprimands for the privacy of a closed room? How do you facilitate respect and equality amongst your team, regardless of position or rank? Lastly, how do you promote a free work environment where staff members have a certain degree of autonomy, enough to make them confident in handling their duties?

Those four covered brings us back to the pinnacle – actualization. The key to remember here is that for a person to even contemplate actualization goals, they must first satisfy goals in areas below. After all, how can someone develop a love for hospitality when they are constantly worried about their health or living conditions?

It's critical to acknowledge that all four underpinning levels contribute towards an individual's actualization, especially as you move up the ladder. Many aspects of esteem are large contributors to the fifth stage. For example, independence bestows employees with the liberty to decide for themselves whether they are on the right career trajectory, while recognition gives people relevance or a feeling that someone is important to society. A good question to ask during your heart to hearts is what can I do to give you more freedom at work?

One of the last key words mentioned – relevance – is deceivingly more vital to fostering a self-motivated team than many give it credit for. In today's world, it's easy to feel lost, insignificant or directionless, especially amongst millennials who are more than likely to comprise the next new entrants to your organization. There are so many great opportunities in this world, which makes it increasingly hard for someone to settle into one dedicated pursuit.

Hence, any actions you can take to quell feelings of insignificance – by bringing them into your hotel family or by praising their work, for instance – will act as great motivators for future successes in all areas, guest service included. Make your employees confident that their work is relevant and that it is significant to others far beyond the people they see on a day-to-day basis.

And Everything Else Connects to Actualization

Two other key motivation tactics worthy of utilization are empowerment and mentorship. The former ties directly into the esteem category as empowerment – otherwise known as inclusive decision making – will allow your team to fully explore what direction they want to take. The adage of 'learning to love' applies here whereby if you give employees autonomy and freedom, they will discover how wonderful leadership roles in hospitality are and aspire to make this field their career choice. Without empowerment, you run the risk of turning your staff into drones who will wake up one day and leave in pursuit of that freedom they feel they deserve.

Mentorship is a practice that has vast potential for the overall development of your team. Become a beacon of wisdom for your team and give them whatever career advice you can, whether it leads them deeper into the hospitality world or someplace else. You can't control people anymore, and if their hearts aren't fully committed to hospitality, then let them spread their wings. Actualization isn't something you can force onto people; it is something that grows and burns within every one of us. The most you can do, as managers, is smile, be kind and lend a helping hand, just as you would to any guest that crosses your path.

The Subtle and Overlooked Benefit of Welcome Baskets

"Welcome to our hotel! Help yourself to some complimentary drinks and snacks." This is what's being communicated on the surface whenever a guest arrives at his or her room and is delightfully surprised by a welcome bag or basket of food and beverages. But beneath the surface, it sounds a lot more like this: "Your business is truly appreciated. We understand that you're tired and perhaps mildly stressed from traveling, so relax and recharge your system in the tranquility of your own room while you plan your next move."

In this sense, free in-room welcome baskets go a long way to build rapport with guests. As shown by the under-the-surface inner monologue above, such snacks demonstrate that your hotel is highly empathetic to the plight of travelers. And the explanation for why a paltry-sized chocolate candy, granola bar or handful of potato chips works so well has to do with the principle of 'decision fatigue'.

Yes, guests can be just straight-up fatigued when they arrive and the complimentary sugar hit will be much appreciated for that alone, but decision fatigue encompasses far more. Assessing and choosing amongst multiple options requires the most brainpower of any operation your cranium can perform, thus depleting your energy stores the fastest. And low energy means depressed mood and the stirring of negative emotions – mindsets we don't want to be transferred to the property.

So, what's one of the first actions a consumer takes when he or she first steps into the room and unpacks? They plan what they are going to do, and that means making decisions. If it's business, then that step is simpler, but such a guest will still have to review the pre-established logistics of scheduled meetings, mentally prepare for new client pitches or unwind before the onslaught of rapid-fire networking chitchat at the upcoming tradeshow.

And if it's leisure, there are obviously fewer monetary bones in the game, but deciding what to do in a limited amount of time (when there aren't mandatory events already allocated) is also challenging. This is especially true nowadays with the internet opening our eyes to a multitude of previously underexposed tourist opportunities – the more choices, the harder the final verdict. Either way, a free snack helps reduce decision fatigue and elevate the mood.

Moreover, this is an opportunity to exhibit products from local vendors, be they fancy snacks, wine, beer, cheeses, other regional delicacies or indigenous fruits. On the other hand, you might also want to showcase your brand as forward-thinking by offering a healthy array of organic snacks. As well, a welcome gift isn't just food; feel free to include little mementos. Even though they won't work to counteract fatigue, they have a good chance of becoming souvenirs that will be remembered for much longer than the intended trip.

In terms of the actual costs for such an amuse bouche and a positivity generator, you'd be hard-pressed to get more bang for your buck anywhere else. It's cheaper than upgrading the bathrooms or hiring more staff members. I highly doubt that a reasonably adequate welcome bag would cost you a penny over $10, even with fancy local goods. If it's a real concern, find a way to hide it in the room rate as most customers won't notice an increase of $6 or $8.

Along these lines, most consumers hate being price-gouged with those $5 bottles of tepid water left by the television. Fix this annoyance by simply giving guests a bottle or two for free upon arrival. After all, bottled water is palpably softer on the tongue than that from a tap, so complimentary fluid in this regard will boost the mood, even if subtly.

Second Assurances

The funny and scary thing about first impressions is that you only get one. One chance to nail that perfect handshake at the start of a job interview. One chance to flash that smile at a girl you're attracted to. One chance to set the mood for an outstanding hospitality experience upon guest arrival.

In an earlier book, I penned an article called "First Assurances" where I equated an excellent first impression of a hotel to that of a subconscious assurance to guests that they are in good hands – that they will be safe within the confines of the property, that their needs will be tended to and that they are about to experience something great. There are many aspects involved in a first impression, from cleanliness and striking décor to fast check-in and attentive staff. They all must be honed and flawless because, again, you only get one.

But is it possible to recover from a first impression fumble? Furthermore, once you've impressed on the first pass, is your work done, or must you continue to uphold your end of the bargain at each point of interaction?

Glass half full, my belief is that, yes, you can recuperate from a mediocre first impression. The initial point of interaction between guest and hotel is not the sole determinant of one's judgment. It's better to think of it as establishing a baseline for what to expect. And if the bar is set a tad lower than you'd want it, then doubling your efforts for the second impression will come as a highly positive shock to the system, quelling doubts and reassuring the guest that your hotel is full of surprises.

The key with second impressions and second assurances is that you must try extra hard to elevate the guest's feelings above the pre-established baseline. To draw upon another golden oldie, again from an earlier book, I wrote on the topic of 'double deviations', arguing that guests are willing to let one light to moderate mistake go by – we're all human after all! But, when the second error occurs, that's when guests turn against you because, as a repeat offender, it's proof that you are not acting as genuine hospitality professionals.

Therefore, if we account for the theory behind double deviations, then it should be readily clear that in a hotel capacity second impressions may be as important or even more important than their predecessors. Singular grievances should be flagged and any associated guests marked for special treatment, lest said customers suffer through another pratfall and become irreversibly infuriated. In other words, it's okay to screw up...once! But when you do, it's all hands-on-deck to steer the ship back on course.

In terms of ameliorative actions beyond the work of a very helpful staff member, my first thoughts run to F&B. Maybe you find out that the guest is dining at your restaurant that night and you decide to surprise them with a complimentary dessert. Or, they arrive back in their room and a bottle of sparkling wine with sliced fruit accompaniment is waiting for them. Sometimes even an earnest handwritten note from the manager can do wonders, especially when parallel actions are taken to mitigate the cause of the error in the first place.

Guests who feel wronged or slighted are not your enemies. They can be won over through the subsequent actions that you and your staff take.

The Power of 'I Don't Know'

Presently, the hospitality industry is facing some highly complex issues with no obvious answers – the OTAs, third-party review sites, Airbnb, dilutive brand expansions, thrifty millennial purchasing habits and many more. Take your pick; there's always something to groan about with colleagues and fellow hoteliers. And yet, managers and consultants are still under the gun, expected to weather these storms like a titanium-hull icebreaker with a clear trajectory that cracks through any obstacle.

While it would be great to have a crystal ball and speak with absolute confidence as to how events will unfold, alas that is never the case. We're humans not gods, after all. We mortals can never say for certain that a given strategy will work or that certain actions will guarantee a specific outcome. As such, when probed about the abovementioned threats to our business practices, there is a power to being honest and blunt when the expectation is for you to deliver sagacious responses to every question asked.

Are the OTAs stealing our customers in the long run? I don't know.

Is Airbnb simply opening doors to new travelers or is it disrupting our business model? I'm inclined to believe the latter, but I can't say for certain.

Will the millennials stay parsimonious or will they eventually grow up to realize the benefits of loyalty programs and upscale service delivery for a reasonable price? I certainly hope so, but only time will tell.

Declaring a lack of knowledge in these instances demonstrates a different form of confidence because you are leaving yourself vulnerable. It's an admirable quality to be able to admit fault or ignorance in certain situations.

A person who is saying those three golden words is always preferable to the businessperson who is the spitting image of genius and bravura with definitive answers to every scenario imaginable. This is because a voice of unwavering poise and foresight leaves no room for second options or creative solutions. Whereas an

'I don't know' opens the doors to a constructive, back-and-forth conversation, an 'I have all the answers' approach prevents an even better resolution from surfacing.

That said, there are many ways to utter, "I don't know," and only a few are useful. It comes down to body language and continuing to move the ball forward, even if it's only inches. For instance, a blasé, "I dunno," accompanied by an equally apathetic shoulder shrug is not helpful because it stalls the discussion. A firm, "I don't know," spoken with care and concern, and matched with a follow-up statement, can be highly productive, however.

Try these two on for size: "I don't know. I'm trying to understand the problem myself and I think about it every day. While I don't have a definitive answer, here's what I do know..." or "I can't answer that right now, but let me do some more research and get back to you in a few days with some actionable ideas."

Both are constructive and help to eliminate any vagary associated with speaking those three titular words. Whether you are discussing ways to convert OTA customers or counteract Airbnb, sometimes starting off from a place of naiveté will help you reach an answer that satisfies most parties. So, next time you're in a situation where the next steps are unclear, understand that 'I don't know' isn't a death knell – far from it, in fact, when stated correctly.

The Power of Hello

Hello. Bonjour. Hola. Buongiorno. Ni hao. As Salaam Alaykum.

A basic greeting from hotel staffer to hotel guest can never go wrong. It's easy; it's fast; it's a sign that you are always welcome. Even better would be to follow-up the salutation with a simple, "How are you?" or "Can I help you with anything?"

And yet, at many establishments outside of the five-star or ultra-luxury bracket, the only hello I get is the perfunctory one at check-in – an instance where I approach the front desk and not the other way around where an employee goes out of his or her way to offer assistance. While I wouldn't expect a housekeeper or maintenance worker to drop everything to cater to my every immediate whim, stopping for a second to greet me is nonetheless uplifting. Questions without a 'yes' or 'no' answer are even better as they imply a more descriptive response.

You say all the right things with a quick and warm salutation. It demonstrates that your staff are both friendly and ready to help. As mentioned above, it elevates guests' moods, letting them know that their patronage is valued and that your hotel is committed to bona fide hospitality. Saying hello also carries with it a profound sense of veneration – that each guest commands enough respect to be welcomed at every instance.

Importantly, the saying 'You never know until you ask' is readily applicable to these routine interactions. Not every guest is an effusive extrovert, and often when there is a grievance it will be go unstated until said introvert gets around to telling friends about the stay or reviewing your property on TripAdvisor. In fact, there is always something a hotel employee can do to improve a customer's stay, even if it is just a reminder that the staff member is kind and thoughtful enough to ask.

To recap, always initiate conversation and greet guests everywhere, not just at check-in, on approach to the concierge desk or when seated at a restaurant. A quick training refresher should cover this. But more so than speaking the words, the true power of hello lies in how the word and any subsequent questions are spoken.

For this, the attribute of warmth cannot be understated. Speak slowly, eloquently and with a smile. Above all, though, the drive to serve a guest must come from within. This isn't something you teach so much as something you screen during the hiring phase. Beyond that, make a guest feel welcome with every encounter as an unassuming trick to boost guest satisfaction.

What James Bond Teaches Us About Hotels

The 24th James Bond film – *Spectre* – delivered the expected mega-dollar box office receipts, and it seems only fitting that we discuss this iconic character in a hospitality context. Ever the intrepid jetsetter, Agent 007 has stayed at some of the most immaculate hotel and resort properties around the globe on his missions for Queen and Country.

In fact, you'd be hard-pressed to name a movie in this series that doesn't involve a hotel! As a quick google search of 'James Bond hotels' will yield dozens of websites listing spectacular examples of where our favorite gentleman spy has absconded, I'll be avoiding specific references. Of note, my two favorites are the Fontainebleau in *Goldfinger* (a landmark property defining Ocean Drive in Miami Beach) and the Taj Lake Palace in *Octopussy* (uniquely Indian and on my bucket list).

The persona that is James Bond exudes class and his taste in hospitality is top notch. As such, he only picks the best places to rest his head, and he demands the best in every ounce of service delivery. For a hotel to appear in a high brow spy thriller is a badge of honor and one that marks your property as one with an exceptional location and an extraordinary sense of place. Watching this film series over the years, here are five lessons that you should consider if you want to be 'Bond worthy'.

Sophistication Never Goes Out of Style

When James Bond crosses his legs and sips his martini in the lobby lounge, it isn't just any lobby lounge that he chooses. The setting he selects for relaxation – or for the guise of relaxation but in reality, some form of espionage – is always exemplary in very specific ways. It may the ornate leather-backed chairs, the polished marble balustrade behind said chairs, his dazzling tux, the crisp staff uniforms, the elaborate flower decorations next to the front desk or even the slight glimmer off his crystal glassware.

In any case, there is always something intricate and highly cosmopolitan about the framing of the picture. And what James does, so too must your hotel emulate. Bond is fluent in numerous languages – do you have bilingual or trilingual employees? Bond attends the most lavish of parties – what royal galas have you hosted within the past year? Oh yes, and his bartender always knows the difference between 'shaken' and 'stirred.'

Manners Maketh the Man

What does it mean to be a 'gentle' man (or woman) spy? I was reminded of this adage by the movie crowd-pleaser *Kingsmen*, which isn't a Bond entry. However, this subheading is also the motto of New College at Oxford University, which has this movie beat by more than a few centuries.

Either way the result is the same: the James Bond-style hero is elegant, suave and proper (except when he has to use that license to kill of his). In turn, the hotel staffers match his demeanor; they are ever attentive and always respectful to their guest's requests. And even when our urbane protagonist has one of his bouts of violence, the team never falters from anything but genteel behavior. That's part of the job requirement after all – you can't be a gentleman without a strict adherence to manners. This requirement also applies to the new 'lifestyle' segment of hotel properties.

Impeccable Service

Building on the last point, yes, manners maketh hotel staff, but if you watch closely, you'll see that they always give a little extra in their service delivery. Property employees are often anticipating Bond's needs or taking care of requests that are far beyond what they have been trained to handle. Furthermore, they do so with a smile and are grateful to be of help. They are dedicated to serving their guests.

Given that these marquis operatives are lodged in guestrooms with ADRs frequently north of $1,000 per night, it seems only fitting that the staff 'earn' their price tags! If you hope to command such a lofty ADR one day, it all starts with the right team attitude.

Classic F&B, with Perfect Execution

James Bond knows his food and he knows his liquor. He dines at the best restaurants and he uses his refined palate to woo his colleagues as well as any persons of interest or a femme fatale. Moreover, his tastes are mostly old school – a vodka martini straight up, meat and potatoes prepared to perfection or a nice bottle of French wine.

There's something to be said about, say, a simple gin and tonic as made with only the highest of quality in both liquid components, or a straightforward roast prime rib au jus recipe that's been honed over the decades by world-class chefs. Yes, be inventive with your food, but respect the staples. And whatever you do end up cooking, pay the utmost attention to the details.

Undeniable Sense of Place

Every hotel that the spy of spies visits is worthy of the silver screen and is a quintessential match for what an audience member would expect from the showcased region. For instance, a laidback Caribbean resort is immediately distinguishable from a palatial Muscovite hangout, and yet both are places you'll dream of visiting! Each location this titular secret agent journeys to must be exceptional to the point where it is easily discernible from other sequences in the movie as well as all others throughout the Bond oeuvre. Ask yourself how you are creating a space that guests will not only relish but will identify as unlike any other in the whole wide world.

Loyalty Through Adversity

Angry guests with insurmountable problems; we've all encountered them. Rivalry, opposition, antagonism, conflict or whatever other synonym you deploy to convey these kinds of obstacles in the workplace would be better viewed as helping your business goals instead of detracting from them. What doesn't kill you makes you stronger, right?

When applying this adage to guest-staff interactions, it's all too easy to deem livid, annoying, testy, arrogant, needy, rude or whining guests as enemies to your organizational goals which are likely to be high guest satisfaction scores and the pursuit of increased occupancies for greater profits. When we are confronted with opposition of this nature, our first thoughts might run to something like, "This person is being unnecessarily irate; he's asking us to perform tasks that are far beyond what we normally do for our guests." It's a little trickier, however, to identify how such opposition can improve your operations.

Negatives are Not Necessarily Obstacles

To start, a good practice is to view your negative-minded guests not as obstacles to your chosen path but as opportunities to learn, grow and better define the path that you are on.

To help explain this, I'm drawn to movies and television where, as you probably already know, conflict and its thespian equivalent, drama, are the essence of quality screen time. Without them, a show or film quickly becomes a yawn-fest. Drilling down to a specific film genre, take, for example, the buddy cop archetype. In successful movies of this type, the story usually finds two central characters with diametrically opposed outlooks on life, forced to work together for the same goal. They argue and they squabble, but in the end, they realize that their commonalities outweigh their differences.

In fact, their relationship is often on more solid ground because they went through hell and back to reach the finish line. It's this adversity, and the fact that they conquered it, that helps form their solid and sincere bond. Meeting challenges makes their friendship stronger.

21

Guest Application

Apply this paradigm to your team's communication efforts with distraught guests. Both sides have the same goal – the best experience possible for the guest – and yet they have vastly different emotional states of mind entering the interaction. The staff member is trained to be calm, attentive and perhaps even a tad subservient while the guest is, more often than not, irascible, demanding and more than a bit anxious. It's one thing for a staffer to apologize and leave it at that; it's something else entirely when the staffer rises to the challenge, recognizing that the guest's emotional state is temporary, and that if they work together to solve the problem, their bond will become even stronger.

I'd go so far as to argue that the distraught customers to whom you do give that extra oomph to ameliorate their grievances will become your biggest advocates. That's where the 'loyalty' part of this article's title comes in. Very few people connect with a mediocre or above average experience at a hotel. But you would remember a place where the team members gave it everything they had to solve a percolating crisis.

The Chicken is Dry

To give you a comparative example, I have a friend who derives a mild sense of pleasure by testing the wait staff at new restaurants. He usually orders the chicken, and when the server returns to ask, "How is everything tasting?" he will automatically reply, "The chicken is dry." Having cooked chicken myself consistently over my lifetime and knowing roughly what methods a professional chef might utilize – sous-vide, deep frying, 24-hour marinades, dry roasting at a low temperature – I can say with certainty that chicken is quite hard to botch.

But my interloping friend's motivation isn't to identify the chicken as dehydrated or not. He's testing the server's reaction. Do they simply apologize with a faux frown and walk away? Or does the server ask forgiveness then prod deeper with follow-up questions to generate rapport and find the actual issue at heart? Does the restaurant give him a little extra as compensation, like a free drink or a complimentary dessert? Or does the server bring out the chef so that a real conversation can ensue?

Corporate Culture

This thought process can help augment the way guests see your hotel, but it can also aid with your corporate culture. Competition at work should not be enveloped in negative energy; your rivals and their actions are simply more fuel for self-improvement.

Moreover, returning to something I said previously, this affects your intrapreneurs. Often these are the people who ask a lot of questions, get emotional about having their way and are the designated devil's advocates on proposed ideas. What might be perceived as rigidity to progress should instead be viewed as a chance for enhancement. After all, this perceived antagonism is much better than the opposite whereby poor ideas may be implemented because everyone was too afraid or apathetic to raise their hands during the planning meetings.

Silence in these instances, and when it comes to guest interactions, is never golden. Confront hard situations, get people talking and conquer adversity in pursuit of better operations.

When Hoteliers Become Heroes

Don't dismiss this so hastily; it could happen to you.

On an unusually warm spring night at New York's Hotel Pennsylvania, Security Supervisor Ruben Hernandez had just begun his shift when he received an urgent call for help. The call was for an unconscious male, not breathing and not showing a pulse. Ruben immediately removed the onsite automated external defibrillator (AED) from its box and responded to the location.

Upon arrival, he and fellow security officer, Danny Sandoval began administering CPR (cardiopulmonary resuscitation). After numerous attempts failed to revive the guest, Ruben made the decision to activate the AED and follow the steps given to him by the apparatus and from his training. After three attempts with the AED, Ruben was able to resuscitate the guest and stabilize him until the medics arrived.

The guest then went into recovery at a hospital where he received a pacemaker. For their actions, both Ruben and Danny received Hotel Pennsylvania 'Superhero' trophies, and Ruben also received a generous gift certificate to replace his clothing which had to be destroyed after the life-saving efforts.

I've long been friends with many senior managers at this hotel, including GM Eugene Nicotra, and I've been saving this story until the time was just right. This tale goes to show that hospitality comes with an implicit duty of care. When guests enter our halls, it is our responsibility to ensure their safety, whether that comes in the form of security, hygienic rooms, cleanly prepared food or commencing procedures to save someone's life.

It is especially important to train all team members appropriately in a large hotel with hundreds or thousands of guests (like Hotel Pennsylvania) because the professionals might not be able to reach an ailing guest in a timely manner. This is doubly true for sprawling resorts tucked away from urban centers down narrow, winding roads.

There are three immediate steps you can take in this regard. Start by getting your team trained in CPR and use of the AED. CPR training should be reviewed annually as the science behind it is constantly being updated and undoubtedly we could all benefit from a quick reminder. Next, do drills to prepare your staff, and be sure to check response times to see if you are improving in the long run. Last, review your crisis management protocols and lines of communication so that emergency cases don't disrupt operations or cause additional turmoil.

We are all hoteliers, but every once in a while, we may be called upon to be heroes. Do right by your guests and ensure that your staff is properly trained to handle these emergencies.

Larry Mogelonsky

What Women Want and Ten Ways to Give Them Just That

My dear bride of some 37+ years travels with me for leisure, and sometimes business. As can be expected, my work activities tend to carry over into dinnertime conversations, so this hybrid mode of travel makes sense. With her critical input, we've come up with a short list of ideas that focus on women's hotel needs.

Travel research indicates that the female head of household makes the bulk of leisure travel decisions – either directly or through a 'grocery list' provided to a male counterpart. So, while we're fussing over our operating costs to the barebones, we may be cutting corners that cost occupancy and loyalty. If you are targeting the premium/luxury segment, or are a fully independent operator, you can easily capitalize on these suggestions, which are not presented in any order of importance or cost to your operation.

Choose Your Bathroom Amenities Carefully

Whereas most males can't tell the good from the ugly, women know instantly. It's more than improved packaging; it's what's inside those mini-bottles that counts. Great brand names are not privately labeled – they don't have to be! Brands like Clarins or Molton Brown charge more for their amenity programs because they provide instant recognition. Lastly, size does count. Make sure the bottle size is at least enough for two. A 50mL bottle should be the minimum; the perfunctory 30mL size is insufficient for double occupancy.

Fresh Flowers Make a Statement

Flowers are more than just lush colors and pleasant fragrances. A single fresh flower in a bud vase indicates a degree of care for the room and a link to nature. Plan at least one floral display for the bathroom and another for next to the bed.

Make Sure There Are Enough Hangers

Somehow there are never enough hangers for all the suits, skirts, pants and other items that remarkably spring out from a single suitcase. Whereas most guys will hang up a suit, leaving everything else packed (how barbaric!), women will want to place everything in drawers and the closet so that there are fewer fold lines and so they can better coordinate apparel for the next event.

Source High Quality Bed Linens and Ensure Beds Are Made Properly

There is no excuse for an improperly made bed, except a lack of training of your housekeeping staff or poor supervision. As for bed sheets, the quality is immediately noticeable. Better linens will last longer and finish better, giving you a further return on your investment.

Bathrobes that Fit

I tend to agree, the opposite way. Too often bathrobes in hotels are 'one size fits all' which means that they are 'one size fits nobody'. For those who haven't met me, I'm 6'4". What works for me is too long for my wife. Ever consider two sizes per bathroom or, at the very least, the ability to call the front desk and request different sizes?

Where Is the Padded Tray to Store Jewelry?

I take off my watch and place it bedside. My wife has earrings, a bracelet or two, watch and necklace that all must find a home in the wee hours of the evening. Yes, they go in the safe when at the pool or when not being worn. Some room safes have velvet trays to hold these items. On the other hand, many hotels overlook this nuance, which adds the constantly gnawing stress of losing an earring to the experience.

Towels That Have Not Died in the Laundry

Towels have a laundering life. Don't try to squeeze the last few uses out of an old towel. Simply replace it.

Provide a Bag for a Wet Swimsuit

You go for a swim, and then you must leave the next day but the swimsuit has not dried out yet. Thank goodness you can take a laundry bag. Wait, that's for your dirty clothes. So, where does the swimsuit go? Help!

Housekeeping That Is Flawless

Nothing is a greater turnoff than a room that is anything less than perfect in this regard. Any variation here cannot be tolerated for the simple reason that it presages deeper problems under the surface. Make a good first impression with your guestrooms and don't give anyone a reason to doubt your services.

Makeup Mirrors Need to be Illuminated and Ideally Magnifying

While this one will require CAPEX, complaints nonetheless mount when the makeup mirror lacks adjustability, magnifying and its own illumination. There are many brands available, and costs have gone down considerably, so the choice is yours.

To Tie One On Or Knot?

What is future for staff uniforms and how will any such changes affect guests' perceptions or expectations? There's much to consider in uniform design and what it means for a brand, so for now let's focus on one piece of apparel: the neck tie.

Keep in mind that as a baby boomer who has spent most of his days living in and around the Eastern Seaboard of North America, I have perhaps a highly traditional opinion on hospitality neckwear. It used to be that anyone in hotel management wore a necktie, with exceptions being few and far between. And, even on those rare holiday outings, it was not surprising to see the general manager sporting a tie. Nowadays, the diminishing presence of the tie – or oftentimes the total lack thereof – in our industry is cause for alarm.

It's hard for me pinpoint exactly when the tie disappeared from the GM wardrobe. Beginning at limited service properties then spreading to trendy boutique properties, this new informality was seen as congruous to emerging brands' modi operandi – laidback, approachable and slightly edgy – bringing conventions more or less in line with a 'west coast' philosophy where the tie has not made it out of the closet in decades.

Formalities still exist overseas, though. On a recent trip to Europe, I visited eight properties; not one member of senior staff was seen without a tie. On the continent where our time-honored hospitality customs were written in stone, this makes sense. Furthermore, I can report similar results from last year's Asian foray, where undoubtedly long-held cultural traditions of strict etiquette are a significant factor.

While formal wear has remained unchanged in some regions, this still begs the question: Is the hotel world a better place without neckties? If it serves your brand to forgo this accessory, then all the power to you, but I urge you to not make this decision lightly. The necktie has tremendous symbolic value, combining both authority and an aura of trustworthiness. Business suits worn without a tie are not as suggestive in these aspects, which can reduce guest service perceptions.

At the front desk, employees without ties command less respect from guests: How can they be important if they are not wearing a tie? Moreover, if a businessperson arrives at the front desk wearing a tie, will he or she think less of the front desk's capabilities because of the latter's relative informality?

On the surface, your logical brain might tell you that the absence of a necktie holds no bearing on your opinion of another individual. We live in an age without prejudgment, right? But there's a reason why the phrases 'Everyone loves a man in uniform' and 'Dress for success' are so pervasive; subconsciously we know that a person who can dress himself or herself properly can likewise handle his or her business in a suitable manner. Need evidence of this? Look no further than the military – they learn to correctly dress themselves and to stay clean long before they get anywhere near a rifle. A uniform indicates authority, but also discipline, dedication, honor, prestige.

Call me old-fashioned. My feeling is that the general manager should always wear a tie, as should everyone else with seniority or in a line staff position that deals directly with guests. By wearing a tie, we demonstrate a degree of professionalism towards our guests and to the traditions of hospitality. The disappearance of this fashion piece in other industries is yet another in a long list of those that make being in hospitality truly special.

When I open my closet and stare at the rows of Italian masterpieces created by Gucci, Salvatore Ferragamo and Brioni, I can't help but think that this neck apparel used to form the mainstay of my daily wardrobe. Now my ties serve as relics of an old-world formality reserved for weddings, funerals, speaking engagements and other such major, life-defining moments. Outside of those occasions, I can count the number of times I wore a tie last year. Sad to say, I miss those days.

Lessons for Hotels from Puebla, Mexico

Feliz cinco de mayo a todos mis colegas hoteleras! I began a recent talk with this greeting, asking the audience to forgive me for any grammatical mistakes – Spanish is not my first or even my second language.

However, since the talk in question took place on one of the country's most important holidays, I thought it crucial to highlight the nation of Mexico – and all native Spanish speakers for that matter. But first, a history lesson.

The significance of May the 5th stems from the city of Puebla where, on this day in 1862, the Mexican partisans defeated the French forces on the road to regaining sovereign control of their land. Wait, the French? But, they're an ocean away.

Yes, well, as it turns out, while America was busy slaughtering itself over the issue of slavery, the French, ruled at the time by the emperor Napoleon III, Napoleon Bonaparte's nephew, decided to 'intervene' in Mexican affairs over some unpaid debts. And by intervene, I mean send around 40,000 troops to the port of Veracruz and install the younger brother of the Austrian emperor, Maximilian, as ruler.

Shocker: the Mexican people were none too pleased over this turn of events, promptly raising their own armies and launching their own forms of guerilla warfare against the foreign usurpers who had neither the justification nor any cultural links to warrant such an invasion. It all came to a head on May 5, 1862 outside of Puebla where the Mexican forces were able to claim the day. Although not the most instrumental battle in driving the French back across the Atlantic – the whole affair didn't end until Maximilian's execution in 1866 – it was a rallying cry for the remainder of the war and has since become an important national holiday.

Well, the obvious question is: What does this have to do with running a hotel?

First, knowing a bit about a nation's history and culture has never hurt anyone, and in this case some of the actual celebrations for Cinco de Mayo are so outlandishly fun, exciting and downright tasty! Second, it serves as a reminder of the growing interconnectedness between the United States and its southern neighbor.

A cursory glance at the changing dynamics of the population of America will reveal that the proportions of people of Mexican descent and native Spanish speakers are both on the rise. As such, it's becoming increasingly vital that frontline hotel staff as well as members of senior management speak Spanish and have at least a rudimentary understanding of many of the unique cultural traditions of not only Mexico but also the Latin world in general.

Do you have Spanish speakers on staff? What positions do they occupy? Do they cover all shifts? Are Spanish counterparts readily available for all pamphlets, brochures, menus, tent cards and all other sales documents? These are just a few opening questions to ask. On a more personal level, do you speak Spanish fluently? If not, do you have any plans to learn?

The imperative for a greater Spanish presence extends not only to Mexico but also the rapidly gentrifying nations of Central America and South America where Spanish is the national language in all countries but Brazil. Cinco de Mayo is a Mexican holiday, but the ideas put forward here are translatable to the rest of Latin America. As these nations prosper, there is likewise an increase in outbound travel, much of which will end up on North American lands.

For this, I like to trust in the old expression, "Do unto others as you would have others do to you." Just as it would humble you to encounter English speakers at a hotel in Buenos Aires, Bogota or Puebla, so too would it be comforting for a Spanish speaker to encounter an American hotelier who can converse in his or her native tongue. Given the influence of the Spanish world on the US economy, it should almost be a mandate to have Spanish-speaking staff members.

As a final note on appealing to changing tastes, cultures and demographics, might I also suggest incorporating more Mexican cuisine ingredients on the menu? I've written in the past about comfort foods or congee and how familiar foods tap into positive emotions, so let's extend this reasoning with a healthy infusion of tomatillos, pico de gallo, salsa guaca or morita peppers. And then, just as before, think broader in terms of incorporating other Spanish-world staples like a quality ceviche or fried plantains.

How Addictive Is Your Property?

To give you a new perspective on your guest service operations, let's reframe a person's hotel experience in terms of chemicals – specifically, how a brain responds to micro-and macro-interactions by releasing certain neurotransmitters. For those of us lacking a medical degree, neurotransmitters are the molecules your nervous system releases to dictate further bodily actions and emotional states. (If you want to learn some more about how and where they work, consult a Wikipedia page near you.)

Although there are dozens of these brain chemicals that have been identified, we're going to focus on five widespread and powerful neurotransmitters as they relate to guest-staff relations – four good and one bad. On the positive end of the spectrum, I remember them by asking the simple, relevant and acronym-tinged question: How DOES a hotel elicit positive emotions from its guests? In this case, the 'DOES' stands for dopamine, oxytocin, endorphins and serotonin. On the opposite end is cortisol, which, although technically a hormone, is a must to avoid.

The reason why we as hoteliers should know a thing or two about neurotransmitters is because they are instrumental in reward-seeking and affection-seeking behavior. Dopamine is most directly associated with adventurous or reward-motivated behavior; when we find something we like, dopamine is released. Oxytocin is the 'bonding hormone', released after we encounter any displays of kindness, warmth or empathy. Endorphins are a series of naturally occurring opiates that inhibit pain and induce feelings of euphoria. Serotonin is the 'feel good' chemical, contributing to feelings of happiness, belonging, self-assurance, satiety and many others. Lastly, cortisol is the stress hormone and counteracts the release of several 'positive' neurotransmitters on top of its own metabolic and emotional effects.

To start, here's a simple example without looking too much 'under the hood': you are offered a free cookie by a friend (oxytocin); the cookie tastes good (dopamine and serotonin); your brain records that the cookie tastes good and remembers this encounter for future reference. In this instance, the cookie is provoking a positive feedback loop to reinforce the behavior of eating more cookies.

Now consider one involving a front desk clerk handling the check-in process with a male guest. It starts with the guest arriving and the clerk smiling in return and offering a warm greeting (oxytocin). After a speedy check-in where the employee continues to talk and ask questions in a soothing yet confident tone (oxytocin and serotonin), the clerk gives the guest a complimentary spa treatment because he has attained a certain milestone within the hotel company's loyalty program (dopamine and serotonin).

Upon redeeming his reward – an invigorating back massage – said guest feels a strong sense of relaxation and bliss (endorphins). Unfortunately, there was a minor spill in the spa entrance area and the guest nearly slipped while leaving (cortisol). He calmed down after the receptionist rushed to assist him and apologized profusely (oxytocin).

When asking how addictive a hotel is, we are pondering what we can do to increase the release of the DOES neurotransmitters in our guests' brains. The above example is rather uncomplicated, but it nonetheless effectively demonstrates the all-encompassing role that these chemicals have as we go about our days. The case goes to show that are there many straightforward ways to increase the impact of how a hotel is perceived. It also illustrates how micro-interactions can act in succession to generate a far stronger and longer-lasting sentiment towards a person, place or object.

Considering that micro-feelings are the building blocks for macro-sentiments and the lasting emotional resonance your hotel will have with its guests, here is a short list of potentially positive interactions and the inscribed neurotransmitter that's released:

- Warm, confident eye contact (oxytocin)
- Firm handshake, hug or other physical show of camaraderie (oxytocin and serotonin)
- Remembering a loyal guest's name (oxytocin and serotonin)
- Witnessing a staff member happily assist another guest (oxytocin and serotonin)

- Briefly chatting with a manager in the lobby (oxytocin)
- Dynamic, vibrant artwork in lobby or corridors (dopamine)
- Carrying a guest's bags to his or her room (serotonin)
- Helping a guest plan his or her day (oxytocin and serotonin)
- Encouraging a guest to try a new activity (dopamine)
- Cooperation between guest and staff towards a common goal (oxytocin)
- Exercise, yoga or pilates (endorphins)
- Revitalizing spa treatment (endorphins and oxytocin)
- Winning a sports match (dopamine)
- New milestone reached in training regimen (dopamine and endorphins)
- Comfortable restaurant seating (oxytocin)
- Lively restaurant atmosphere (serotonin)
- Bold, new food or beverage that's also quite tasty (dopamine and serotonin)
- Jovial and attentive attitude of servers and bartenders (oxytocin)
- Live music (dopamine and serotonin)

I could go on. The pattern you should see amongst all these neurotransmitter-inducing scenarios is that those involving staff-guest interactions lean towards the chemicals (oxytocin and serotonin) responsible for generating feelings of affinity for a hotel, whereas property features that lead to novel or active experiences are more likely to activate dopamine and endorphins.

Although the former two can inscribe severe habit-forming behaviors, you merely need to look at two of the most rampant narcotic scourges of modern society – cocaine, a dopamine provocateur, and heroin, an opiate that mimics the actions of endorphins – to realize the value in stimulating these same reward-based pathways through the enterprises of your hotel and staff. No, I'm not telling you to hand out free drugs in the lobby. But I am urging you to look at your hotel's features to assess how they can better imitate these two highly addictive substances.

How does your hotel excite the senses? What physical objects can you place in the lobby, restaurants, bars or guestroom corridors to provide your guests with a palpably distinctive space? What features or amenities do you offer that would be considered exceptionally rare amongst your average guests? More to the point, what do you offer in terms of exciting and novel experiences? Responding to these questions and adjusting your operations accordingly will have powerful subconscious effects on your clientele.

Before I sign off, a word on cortisol is required. This hormone is the antithesis of what you want. Along with adrenaline, it helps put you in 'fight or flight' mode, arresting restive bodily functions in response to stress or some other external hazard. As part of our evolutionary development, we are built to vividly remember dangerous encounters so that we can do our best to avoid them in the future. In this sense, we often recall incidents of pain or suffering in far greater detail than those with the opposite circumstances.

Cortisol is also partly responsible for our visceral reaction to seemingly unsafe or unhygienic conditions – what our primitive brains interpret as precursors to danger. It is a powerful hormone and one you must do your best to avoid because one cortisol-inducing event may be enough to counteract a dozen others that promote serotonin or dopamine. As such, if you are hoping to deliver an 'addictive' experience, start by eliminating any perceived negatives, and then, and only then, build in your positive.

BRANDING

The Four Seasons Resort Orlando at Walt Disney World was built with separate pool areas and lobby flatscreens at children's heights to specifically cater to different age groups.

Photos copyright of the hotel and cannot be reproduced without its permission.

Larry Mogelonsky

Another Day Another Brand

It seems that you cannot read an industry periodical without perusing an article about another brand being launched within the hotel industry. Off the top of my head, here are a few: Centric, OE Collection, Ritz Reserve, Canopy, Tru, Moxie – need I go on? Why is all this happening now, and what does this foretell for our industry? Here is my take on this cavalcade of marketplace shuffles and shifts.

Let's look at this from a purely economic sense with, of course, a healthy dose of financial and marketing considerations. From basic business theory, we know that there are economies of scale that can be attributed to larger entities. In our industry, the more rooms in the fold, the easier it is to spread corporate overhead costs – that's straightforward.

To a certain extent, the same rationale applies to product awareness: the more properties you have, the easier it is for customers to recognize the brand and its attributes. As well, the more properties you have, the greater the strength of your loyalty program (at least for those looking to visit more than one city or region in their lifetimes).

This has always been the struggle facing the independents: how does a relatively unknown property fare when compared to the branding power of the chain down the block? This lack of familiarity was the impetus to create associations such as Preferred or Leading Hotels, whose relationships and seal of quality have provided a steady stream of customers coming to their independent members' doors. It's also been a driving force behind the more recent trend towards independent hotel networks within a larger portfolio such as Marriott/Starwood's Luxury Collection and Autograph Collection.

This 'networking power' that the major brands have seems, on the surface, to be at odds with their current actions. That is, why would a recognized name in the industry branch out and create – and potentially cannibalize – new progeny with dissociated names? My thoughts and hypotheses, for discussion, are these:

1. Their own brand names are tarnished or have suffered irreparable harm through years of failing to properly support every brand constituent. Asked somewhat naively: What does Hilton, Sheraton or Westin mean to a customer? Maybe those great brand names are cast too closely to an old-world business model that is just too hard or entrenched to refresh.

2. Many think it is easier to create a new brand than to invest in regenerating interest in one that's established. I don't necessarily agree with this. Think of the car industry and its numerous examples of brands or series models (Volkswagen and the Chevrolet Camaro to name two) brought back from near death by making them relevant to today's customers. Then again, we have yet to see anyone consider bringing back Ford's Pinto or Maverick.

3. A new brand means new rules for franchisees. Room standards change over time. Many of these changes require a capital investment. It's often hard to move a brand standard 'up' and convince a franchisee to invest in this higher-level product. A new brand is not encumbered with these issues.

4. New hotel brands provide a broader selection of products for the consumer under the same umbrella brand. For example, say you're a Hilton loyalist and are impressed by their excellent HHonors reward program. By adding brands, the thought is that this hospitality behemoth will keep you in the family no matter what your travel motivations are or how your tastes will change over time.

5. Hotels don't spend much on advertising; so, adding brands is a way of getting creative. While this sounds absurd, additional products and brands add to the marketing department's responsibilities and feather the CMO's nest. New hotel openings, groundbreakings and brand announcements always make for a good media splash, filling the left-hand editorial content with something hospitality related while the right-hand page changes from a full-page branded hotel promotion to an ad for the latest mobile-based tech startup.

Whatever the reason, for my money, there has never been a better time to be an independent, especially in the premium tier. With every new brand launched, the clout of each individual brand diminishes. The human memory is only so big and the more brands you try and cram in there, the less space each individual name will occupy.

Your standalone property now competes with other 'almost-stand-alone' properties being launched by the major hotel brands. With fractured support from headquarters, they need to fend more for themselves in their respective marketplaces than ever before. In the end, this gives the advantage to independents because they stand a better chance at developing emotional connections with guests.

It remains to be seen if this 'a brand for everyone' strategy will improve business or only lead to a further dilution of major hotel networks' already under-supported core businesses. I'm skeptical of its long-term success and, before you run off to split off another hotel concept or add a soft brand to an existing portfolio, give some thought to what's been addressed above.

One Love: Keeping Brands United and Limiting Consumer Choice

A recent trend in our industry that I'm quite suspicious of has been the vast proliferation of new brands, sub-brands and soft brands. Starting my career off at Procter & Gamble, effective branding is in my DNA, and it makes my blood boil to see these events unfold, as they will certainly have a dilutive effect on customer awareness.

The solution nowadays to any brand problem is to simply make a new brand. How can we in all honesty believe this to be the best option for every situation? Fuming with anger, I switch on the satellite radio and on comes the perfect song for this moment – "One Love" by Bob Marley. I doubt this 1977 reggae legend had the hospitality industry in mind when he wrote this classic, even if it makes for the perfect title to this diatribe.

While I acknowledge that only the big corporate bigwigs have any real say in the direction a brand takes, it's nonetheless vital that every hotelier have a basic understanding of the underlying principle that explains why a multitude of brands hurts us all in the grand scheme of things. After all, you may soon be promoted to bigwig status, where you will have an opportunity to shape top-down ventures such as rebranding initiatives.

Yes, there are extenuating circumstances that are contributing to this issue – like owners' gross capitalization or market saturation – but that shouldn't preclude you from knowing the fundamental rationale behind the problem. And if you are an independent or small chain operator, this forthcoming tenet has immediate applications in hotels from F&B menu design and amenity packages right through to the types of guestrooms you offer and how many promotions you should run at any single time.

It's called the 'Paradox of Choice' and it governs how consumers sift through the noise to find exactly what they want in as little time as possible. When you give customers too many options, it makes the sales process more grueling and intimidating, so much so that it can halt the process altogether.

A classic example: when you buy most vehicles, your options for paint colors are limited to two, three, four or sometimes five colors (special, higher priced metallic options excepted). Manufacturers do this even though nowadays with robotic sprayers it would be easy to offer a plethora of options. The fact is that cars cost a lot of money, and dealerships want to reduce any hiccups in the sales process so that potential buyers don't get cold feet.

Like automobiles, hotel rooms are a big investment for the average person, especially when you factor in other traveling expenses like airfare, car rentals, time off work and food. Because of the stakes involved, hotel purchases are thus highly emotional, meaning that customers can be easily dissuaded from following through with an acquisition up to the point where they must provide their credit card information. The more choice you give customers, the more they will look for ways to 'cut through the noise' and simplify this decision-making process.

In this sense, whenever a brand splits or a new hotel product enters the fold, we are only making 'streamlined' services like Airbnb and OTA websites even more powerful. Think about it: instead of a guest having to peruse the differentiated brand standards of all the major chains and their sub-brands, he or she need only do a city-wide query on his or her favorite OTA, and then find a property with decent reviews and an affordable price point. Similarly, for Airbnb one need only know the name of the travel destination and desired price range, then everything else will be populated to meet those criteria.

On a microcosmic level, consider how this paradox of choice applies to your own branded website, your booking engine and what types of rooms you offer. How are you making the process easy for customers by funneling them towards the credit card input or booking screen? Are promotions and products clearly labeled to immediately infer what guests will receive? For instance, instead of giving fancy names to each room type, why not just call them 'Gold', 'Silver' and 'Bronze'? I know, a very crude example, but it nonetheless demonstrates how we should be simplifying the sales process to help speed it along.

This paradox of choice is so foundational to how we operate that it can be applied to nearly any operation at your hotel. Is your food menu too long, thereby forcing people to select the safest option or, worse, reducing the number of turns? Does your spa menu list so many treatment options that consumers are deterred from making a purchase in the first place? Are you offering so many different promotions on your website that customers can't decide which one to buy?

And for all those naysayers, consider Coca-Cola – yes, THE Coca-Cola, one of the largest beverage companies in the world – which around this time last year felt compelled to consolidate and streamline their four main product labels by reducing the text on the can and color-coding each: classic is red, light is silver, zero is black, life is green. This change makes it extremely easy for customers to get what they want – all they need to know is which of the four colors they enjoy!

If Coca-Cola is factoring in these psychological principles into what products it offers, then why aren't you? As a happily married man for over 37 years, I can proudly support Bob Marley's "One Love" philosophy. Real men only have time for one woman in their lives, and all of us only have time to care about a select few brands or product lines. So, do us a favor and limit our options so that we can make the right decision instead of no decision at all.

Consistency in Quality is the Modern Credibility

Soft branding is a popular trend these days, showing no signs of slowing down in the face of billion-dollar mergers and acquisitions. Unquestionably, soft brands fill a specific demand within the traveler mindset – the desire for an independent property to add an extra layer of exclusivity to a trip combined with the expectation that certain standards will be upheld. It's a fascinating space and one that has yet to reach full maturity or capacity.

Tapping in for a phone interview to elucidate how properties can succeed within a soft branded space is Filip Boyen, the CEO of Small Luxury Hotels of the World (SLH) and formerly the COO of Belmond who helped shepherd that organization through the Orient-Express rebrand. With its 520+ properties spread across 80 countries, I've heretofore considered SLH to be somewhat of the 'fourth flower' in this arena alongside Preferred & Resorts, Relais & Chateaux and Leading Hotels of the World. SLH doesn't quite have the same degree of brand awareness of the other three, but don't let Boyen's ebullient Belgian accent deceive you; the company has a strong vision to boost this awareness on its way to becoming numero uno in soft brand associations.

To start, SLH unveiled a new logo to generate excitement for activities including a holistic update to its loyalty program 'The Club', which has 400,000+ members. Currently underrepresented in the Americas, the association's primary goal is to thoroughly penetrate the US market and emerging South American destinations as well as gateway cities in Asia.

But what is SLH doing to improve the state of affairs in the hospitality industry and to elevate the bar for others to follow? I nodded and grinned profusely when Boyen confidently stated that SLH isn't trying to be everything for everyone. Their USP is to connect independently spirited hotels with independently minded customers, not necessarily to go head-to-head with a major chain or generate trial through discounted promotions. In this sense, SLH constituents' largest competitor is now Airbnb, and Boyen certainly had strong words on that matter.

Airbnb is here to stay, as everyone knows. But now that the alternative lodging provider offers foodservice options, they are encroaching ever closer on the luxury accommodations segment which prides itself on its robust amenities. Boyen sees it as an ongoing arms race, and the only road to success is to be better and make each property even more exceptional.

After all, to the uninitiated, the SLH name means very little; it's only after guests have experienced a property's unique sensibility and the association's 720 heavily enforced brand standards that they might choose to stay within SLH instead of Airbnb or booking through an OTA. Boyen placed special emphasis on the enforcement of these standards because reputations are so fragile these days that the only path to long-term success is through a consistent delivery of quality service, even at the independent and semi-independent levels.

As an interesting aside, two-thirds of SLH's bookings still come through traditional travel agents. From this statistic alone, any hotelier can infer that there is a sizeable buffer between the target demographic of associations and that of Airbnb, and even the OTAs for that matter. As part of the strategy to widen this gap and become a niche leader, Boyen aims to drive greater levels of suite business (very high ADR guestrooms) and to work hard at the property level to become a facilitator for each destination – that is, developing programs to serve the local authentic guest experience and heighten guest education.

Still, Boyen recognizes the need to gain traction amongst the millennials well before they are at a point in their lives where they are ready to adhere to one brand over another. It's a long-term effort that requires continual attention. The revitalized loyalty program will help by increasing engagement with guests and fans. The real 'meat' for this objective will come by creating special and specific guest experiences that connect with local communities while also not succumbing to 'big brand creep'.

At a glance, these initiatives may not appear to be anything revolutionary. It is their execution that will distinguish SLH over the coming months and years. "We steal with pride," remarked Boyen.

He isn't ashamed in the least to source the best ideas already being successfully utilized within the hospitality space, and then adapt them to SLH properties. Even though the soft branding phenomenon may have overextended itself in the past few years, Boyen makes a very solid argument to support the notion that now is indeed the time for soft branding.

Full Service Versus Limited Service: Who is the Real Winner?

While travelling on business earlier this month, I had the opportunity to compare two outlets of a major chain – one part of their full-service collection, the other being one of their limited service brands. In both instances, I was alone and my stay was merely for a night and breakfast, arriving after dinner and departing the next morning. Accordingly, my comments relate mostly to a typical business traveler who sees the hotel as an accommodation necessity, rather than the leisure traveler who may be more inclined to indulge in the multi-faceted operational elements such as a spa, pool, bar, concierge and upscale dining.

Full Service

Arriving in the early evening, there were several front desk receptionists. I was welcomed immediately and, after the perfunctory greeting and credit card swipe, was given a room key and told where the elevators were. I did not see a bell-staffer or evidence that one was on duty, nor was the concierge at his or her station. Arriving in the room, it was well-polished, with numerous tent cards and other printed elements encouraging me to take advantage of extra cost services. The internet connection was complex, with a daily rate of $10 to connect.

The bed was comfortable, the room quiet. The bathroom had the usual amenity tray with five items. However, the shampoo bottle was so small that it would be insufficient for two. Towels were adequate and there were two bathrobes.

Breakfast the next morning was available starting at 7am with a $20 buffet or a la carte alternative. Valet parking was $30 for the night. A checkout folio was inserted under the door in the morning.

Limited Service

There was only one person at the front desk and I waited about two minutes until the receptionist was available. Her greeting included instructions on the free WiFi, free breakfast and free parking.

Obviously, there was no bellman or concierge, but the receptionist told me about a great restaurant nearby as well as a caution about road construction in the area.

The room itself was very similar to the full-service twin. The décor was different; upon close inspection, you could see that the furniture was not quite up to the same standard. Interestingly, the television set was larger. Internet was easy to access with no revenue gateway. The air conditioner unit had a bit of annoying fan noise so I shut it off before bed. The drapes did not have the same light cancelling quality.

The bathroom was actually larger than the full-service counterpart. The shower had an insert rather than tiles and the vanity was plastic rather than made of stone or another premium material. The shampoo bottle was larger (there were only three amenities available) and the showerhead provided ample coverage. Lastly, I did not spot any bathrobes.

In the morning, the breakfast buffet was ample and I took an extra coffee for the road in a Styrofoam cup. Parking was free and I was efficiently off to my next meeting.

The Winner?

Limited service hotels are clearly the businessman's friend. They're no nonsense – you're in and out with a minimum of fuss and cost. If I am staying less than 12 hours on property, this seems to be the right choice.

But it does not have to be. If you manage a full-service property, have you ever considered creating a package or price-point that caters specifically to the business travel market? Restrict it to one night only, allot your smallest room, limit it to single occupancy, include breakfast and parking, and give it one fixed price. Importantly, offer it only on your website through direct booking, eliminating OTA commission costs. Call it 'for the road'.

Just What is a Lifestyle Hotel?

A short detour through Southern California brought me to an independent property advertising itself as a 'lifestyle hotel'. Not knowing the specifics of what this meant in a West Coast context, who exactly this hotel was targeting or how the property was differentiating itself to substantiate this modifier, I was curious and excited to try it out.

Withholding its name so we can keep this discussion neutral, the property itself was a one-time Hyatt that had seen a recent – and, from what I am told, extensive – renovation. The open concept lobby's enormous size was augmented by its sleek, reflective tile surfaces and made only more inviting by the vibrant reddish orange hues utilized in the sparse décor. The patchwork lighting was eclectic and moody, as was the labyrinthine juxtaposition of the lobby furniture and bar area. Furthermore, a large grab-and-go outlet reminiscent of a humble, luxury-goods-oriented airport duty free shop dominated one side of the lobby just before the entrance to the restaurant. The overall feel was relaxed and inviting yet also animated and hip.

The front desk staff was no different than what one would expect in a traditional hotel, except for a somewhat disconcerting lack of name badges. The property was very busy, and I was advised by the desk clerk that they were expecting to sell out that evening. Looking around my double queen guestroom, I noticed the traditional binder of statistics, safety data, TV channels, conference space maps and room service listings had been replaced by a bound, well curated series of cardboard flip charts, each one depicting an element of the property's features. All was presented in a laid back, millennial-seeking lexicon.

Apart from this element, the bedroom and bathroom were traditional in every other way. Towels, amenities, bed linens, soft goods and case goods looked catalog-familiar. The neutral brown color selections and bland interior design elements lacked clear-cut distinctiveness. Writing about it just one week later, I had a hard time remembering the specific combination of textures and shades which served create any sort of 'lifestyle roar'.

So, what is it that differentiates or allows your property to be described as a lifestyle brand? One would expect – or at least a traveling boomer such as myself would surmise – that a strong sense of place would be a key factor contributing to this descriptor. After all, lifestyle's dictionary meaning pertains to the ways in which a person or group lives. And aren't our surroundings an important influence on our behavior or livelihoods? Moreover, shouldn't lifestyle hotels work to enrich or improve our lives in ways that other standardized hotels simply cannot do? A lobby bar and c-store are not enough.

From this example, I would say that lifestyle means a younger, less formal attitude, which translates into youthful front desk staff, lax uniform code, irreverent guest communications, creative use of print elements and a lively website. Perhaps the word 'lifestyle' just isn't meant for those of us over the age of 45.

Not to seem jaded, but from this experience and others it would seem as though the promise of a lifestyle property has been hijacked by savvy marketers hoping to fully reposition a hotel without changing all that much in terms of appearance or operations. My token of advice if you are currently operating a lifestyle hotel or are thinking of moving in that direction is to give some serious thought as to how exactly you will transform your property to make it not only truly distinctive but also better than your competitors.

Every Brand is Now a Lifestyle Brand

Did you read the news this morning? Hilton, Hyatt, InterContinental and Marriott just announced that they are reinvesting in their core brands by folding all the new names in their respective houses and transforming their hotels into lifestyle brands. Hilton's Canopy is no longer; Hyatt has sent Andaz packing; InterContinental is giving Hotel Indigo the heave-ho; Edition has been excised by Marriott; and Aloft and Element are no longer members of the family.

United these corporations stand with a 'one brand, one name' policy. As a house of brands, Corporate's position on this is a tad more complex, but that's nothing a few Chinese investors can't fix!

Gone are the days of niche sub-brands with cool yet ambiguous names and fewer than ten properties worldwide. Every hotel will now experience the benefits of having 'lifestyle' features no matter if they appeal to millennials demanding perfection for bargain basement prices or boomers craving the inky touch of a physical, environmentally unfriendly magazine.

In case you haven't guessed it by now, this is a joke. The major chains are currently in the process of diluting their core brands through successive new product announcements. All these sub-brand launches, no matter what target demographic that market researchers have found to be 'underserved', in the grand scheme of things only serve to complicate the travel research phase for the average consumer.

When you give people too many options, they will look for ways to simplify the decision-making process. Make a restaurant menu too long and patrons will spend more time perusing the options only to ultimately end by asking the server for his or her recommendation. Give prospective car buyers too many colors to choose from and they won't make their purchase from your dealership. Present customers with an armada of flavors to try and they'll buy the competitor's brand of soda, the one that offers only a few clearly labeled and easily differentiated options. Other examples abound in any industry that cares about actually selling to its consumers.

In the realm of hospitality, the OTAs help alleviate this pain point as all you need to know is the location you want to visit and your budget, brands be damned. Ditto for Airbnb. Despite all the official rationales from the major chains for why these new sub-brand creations are justified, not one comes close to solving this 'paradox of choice' problem. So, if you are contemplating spinning off a product with a new name, do so at your own risk and know that human genetics are not on your side.

My second gripe with all these brand launches comes via the lazy usage of the already vague 'lifestyle' modifier, which is meant to denote forward-thinking hotels with an eye for contemporary, ergonomic and intimate design as well as health and wellness. Creating a new sub-brand to fit this trend shouldn't be a crutch to resuscitate the parent company.

Instead, lifestyle attributes should be applied across the board. Give all your hotels a modern makeover. Transform every lobby into a functional third space with grab-and-go dining options. Upgrade your health and wellness amenities regardless of whether the average customer is a millennial, Gen Xer or baby boomer. After all, just because a brand is old and established doesn't mean it is immune to change. Brand evolution should be holistically embraced as, in this case, I'm sure most customers would love to experience some of the features that demarcate such lifestyle brands without having to try an entirely new product.

Yes, there is the argument to be made that people want to try new things. And this point is spot on. People do indeed try new hotels...by traveling to different locales around the world!

But maybe, just maybe, if you let them know that your hotel brand is a singular entity with many different properties in many different locations, such travelers may decide to check out where your other constituent hotels are situated and let that grouping determine where to visit next.

Would the Real St. Regis Please Stand Up

Here's an interesting case study for you. The St. Regis Hotel in the heart of downtown Vancouver, British Columbia, is an independent property and not part of the international St. Regis brand in the Starwood family. Copyright claims are nullified by the fact that the St. Regis Hotel in Vancouver – established in 1913 – predates the latter's brand launch.

After visiting, the argument can be made that no matter what, you can't bank on your name. You have to deliver and exceed on consumers' expectations. Here to help offer some insights is the property's General Manager, Jeremy Roncoroni.

Give us a very brief property overview.
65 rooms: 15 suites, 10 kings, 30 queens, 10 doubles. Built in 1913, boutique in style, $12 million (Canadian) renovation in 2008 by acclaimed interior designer Elaine Thorsell.

You manage the St. Regis Hotel, but it is NOT a St. Regis Property.
Oh, but it is truly 'St Regis'! In 1990, this was challenged by Starwood/Marriott Hotels without success. We own the brand in the lower mainland of British Columbia.

Has guest confusion ever ensued?
All the time! To this day I still clarify that we are not a Marriott-Starwood property and that we cannot honor their loyalty program's points. We are, however, a member of the reward program VOILA Hotel Rewards which offers worldwide redemptions.

The property delivers incredible guest service. What's your philosophy here?
We make a living from our guest; so let's give them more that they expect and let's not nickel and dime them in the process. Unless you order room service or utilize our St. Regis Bar & Grill or the iconic Gotham Steak House and Cocktail Bar, there will be no additional

charges. We are one of the only all-inclusive city hotels in North America, from free internet access to full cook to order breakfast (for two) and worldwide calling as well as other basic amenities like complimentary in-room bottled water and 200 HD channels including movie central. Parking is the only item that's not included.

Tell me a little but about your business approach.
We are in the business of providing a good night sleep and if we fail to do so, we will look after you. Why allow a guest to leave unhappy? Do you know how many people they are going to tell? Or, even worse, it might create a social media nightmare. I personally thank every guest that stays with us via a handwritten note asking them to call me if I can do anything for them. As a recent example, we had an issue with one of our fire detectors and the guest did not sleep well, so I removed the room charge – an obvious error on our part and sometimes the simplest solution is the best.

Can you expand to more St. Regis properties elsewhere?
Starwood owns the St. Regis name outside of our region. But that hasn't stopped us. We have The Plaza Hotel in Kamloops that has taken our same approach of inclusion – also boutique in style, also a heritage property and, of course, a steakhouse, Fireside Steak House & Bar. It's not our name that has made us successful but our product delivery, maintenance of the property and our friendly service.

What advice do you give other luxury hotel operators?
Don't ever lose touch with the final product; inspect it every single day. I personally attend housekeeping and front desk daily meetings, and then inspect about 4,000 to 5,000 rooms a year.

Anything else you want to add?
After six years in the marketplace, we are seeing many properties start to play with their inclusion. The future will see more inclusion

coming the consumer way. The idea is that the bill should never be more than one page long. It took three years for the average customer to understand our inclusions; once they did, they kept coming back. The most frequent complaint I have heard in the last ten years especially is all the charges on top of the room, especially unspecific 'resort' or 'facility' fees. I understand that revenue is important, but creating new fees to generate streams of revenue? Come on, that would make us just as greedy as the airlines!

Larry Mogelonsky

Building Your Hotelerati By Promoting Your Hotel Personalities

People buy from other people, not from corporations. This mantra – or any other version of it – has existed for almost as long as the craft of salesmanship itself. And it makes sense, too. We build rapport far easier in person than over the phone or via the internet. Furthermore, human beings are genetically programmed to constantly read faces and facial expressions as a means of analyzing social cues or forming emotional bonds with the opposite party. We mentally connect with and remember faces much quicker than objects, places, symbols or words.

This makes it hard for companies, which are inherently faceless. It also explains why corporations spend billions of dollars each year in advertising to try to develop a 'face' that people will recognize. More recently, particularly with the widespread adoption of social media, companies have started to promote select employees to publicly, and often effectively, represent their brands through their individual accounts.

For instance, instead of responding to guest requests on Twitter through the company's generic handle, select managers will reply on behalf of the hotel. A guest asks a question in the comments section of a recent post on a resort's Facebook fan page and a manager answers through his or her own profile instead of through the resort's administration account. These seemingly miniscule changes go a long way to furthering the rapport between hotels and consumers by gently amplifying the degree of personable communications.

As places that serve a multitude of public functions and services, hotels and resorts should be especially receptive to the idea of promoting members of the senior staff to the status of ambassador or public relations correspondent. This isn't anything new, though, and indeed I've been a proponent of heightening face-to-face, passive marketing tactics like this for years. I consider it 'passive' and largely experiential as well because its effects aren't straightforwardly quantifiable and direct calls-to-action aren't often applicable. Rather than repeat what's already widely known, let's take it a step further and transform your executive team into celebrities.

Celebrity Theory

Why are we so interested in the daily minutia of the lives of celebrities? Why do we care about gossip like who a person we've never met is dating? For some reason, there are a plethora of magazines, internet sites and television news programs devoted to just this. An iota of this 'news' is fascinating, another slice serves as part of a grand self-promotion strategy and the bulk of it is pure, unadulterated crap.

Living in the age of media bombardment also means living in the age of celebrity-dom. We have immediate, and bordering on invasive, access to the lifestyles of the rich and the famous. It's reached the point where it's near impossible to avoid these sorts of 'titillating' details. Moreover, some people will do just about anything to be of renown and to be identifiable by the public. But why? What would drive someone to seek out fame at all costs? More importantly, why are we so enamored with celebrities?

Much has been written on this topic of recently, coming from people far smarter than me who are active in fields like psychology, anthropology, economics, biology and sociology. Although the findings are varied, the most common conclusion is that celebrity bestows people with a certain degree of exclusivity. Dishing on celebrity gossip makes you appear more knowledgeable. Spotting or meeting a celebrity tells people that you are attending the proper events, traveling to the right destinations or dining at the best restaurants. And being a celebrity? Well, you are in for a lifetime of sycophants jockeying for positions in close orbit just to feed off your aura.

In a world with over seven billion people, it's becoming progressively harder for any single person to be totally unique or exclusive in some way, shape or form. All pessimism aside, it's the truth; you're competing against seven billion people trying to do the same thing! Celebrity, even in as innocuous a form as a name drop or a prominent hotelier refashioning his Facebook profile, is used by all of us to make ourselves feel special and important.

But the idea of celebrity encompasses more than just actors, athletes, musicians and the British Royal Family. There are also local celebrities – people who are well-known and cherished within their own communities. These can be mayors, multimillionaires, police officers, critics, doctors, journalists, restaurateurs or barbers – anyone who has a well-regarded reputation that extends beyond the immediate circle of family, friends and friends of friends. This is where hoteliers should aim to harness the power of celebrity, not all the glitz and glam that comes with the high-profile counterpart.

Hotelerati

Knowing the why behind celebrity can help guide you in the ways of elevating your own in-house personalities to the status of local celebrities. By doing so, you will greatly expand the attention that your 'hotel faces' can command and further the level of trust with which consumers view you. Of course, no concept should be without a catchy or contrite buzz phrase to describe it, hence I concocted the word 'hotelerati' to denote these staffers, styled in the same vein as other Latin adaptations like literati, illuminati and glitterati.

As an aside, put your consumer shoes on for a moment and ask yourself: Has the presence of a particularly friendly or charming hotel manager ever influenced your choice of hotel? Moreover, when was the last time you heard a person lauding a great executive they met while at a hotel? As it pertains to celebrity, we are not only attempting to raise the clout and renown of our properties, but we are also transforming specific employee positions into 'features' and key selling points. And while the idea of celebrity infers a strong sense of individualism, it's best to think of your hotelerati as a team culture composed of strong personalities, all managed through well-defined tasks, regular meetings and long-term objectives that everyone can get behind.

Certain roles within the property hierarchy make for the perfect hotelerati to flaunt about onsite and online. Start with ones that are already somewhat in the spotlight like executive chefs, golf pros, general managers, spa directors or concierges. Then, look to cultivate, or dare I say, celebrate the diversity of your hotelerati by empowering others who regularly interact with guests like front desk clerks or bartenders. The 'Employee of the Month' concept shares many similarities with this. A third option is to recruit external celebrities who are tangentially related to your property – the famous interior designer hired for your latest round of renovations or an acclaimed nutritionist who contributed to the restaurant menu design.

Here are three examples to clue you in on what to look for. First up are your bartenders, who are best thought of as ambassadors to your restaurant. Good barkeeps can do a lot with a "What do you recommend?" question thrown their way. Not only can they surprise patrons with some well-crafted mixology but they can nurture a homelier atmosphere by cutting in at the right moments, playing the middleman by introducing different groups around the bar and livening the spirits of all through a vivacious attitude. Are popular bartenders worth promoting beyond the four walls of the restaurant? You bet!

Next up is the resident golf pro. For decades, people in this role have been sought out for lessons and course advice, but now with the power of social media and content management systems, these pros connect with a far larger audience. If you have such people on staff, encourage them to embrace their avid fan bases through regular updates and by posting insider information – those little factoids that can only come from someone who knows the course inside and out. Beyond this, ensure that guests know a golf pro is available for a quick chat, whether it's through rich website copy or on-property signage.

Third but not least is an especially rare case but nonetheless significant for the overall point – an acclaimed executive chef at a Michelin-rated restaurant within a hotel. It goes without saying that attaining a Michelin star is an incredible feat, and the chefs who reach this echelon are nothing short of geniuses in the kitchen. This genius is something that you should celebrate, starting with simple pursuits like food pictures on Instagram or Pinterest and extending to well-curated pages on the website and prearranged magazine interviews.

Keys to the Hotelerati Kingdom

There's a big difference between being a fully attentive servant who's able to complete requests flawlessly and a team member with local celebrity status. It all comes down to personality, of course, so let's break down some of the characteristics or skills that you can imbue your staff with to heighten their hotelerati presence.

The cardinal trait all budding hotelerati must have is the desire to give value to visitors. This goes above and beyond simply being amenable, responsive and anticipatory to guests' needs; it means tactfully going out of your way to maximize the guest experience. And much of this 'value' isn't what we typically ascribe to the word in the form of complimentary gifts, rewards, vouchers and other physical objects. Let that extra value that you give come from within – from the personality of your team.

For instance, humor is a form of value – you are giving people the gift of laughter. Although this isn't something you can teach (apart from sending people to improv classes), what you, as a manager, can do is provide your team with a loving, comfortable environment that allows a staff member's goodhearted qualities to shine through. A stressful workplace isn't conducive to humor, nor is hostility from colleagues and bosses.

Building on this notion of intrinsic staff characteristics that you can hone rather than produce out of thin air, another value-add is speaking with authority. Guests are arriving from all over the world and they may be slightly timid, especially if they aren't native speakers, fatigued from a long flight or confused as to the ebb and flow of the local environment. A strong voice and confidence from property employees reassures such visitors and reduces stress. And the great thing here is that this can be trained! Educate your staff on proper body language, and then quiz them thoroughly on hotel operations, attractions and happenings in the region so that they have the up-to-date knowledge base to underpin a commanding presence.

Somewhere on the spectrum between humor and confidence lays the mercurial and mysterious trait we call charisma. It's something that indeed all celebrities of some renown do possess, and it is something that your hotelerati should strive to bolster as well. Charisma can be taught to a degree via instruction on proper body language, vocal tonality and charm. Two other forces that help define one's charisma are humility and compassion — both I cannot emphasize enough as pillars for any solid customer interaction. You must be able to empathize with guests' plights and have enough modesty to apologize when necessary.

I'm not suggesting that these minor adjustments will transform each team member overnight, but imbuing your hotel with a strong culture of personalities will work in the long-term towards building a community of new and returning guests. This is particularly critical if you can fathom that the oldest members of the tech-fluent Generation Z will reach the age of majority in five years' time. They are growing up in an age of internet-born celebritydom and they'll soon be looking to hoteliers for personal connections as they start to travel the globe as independent business and leisure travelers. Aim to gradually convert select hoteliers into hotelerati and watch this rising tide lift the profile of everyone else associated with the property.

Larry Mogelonsky

Brooklynize Your Property

We live in an era of buzz phrases and neologisms that represent just about anything the human mind can imagine. More specific to hotels, we are also living in an age of embracing the 'local authentic experience' and all that that infers. Combine these two ideas and we arrive at the word 'Brooklynization' which has recently been making waves in the more erudite presses. This catch-all can mean a lot of different things depending on the context, so let's make sure we are on the same page regarding its meaning for hospitality.

To start, why Brooklyn? It's less about the historical relevance of this two-and-a-half-million-strong borough and more about what it stands in the shadow of – Manhattan. With the nearby island as an archetypical representation of capitalism, corporate imperialism and unchecked greed, Brooklyn has sought to be the exact opposite with a focus on small-batch production, artisanal craftsmanship and all-round bohemian vibes. Brooklyn as a brand also connotes local sourcing, manufacturing by hand and niche hobbyist entrepreneurship.

This has, of course, only been made possible by the mass migration of the creative classes out of Manhattan and onto Long Island neighborhoods with significantly cheaper costs of living. A similar pattern of exodus has been documented from San Francisco to Oakland and, closer to home for yours truly, Toronto to Hamilton, with countless other past and present examples occurring all around the world. That said, this trend didn't start in New York City; but given the borough's dense clustering of artistic folk and its recognition as a cultural nexus, nobody does Brooklynization better than Brooklyn itself.

While you would be remiss to adorn a giant "Made in Brooklyn" label atop your hotel and on your website unless you are in fact located in the borough, the Brooklynization trend is one that flows from the same source as the current push for property differentiation via the embrace of the authentic local experience. For starters, performing a Brooklynizing audit on your hotel will reveal aspects both large and small where you can transform the ordinary or cookie-cutter into something chic and a little edgy. Local producers should be on your radar as sources for restaurant ingredients, the gift shop, lobby art, in-room décor and spa inventory.

But the spirit of Brooklynization is more than just shifting contracts from one massive producer to a much smaller one. It also denotes the empowerment of the creative class in your area to help grow your local identity. That is, a hotel property has the resources to be an active community leader and a champion of the young entrepreneurship that will shape the future. This means opening your doors to the neighborhood for events – for instance, a local tech business social in your banquet hall or a farmers' market in a cordoned-off area of the parking lot. This also means hiring visionary young minds, and then giving them a bit of leeway to help steer the ship towards what's functional and 'cool'.

Many of us are already well on our way towards a process of internal Brooklynization under the guise of boutique or lifestyle branding or the semblance of an artisanal, crafted, curated or local hotel environment. Guests increasingly yearn for these authentic experiences, so keep heading in that direction, and when in doubt about where else you can differentiate, look to the Long Island city that epitomized the movement.

Brands are More Than a Promise: They are a Guarantee

Right now, the hotel industry is experiencing a virtual gusher of new brands. There are so many new faces on the logo tree that even as a keen observer of our niche in the world, I am having difficulty placing what brand goes with what house. I imagine that launching a new brand registers some excitement in the corporate head office, giving c-suite executives a somewhat pleasant diversion from the real work of fighting issues such as the encroachment of alternate lodging providers, elusive millennial travel desires, waning loyalty or the market domination of the OTAs.

While these new brands offer intriguing 'lifestyle' bolt-ons such as improved lobbies, fancy cappuccino makers and shiny exercise facilities, lost in the designer mirage is the need to focus on the brands that got us to this point in the first place. For a moment, let's address those at the core: Marriott/Starwood, Hilton, Intercontinental, Wyndham and so on. These are all well-known, consumer trusted and proven products.

Is it just me, or is the hotel industry hoping that these established brands will just go away? When was the last time we heard of a refocus on these venerable 'core' brands rather than the new 'toy' brands? My issue is that brands like Hilton already have a 50-year head start, and in this fast and crazy world we live in, attempting to introduce something new is incredibly hard. For example, ask any non-hotelier what a Tru or a Centric property is and you will likely get a puzzled look. Better the devil you know...

Ergo, here are some of my suggestions for the corporate hotel world. I make these unilaterally, as I am not in any way connected with any of these concerns. I don't even own shares in any of these publicly traded companies.

Don't throw out these old brands, reinvest in them.

Some of these brands have 40, 50 or more years in the marketplace. They have attained levels of brand recognition that in today's internet world would be impossible to recreate. Aside from accrued reputation and product awareness, they also have decades of internal wherewithal to build upon.

Hold your brand values sacrosanct.

Simply put, if operators do not live up to the standards, turf them. Period. No exceptions; no grace period. Remove your brand and take the product off your corporate website. Upholding your brand is an imperative now because consumers have so many options that one little slip can mean a lost customer for life. Add to that the fact that a single bad property reflects poorly on all others in the brand and you have yourself a major reason to reassess your franchisee contracts.

Advertise your brand promise.

Advertising creates imagery for the consumer that excites and builds anticipation. Advertising also creates awareness and builds value in the brand. It reinforces with your franchisees the corporate commitment to building revenue.

As the ultimate challenge, I dare a brand to say that they have a money back guarantee. Something like, "If we fail to deliver x, y and z then tell us how we failed, and if you booked through our corporate website, we will refund your accommodations." Of course, let your franchisors know they're on the hook for failing to deliver. Post the guarantee on your site as yet another reason why booking direct is the way to go.

To conclude, it's time to take the corporate gloves off. If we are to survive as an industry and keep our brands intact in the face of so many tech-born disruptors, we need to get serious about our products. Adding new brands is an ingenious corporate smokescreen but ultimately fails to address the needs of the core brands.

These newer toy brands may work in the short-term, but I foresee doom in the long run if we don't collectively reinvest in the core brand names that made our industry great. Brands are designed to be more than just a promise; they're a guarantee of quality. Right now, all we are guaranteeing is that we will confuse the average consumer.

TRADITIONAL MARKETING

*Naples, Florida is a mecca for snowbirds from the norheast
and The Inn on the Fifth caters to this audience with
superbly finished rooms and remarkable service levels.*

*Photos copyright of the hotel and cannot be
reproduced without its permission.*

Larry Mogelonsky

Traditional Marketing Section Introduction

The advent of the World Wide Web has forever changed how we conduct business and the mediums through which we connect with guests. But there are still many ways to reach consumers that are as effective now as they were before the dawn of the internet age. This chapter is dedicated to those traditional and 'old school' marketing tactics, strategies and concepts that have been overshadowed of late by their digital counterparts along with several other lesser-known opportunities that can help heighten sales.

This chapter also includes two subsections devoted to focused subject matter on building revenues from specific time periods and certain demographics. First, the articles on holiday marketing discuss many of the popular and more obscure days of the year that hoteliers can leverage both by capitalizing on consumers' innate desire to travel and by differentiating your marketing presentation. The second section is titled 'Gray is the New Green' and details methods to better target baby boomers – an age group that is currently undergoing a great metamorphosis, with many entering retirement and in possession of excess funds allocated especially for leisure expenditures.

Above all, it is stressed throughout that there are many ways to successfully increase sales that you can effectively utilize simply by being different from your competition. Thus, as businesses become ever more reliant on the internet for the bulk of their revenue generation, incorporating traditional marketing tactics into your overall strategic plan may be just what your hotel needs to gain an edge.

Just Like Home is a Sham

'Feels just like home' or 'Make yourself at home' or any other iteration on this phrase is a common copywriting tool for hotels to create an inviting feeling for prospective travelers. While the intentions are all well and good, there is an underlying problem with this language.

Namely, what does the average home look and feel like? Cramped spaces. Old furniture. Hodgepodges of mismatched art. No cohesive design or vision. Kids toys scattered everywhere. Messy kitchen. Bedsheets changed at a maximum of once a week. Grime in the washrooms. Mediocre garden. Nosy neighbors. Repairs upon repairs.

True, the home is where the heart is. It's where we rest, recharge and reflect, and this is the sentiment that we are all after when we insert a sprinkle of 'just like home' into the marketing prose for our hotels. We are subtly communicating that we want our guests to feel at ease. But 'home' also has quite a few less attractive connotations, starting with those mentioned above. Combined with the general overuse, it's time to move away from this expression.

It's time to market our hotels as better than home – cleaner, uncluttered, more secure and better serviced. In this sense, we should flip the switch; our guestrooms ought to be aspirational for what our customers' homes could resemble one day. Staying at your property should enlighten your guests as to how they can make their houses feel 'just like a hotel'.

One clear-cut way to become an aspirational hotel is through the furnishings, décor and art that you deploy to fill the front-of-house spaces. This should be obvious for any hotelier who has visited more than ten properties. While you do indeed want to let your interior designers' imaginations run wild to help bestow your property with a unique sense of place, there should still be room for little touches that are readily applicable to any guest's personal domicile. The gift shop can act as a bridge in some ways, but you might also consider drafting a guidebook that details what each piece of art or furniture is and where it was sourced so that if customers like a specific work they can cut out the middleman.

The next two broad routes to becoming an aspirational hotel are through embracing technology and by offering 'sample services'.

The former should be readily understood; guestroom or lobby features that heighten the utility or aesthetics of a space are bound to trickle down to other forms of residence, much like how military and NASA electronics have inevitably found their way to the average consumer in the form of geolocation services, cell phones and a host of other technologies.

What I classify as 'sample services' are ones where guests can try out different products to find what suits their needs best. The entry level to this occurs at the restaurant where you might offer charcuterie boards, cheese plates, wine tastings or fruit samplings, for example, so long as you have your servers identify what each individual component is. You might also have a prix fixe menu with demonstrations on how to make each dish.

Sample services are also appropriate for in-room uses. Think a custom selection of pillows covering a range of soft to firm, or a differentiated towel service comprising a variety of fabrics. Ditto for all other products you put in the washroom, or even the mini-bar for that matter. And building on this, the spa is prime territory for sample services whereby you might offer a discount on treatments for first-timers – with the products available for purchase, of course.

The idea behind sample services is to give guests opportunities to try new things they would not otherwise be able to do at home. Instead of attempting to create what guests already have, help them improve their homes and they will be all thankful for it.

Refocus on the Voice Channel

A long time ago in an article far, far away, I introduced the concept of the 'Communications Hierarchy' which inscribed a certain degree of emotional commitment to each form of contemporary communication, from group emails and direct messages to conference calls and face-to-face meetings. What was made apparent was that the more intimate the form of communication, the better it was for securing business and building rapport.

If it isn't obvious from the title, you should know that I am a staunch proponent of talking to clients and customers over the phone. Yes, email and text messages are often significantly faster, but the written word (outside of novelistic expressions) will always fail to grasp the full inflection, subtle cues, mannerisms and hidden desires of the parties involved. Importantly, the 21st century has seen the proliferation of these digital forms of communication, making phone calls rarer by comparison.

And this presents an opportunity for you. The more atypical voice channels become, the more their use stands to separate you from the pack, whether it's a direct sales call, connecting with a reservationist or following up on a service request. Their relative scarcity nowadays will make people feel validated, especially if you work tactfully to develop a rapport.

While in-person conversations are still the foremost way to reach a meeting of the minds, the telephone is the next best thing. Hearing customers speak will allow you to learn things about them that electronic messaging channels can never provide. This as well as other abovementioned reasons explain why, to this day, voice reservations have the highest satisfaction rate. But to have voice channels perform optimally, here are a few suggestions:

Timing is everything.

You must train staff to judge the best time of day to call and to not be annoying in this regard. Calls first thing in the morning will be dismissed in favor of organizing one's day, whereas calls during dinnertime are considered to be particularly rude. Frequency is likewise to be kept at a minimum.

Inquire about the best time.

People are always busy, or at least they'll say they have more pressing matters to attend to. No worries; simply ask them when is a more appropriate point for a chat and try to firm up a specific time.

Voice mail is your elevator pitch.

In many cases, your first call will get the answering machine. Do not despair; this is your time to shine. Have a prepared speech ready and practiced, one that is personable and delivered with candor. Don't overstay your welcome either; keep it under 30 seconds.

Call then email then call again.

Rather than sound off the elevator pitch when you hit voice mail, send off with an email stating that you will call again at a certain time, keeping the ball in your court while being firm yet respectful with your follow up.

Outbounding.

Ending with a new age marketing term, this describes the process of pursuing inbound calls that don't result in direct sales. While you don't want to be an interloper, persistence is nevertheless a virtue. If you are forthright and earnest when returning an inbound call, you stand a much better chance of converting it into a sale.

I hope these tips illustrate how viable the voice channel can be if you use it correctly. After all, hospitality is still about people connecting with other people, and in this age where texting is the norm and it's hip to be retro-chic, picking up the telephone is now more lucrative than ever.

Use Kairos To Improve Your Voice Channel Sales

I can't speak to the buyer.
I can't reach their event planner.
I can't even get to a hold of a manager!

This article is specifically addressed to your sales team members. Those individuals who are charged with the daunting task of continually filling in your meetings space with group events. In this era of electronic communication, where faceless automated RFPs prevail, the challenge of booking corporate groups has exploded. With the advent of the electronic RFP, the number of actual submissions has increased exponentially, making it incredibly difficult for a single property to standout.

How do sales team members differentiate your property from competitors? How do they express your property's USP in any sort of targeted manner? And most importantly, how do they improve their conversion rate on business presentations?

Now, more than ever, there is a need to go beyond automation and rekindle one-to-one communications. But it's not like you can just show up at someone's office – the days of traveling salespersons are over. Instead, we are seeing the voice channel emerge as a viable intermediary between being lost in the noise of electronic RFPs and landing a personal meeting with a much-vaunted handshake at the end.

Business habits are a tad different nowadays, however. People hide behind their voicemails, so this should be the expectation over top of getting the person on the line right away. Here is a three-step approach you may want to consider:

Preparation

Develop a 75-90 second presentation on your property. This is your 'elevator pitch' and it can't be any longer or else you run into the cognitive drift problem. The appropriate Latin phrase to tape up on the wall is "Ex hoc momento pendet aeternitas," roughly translating to 'Eternity hangs on this one moment'. In other words, you only have one shot at this, so make it count!

Rehearse your presentation so that it sounds sincere and emotive. Next, use it on one of your team member's voicemail. Then play it back over a speakerphone for other members of the sales team. Listen and accept their constructive criticism. Repeat this process until you are comfortable and the team gives you two thumbs up.

Phone Execution

With the appropriate personalization for every execution, follow up every RFP with your short presentation. Even though you are leaving it on voicemail, the odds are that it will get heard by the recipient and quite possibly forwarded to a decision maker. You may not get a phone call back even though you left your return number. That's okay, as the goal here is to get a successful return on your RFP and not necessarily to start a direct conversation or set up a one-on-one meeting.

You should not delegate this to someone who is a junior or who does not have direct sales responsibility. Why? Because occasionally, you hit the jackpot and the recipient picks up! I know, it does happen from time to time, and in such instances with a live client on the line you should be ready to conduct business.

Leaving those trendy Latin business phrases aside for the time being, the ancient Greeks had two words for time that come in handy here: *chronos* and *kairos*. The former denotes all of time or at a lengthy period while the latter is considered only a moment of high importance. Often, a *kairos* equaled 1/40th of an hour or 90 seconds, which happened to be the shortest period that could be measured on a sundial.

So, consider your short speech on the phone to be a *kairos* – a defining moment that proves your point – which is that your property is ideal for that meeting.

A Handwritten Note

Your property has welcome cards left in guestrooms. Steal some for your sales department's use. Write a personal thank you (do not computer print!) for the opportunity to present. Add one key fact to make sure the note is personalized and expressive of your USP. Given that you will be 'snail mailing' this, make sure to get it out the door on the same day as you press 'submit' to the automated RFP.

While the electronic RFP has made it very easy for a planner to add an increasing number of properties to their potential venue list, the effect of each individual proposal ends up being diluted as a result. This three-step plan is but one way for you to continue to differentiate yourself. Give it a try!

Larry Mogelonsky

Marketing Wellness to the Unenlightened

A spa or wellness center can be a tremendous profit maker for a hotel or resort property. Indeed, various estimates put wellness tourism in or around half a trillion US dollars worldwide, more than one-seventh of all travel bucks spent. Hardly a loss leader, but I nonetheless ask: how can wellness tap into the other six-sevenths?

To spa or not to spa – that is the question I've asked travelers in the past, both anecdotally and through dedicated research. Without making this a numbers or methodology debate, let me just say that there is a sizeable percentage of the traveling population that has never utilized a spa or very rarely does so. While rigorously working to retain existing business – that is, those customers who actively seek out spa accommodations – is always a prudent course of action, that six-sevenths is too big to ignore.

Just so it's clear, we aren't discussing wellness travel and those people who are already well aware of the benefits of a spa. We are talking about getting consumers in the opposite camp on board. Putting on my marketing cap for a moment, I wouldn't call people who do not regularly go to the spa 'naïve'. Rather, consider the word 'unenlightened'; it's a positive word that invites you to inform those who haven't tried a spa's, or at least your spa's services yet and just aren't familiar with the great experience on the table.

The fact remains that a wellness center is so much more than just massages, skin-softening ointments and aromatic treatments. Wellness itself encapsulates so many different forms – physical, mental and emotional for starters – all with the overarching goal of helping people achieve their life goals. But no one will come to enjoy these broad benefits if you don't give your spa facility a good hook or angle for the layman to latch onto. Therefore, let's look at several ideas below to see how you might improve this amenity so that it's more inviting to newcomers.

Purposeful Wellness

Spas are no longer just for pampering. The modern guest seeks a more comprehensive wellness experience with palpable long-term benefits, intellectual stimulation and takeaway lessons, be it through nutrition, yoga, meditation, art therapy, acupuncture or mind-body therapies. Key to this is realizing that many consumers are looking for an interactive experience instead of merely a passive one where the therapist does all the work.

A good way to go about transforming a spa menu from passive to dynamic is to integrate fitness regimens, and many facilities are already taking this hybrid approach. But if you haven't, consider partnering with a doctor, physiotherapist, kinesiologist, chiropractor, isometrics specialist or other accredited professional to help you design treatments that are more functional in structure. I'm not insisting you turn your tranquil locale into a full-blown gymnasium, but some advanced rehabilitation equipment would be nice. Think of angle-centric machines built for bodily alignment and stabilization and not ones made for gross muscular strength.

Along these lines, the outdoors and surrounding environments are a wellness center's best friend. For every class that you offer, ask yourself: can this be moved outside? Morning yoga classes along the beach or midday art hikes into the woods are a good start. Crucial to this tactic is to highlight and exploit the exceptional aspects of your local area as much as possible so that your guests experience a level of value unavailable anywhere else.

Go Local

Building on that last alfresco point, it's become apparent in the hospitality industry that being 'authentically local' is mandatory for all properties except for the economy and road warrior sectors. This trend makes sense for businesses and consumers alike. In a world where competition is global and heavily filtered through online distribution channels, properties must be able to distinguish themselves from their neighbors on more than just price. Guests, on the other hand, crave unique experiences that they can't get back at home.

Think regional fragrances, seasonal treatments, artisanal district producers or anything you can offer to lend an authentically local voice to your wellness offerings. Sadly, though, simply having local infusions isn't enough nowadays because everyone else has already caught on to this. Understanding how to market these products is what separates the cats from the kittens.

Although this is something I'd treat on a property-by-property basis, one commonly applicable thread is the notion of specialization and unity. Rather than attempt to convey the full breadth of the region's character to the consumer, focus on just one or two highly appealing features, and then express them through a range of products. For example, suppose your area is known for exclusively growing a certain flower in addition to a dozen other marketable goods. Instead of shoehorning all thirteen in the spa menu, use just the flower and, sourcing problems notwithstanding, use it for everything from facials to manicures, pedicures and rubs.

Friends and Family

Wellness can be a solo adventure, but it can (and should!) also be a shared experience for families to come closer together, for friends to reconnect or even as a respite to enhance a meeting's productivity. The underlying concept here is that, as humans, we are social animals and we can often improve our own well-being and perspective on life by interacting with others in a constructive atmosphere. This starts with romantic couples' packages, but then goes into other less-touched ground: mothers and daughters' packages, corporate or group offerings, prenatal and maternity treatments, or treatments for teenagers. Next, to pump up the social factor, mix these specific wellness packages with F&B...with an emphasis on the beverage!

Spa Samplers

A definite barrier to entry and intimidation factor for the unenlightened is the cost. It's just too expensive for some to try for the first time. While one time-honored workaround for this has been to incorporate spa treatments into room packages and promotions, another tactic is required.

Picture a spa sampler in much the same way as you would for someone working the counter in the cosmetics section of a department store. These individuals often hand out free samples or mini-treatments to help sell their wares. Why can't you do something similar?

Instead of offering, say, a full pedicure or half-hour massage for all passersby, set up a station in the lobby where members of your wellness team can demo certain products to the crowd as well as hand out free samples. You might even consider unfolding a massage table for quick, five-minute sessions or a proper chair for manicures. Whatever 'show' you decide to put on, ensure that you do it in a highly trafficked corridor of your property to generate the most awareness and the most interactivity.

Wellness Room Service

For some, cost is prohibitive. For others, it is the physical act of venturing into an unfamiliar space. It may be a privacy issue or related to hygiene, or the guest might just be downright lazy. Whatever the reason, a small selection of within-the-guestroom treatments will find an audience, but only if you advertise them and actively inform guests that they are available.

The Mobile Massage

Sitting is the new smoking. We've all heard this tossed around of late in one form or another. But what does it mean and what can you do, as a wellness operator, to help guests alleviate their chair-related problems?

For many of us, excessive sitting is the result of too much typing and staring at a computer screen. Most of our jobs involve interacting with a screen on a regular basis and many of us unwind outside of work by surfing the web, going on social media or watching videos off a laptop. Neck protracted, shoulders rolled forward, hip joints flexed, wrists compressed – these are unnatural poses to hold our bodies in for long stretches of time.

In this screen-dominated world, our skeletons have yet to keep up with our minds – that is, the aberrant positions these keyboards, monitors and smartphones force our joints into can induce injury or chronic pain if left untreated. A 'mobile massage' is a catchy title for a method for recruiting businesspeople and other possible carpal tunnel candidates. But this naming can be expanded to target all over-sitters where the chief sources of consternation include the lower back, upper back, neck, shoulders and knees.

Spa Sommelier

Yes, you can't run a successful spa without a spa manager or director of wellness programs who can handle inventory as well as work effectively with other departments. But thinking in terms of a 'sommelier' or other dignified curatorial position such as a 'spa concierge' will help bring an air of sophistication to this amenity. Plus, such an individual helps personalize the spa experience by, for example, catering specific oils and cleansers to match a guest's palate and aroma preferences. Such personalization adds to the uniqueness factor.

And that's what it's all about – being unique. You need not apply all of the above suggestions to your operations, but perhaps one or two pique your interest and can help convert unenlightened guests towards the path of spa and wellness!

The Power of Trees

Undoubtedly you've browsed through more than few articles discussing sustainable designs and how they can save oodles in long-term expenses on top of all the ensuing benefits for our environment. Moreover, you've probably come across several statistics demonstrating that modern consumers, particularly those falling in the younger demographics, are predisposed to like a brand even more if it has shown itself to be environmentally friendly.

These two subjects are worthy of their own lengthy editorials, so I'll leave them for another time. Instead, let's focus on a few smaller topics.

Remembering that there's even a holiday, Arbor Day, truly devoted to trees, I want you to consider all the ways that trees impact our lives. Outside the obvious, in that they look aesthetically appealing, they can also have a powerful effect on people's dispositions. They can calm one's emotional state and, as nature's air purifier, they give off a faint yet pacifying scent. Moreover, green itself has been proven to have a positive influence on mood, motivation and creativity.

Knowing this, how do you currently incorporate trees and other plants into the workplace? Do you have them scattered about the cubicles to accent the otherwise drab color setting? Yes, they require watering and pruning, but the positive outcomes are undeniable. Applied to the front end of a hotel, how do you think the presence of ample trees and plants would impact guests' moods when placed strategically about the lobby, spa, restaurants and rooms? I'll tell you from experience that a well-maintained array of beautiful plants outside the front entrance makes for quite the impressive display for arriving guests.

As a final, minor suggestion, as 'authentic local experiences' are all the rage these days, have you considered incorporating local indigenous flora into your hotel? An F&B outlet might offer more indigenous plants as ingredients on the menu. Fragrant local plants can be blended into specialty spa treatments and products. You might also showcase a particularly esoteric indigenous plant in the lobby for all to see and appreciate.

In closing, whether it's Arbor Day or not, consider planting a tree. And when the holiday rolls around in April, give some thought to making the day an annual team building outing for all your colleagues to enjoy.

Specific Tips to Attract Chinese Travelers

To many in the Western World, cracking the Chinese travel market is a frustrating enigma. There are over a billion souls living in this over-six-thousand-year-old nation with a voraciously widening middle class, and yet a combination of language, cultural and governmental barriers intimidate us away from launching full-fledged awareness campaigns in this market. But this shouldn't be the case, and it's why I've been ever curious these past few years, seeking out individuals who have insights as to how hotels can bridge this gap.

I had the chance recently to interview Evan Saunders, CEO of Attract China, regarding the expectations of Chinese outbound travelers and what hotels can do to better accommodate members of this group. To clue you in on the gravitas of this situation, it's estimated that by 2018-19 China will be the number one nation in terms of visitors to the US and in the top three for most other Western European countries. The main obstacle preventing this from occurring right now has to do with visa issuing.

As of now, the top destinations for Chinese travelers tend to be the foremost tourist cities. They want to experience the best the West offers. In the US, this means New York City, Las Vegas, Los Angeles and San Francisco, while in Europe, it's primarily London, Paris and Rome. However, as more direct flights open and Chinese visitors become acclimatized to international travel, new locations are quickly gaining ground – Boston and Orlando (theme parks being the essential factor here) in the US, and Barcelona, Madrid, Florence, Berlin, Vienna, Prague and Amsterdam in Europe.

A cardinal expectation amongst most Mandarin speakers is that foreigners won't comprehend their language. As such, they come prepared; they've done their homework and research – often starting upwards of six months out from the departure date. They know the specifics of their daily itineraries well before they set foot in another country, and they have near memorized how to get to and from the airport.

In line with this, a hotelier shouldn't expect last minute bookings from this group as they typically complete their reservations at a minimum of one month ahead of time. Free and independent travelers will most likely find your hotel through online resources and they'll reserve online, too, whereas groups will book through a travel agent.

As Saunders points out, this behavior can also be leveraged as a value-add. Properties that have staff members who can converse in Mandarin or properly translated pamphlets and websites will make very powerful impressions with these guests. Like many other aspects of our business, it's all about exceeding expectations.

In fact, any semblance of home will be greatly appreciated. For instance, Chinese travelers aren't expecting a full buffet catering specifically to their indigenous cuisine, but offering select Chinese breakfast items like noodles, dumplings (bao or jiaozi), tofu, rice porridge (congee) or pancakes (bing) will go a long way towards making such guests feel at ease. And once again, the issue of free WiFi rears its bothersome head; given that Mandarin speakers won't be able to vocalize their inquiries, they'll need the internet to find answers in their native tongue.

Other in-room 'gestures of good faith' include slippers and tea kettles as well as toothbrushes and toothpastes. Just imagine how hard it would be to locate these two essential items in a city where you don't know the local language. Welcome letters in Mandarin, or any other translated materials for that matter, also go a long way, as well as dedicated smoking rooms or proper signage to indicate where guests can smoke.

In terms of actual marketing best practices, my conversation with Saunders shifted to the nature of internet usage in China and how its citizens source the web to determine their travel destination. Successful advertising and awareness efforts seem to be shifting away from conventional channels toward those that are peer-reviewed. Think blogs, dedicated travel websites and social networks that are different from those utilized elsewhere in the world.

Our chat concluded with a discussion of DaoDao.com, an online travel entity owned by TripAdvisor. Saunders warned that the website wasn't getting the traffic needed for critical mass because it didn't offer expert reviews, nor did it allow for users to post to their own personal blogs or syndicate to external addresses. As an alternative, Saunders advocates the newly launched XiaoYaoDao.cn, which specializes in expert reviews for popular destinations like New York City, with a rapidly expanding repertoire of appraisals.

Either way, what's vital to know here is that if you want to crack the Chinese outbound travel cipher, you must investigate these third-party review sites alongside other informal channels.

Larry Mogelonsky

The Rise of Indian Outbound Travel

Much attention has been given over the past few years to the rise of Chinese outbound tourism. And rightfully so, as the nation of roughly 1.35 billion souls has undergone profound urbanization and gentrification during the last three decades. Its burgeoning middle class now represents a consumerist powerhouse greatly influencing the future of worldwide tourism. I've written extensively on ways for hoteliers to capitalize on this, but now let's turn our attentions to another part of Asia – the Indian subcontinent.

As the globe's second most populous country, India, has experienced tremendous economic upheavals in recent years. In the flat and outsourced world we live in, this ageless and ethnically diverse democratic nation of 1.2 billion people now has a sizeable tech and telecommunications sector on top of its strong agricultural and manufacturing export industries.

A large economy and population are, however, not immediately synonymous with booming outbound tourism, and indeed there are many factors both for and against India immediately following China's lead in this regard. Rest assured, though, it's a country that hoteliers across the globe must pay attention to, and a thorough examination of present and future conditions will give managers a better idea of how best to approach this fast-growing travel market.

The Present

If I were to liken India to a person, it would be a future hall-of-fame linebacker in the middle of puberty – lots of haphazard growth with erratic hormonal fluctuations and nothing, as of yet, wholly solidified. It's the same with the clear majority of us in our adolescent years, when we are just starting to envision our full potential as we grow into young adults. Only in India's case, when the nation matures, it brings with it the world's largest democracy and over a billion potential consumers.

There's no question of India's growth, but it is still a country with strong ties to its agrarian past. India has deeply entrenched regionalism with numerous religions, languages and ethnicities slowing the road towards total economic synergy. Additional obstacles include a lack of appropriate infrastructure for trade, sluggish bureaucratic systems, corruption and widespread poverty. Since the liberalization of its monetary policies in 1991, however, India has been making consistent-yet-modest strides towards full-fledged free market capitalism, and not even the recent global financial downturn has had a lasting effect in stalling this advance.

Using 2014 as a comparison year, India had around 18 million departures, compared to 60 million from the United Kingdom, 68 million from the United States and just over 90 million from China. India is, however, the second fastest growing nation in gross numbers of outbound travelers behind only China. Nevertheless, according to recent research by the World Bank, India still has a few more glaring conditions which prevent it from reaching its full potential.

For starters, even though the internet has made enormous inroads in the major cities, where service, software and business outsourcing are now staple industries, the clear majority of the country has yet to log in. Less than 10% of homes have broadband access, while amongst the significantly smaller affluent and consumer classes, this statistic is close to reversed. This hiccup in ubiquitous internet adoption has caused further delays in the proliferation of social media usage as well as ecommerce via online travel agencies, which is further compounded by the fact that most Indians don't own a credit card.

All this means that the OTAs are mainly for 'looking rather than booking' with most travel transactions occurring via traditional travel agents, directly with an airline or through a corporate travel department. There are currently over 20,000 active agents throughout the country, but they are dispersed amongst many small tour companies rather than a select few consolidated operators like in the West.

These conditions are in sharp contrast to the largest urban centers where smartphones, social media and OTAs are already seeing extensive adoption with over 165 million active users as of 2014, most of them using Facebook with minor contributions from

Twitter, blogging and YouTube. In fact, this group of cities, which includes Bangalore, Chennai, Delhi, Hyderabad, Kolkata and Mumbai, corresponds to over 90% of recent outbound travelers. Amongst this demographic, the most popular booking websites include Cleartrip.com, Yatra, Travelocity, Expedia, Travelchacha.com, Travelguru.com and MakeMyTrip.

Aside from any internet barriers, the interests of traveling Indians are the same as those people from everywhere in the world. Shopping, sightseeing, museums, history, nightlife, amusement parks and ecotourism lead the pure leisure motivations, while visiting family and business remain as the top two overall. Note that most people departing India for business or a vacation are first-time travelers.

The foremost travel destinations are those within short-haul range – that is, less than a six-hour flight – including the Maldives, Singapore, Thailand, Malaysia, United Arab Emirates and Kuwait. Long-haul tourism – over six-hour flight time – is seeing sizeable growth to the United States, United Kingdom, South Africa, Australia, Indonesia, France, Italy, Switzerland and Canada due in large part to the greater capacity nowadays for low cost travel via the OTAs, even though visa issuing to these countries remains a primary obstacle.

The last key barrier to reaching and influencing outbound Indian travelers has to do with the country's strong indigenous hospitality brands. Unlike China, which lacked a commercial hotel industry for most of the 20th century due to its relative isolation under hardliner communist rule, India's domestic hotel brands are entrenched and thriving. This has prevented a full-blown conquest by the leading international entities, which in turn means it's harder for outside hotel companies to raise awareness and instill their brand values amongst Indian consumers. This hasn't necessarily affected outbound travel per se, only how consumers choose their properties.

The Future

By far the most critical trend affecting India is the rise of its consuming class, which is defined as having an annual household income of greater than $5,000 (US). McKinsey estimates that this largely urban middle class will break the 500 million mark by 2025. This growth in average earnings will translate into 50 million outbound tourists (if the rupee remains stable as a currency) as well as India overtaking the US as the second largest mobile market behind China. Concurrent to this will be further urbanization and recreational spending as well as the development of more secure credit card operations.

By 2025, India will be the world's fifth largest economy behind China, the US, Japan and the Germany. While the nation may have a plethora of Hindu dialects and other spoken languages – the millennia-old Sanskrit is still taught in schools – English is becoming the common go-between and the language of commerce. As with other progressions towards first world conditions, expect longer life spans amongst the Indian population, indicating that there will be an influx of senior travelers. Moreover, women will gain more equality both at home and at the office, translating to more influence in couples and family trip planning as well as more female travelers overall, both for business and leisure.

This economic prowess will also involve many psychographic shifts. As the Indian economy integrates with the rest of the world, we will see bolder vacation decision making to previously unsought long-haul destinations such as Spain, Turkey, China, New Zealand and Germany. Greatly influencing what locales emerge as popular will be direct flight access, or nonstop plus one stop, from India. In this sense, proximity will still be a ruling factor as such destinations will most likely correlate with cheaper costs for travelers and shorter visa-issuing times. All told, travel from India will amount to over $90 billion in worldwide travel expenses by 2030.

Social networks and smartphones will, of course, continue to flourish, with some estimates projecting over 280 million social media users by 2020, making both social shopping platforms and mobile advertising key promotional channels to help motivate consumers. Facebook will continue to be the dominant network, although niche sites such as Instagram and Pinterest will make headway as internet users mature. However, this shift to digital dependence won't be binary, meaning that traditional travel agents, print media, television and word of mouth will still play a central role in travel decisions.

What You Can Do

Caveat: there isn't much you can do to move your property's location – you are where you are. So, if you find yourself in a place where Indian travelers just aren't looking – refer to abovementioned hotspots – then there isn't all that much you can do. Sorry for being blunt, but your resources would be better allocated towards enticing other, more fruitful markets.

If you find yourself situated in a city or region where Indian travelers are or might soon be hankering to visit, then there are a few key efforts you can undertake to raise awareness and draw more eyeballs to lead to more sales down the road. To start, the Indian market is ginormous; you must focus your marketing and advertising efforts. My suggestion is to stick with the main urban centers listed above.

The crux of your efforts, though, will come through tactics in the digital realm. Your website should be the hub for all further activities and social networking. Once a potential guest finds you through a Google search, tourism agency, travel agent or OTA, if they're at all intrigued then they'll be very likely to click over to your brand. com to get a quick sense of your property. With Facebook rapidly solidifying its position as the foremost social site, I'd suggest you spruce this up, if you haven't already. As well, coherent English in all copy is a must.

On this note, targeted social media advertising campaigns present a viable option for reaching this audience, even though they've been proven to be less effective in internet-mature markets like the US or Western Europe. Ultimately, in my opinion, social media for India would best be utilized with the same philosophy as everywhere else – with content that adds value and gets the conversation rolling.

And there's no better form of rich content that facts, images and videos that help tell your property and your area's unique experience. Yes, just like everyone else across the globe, the Indian traveler craves the authentic. So, what makes you unique as a property? What gives your region identity? How can you demonstrate this to guests both onsite and online? Why should citizens of this country spend a minimum of eight hours cramped in an airplane to visit your area? With arguably the most flavorful food in the world, why should an Indian traveler care to try your local cuisine?

Answering these questions will not only help you with potential gains in awareness and sales from the subcontinent, but also from everywhere else. My advice: express your uniqueness and you'll be sure to come up winning either way.

Where Have the Real Hotel Marketers Gone?

In my role as hotel industry consultant, marketer and blogger, I am often asked to provide advice to hoteliers and suppliers. One such call came in a couple of weeks ago. The call's nature provides a keen insight into the current state of hospitality marketing.

The call was from an advertising agency that was tasked with the requirement of building a traditional media plan for a certain hotel chain. The amount was in the multi-millions of dollars, not small change given the meager amounts spent these days. I was asked – pro bono I might add – to see if I could give any recommendations.

My first questions were simple. Who is the target customer for this advertising? What was the message the ads were going to convey? And what were the goals or metrics for the campaign?

The response to my simple questions nearly floored me, and I quote, "[The chain] needs to demonstrate that they have some muscle and can support their franchise holders with visibility in the face of continued pressure from travel agencies. They did not give us any metrics, and the advertising message will be the same as last year's, focusing on their value proposition. They already have a terrific pay-per-click program, and that will remain."

At first blush, I applaud the chain's recognition that advertising is a necessary part of the successful business mix. I also understand the need to respect the needs of franchisees for some muscle or gravitas in the airwaves and in print. But is this the correct approach?

Clear and provocative ideas are the base for any campaign.

This is not a 'chicken or egg' situation. All advertising and promotions start with what you want to tell your customer. And these days, that had better be provocative! Whether in the case of this chain, where millions of dollars are being offered up, or an individual independent property with a much more limited expenditure, advertising is an investment in your brand. For that investment to show a return, there has to be a return, and that return only comes from generating awareness and interest. If this foundation is missing, the advertising will not deliver desire or, ultimately, purchase.

While I applaud the senior chain management in recognizing the need to build brand awareness through advertising, I would be giving two thumbs up to a program that not only had some visibility, but also some viable and provocative messages that would ring true to their target audience.

Who was he/she sleeping with?

Remember the Westin advertising of the early1990s? This very provocative selling line, coupled with some great creative development propelled their multi-media campaign and I suspect, delivered some huge awareness numbers for the corporation.

This was not just a summary of product features and benefits; the line pushed beyond everyday verbiage to communicate in a meaningful and memorable fashion. This work was done by a 'Madison Avenue' advertising agency, and I am sure that it took some brave soul in the Westin marketing department to stick his or her neck out in defiant support for the idea.

On a smaller, local level, I have seen numerous examples of hotels that have worked at differentiating their property through unique and highly differentiated advertising. Calling Google Adwords advertising is a misnomer. Yes, Google Adwords work and are important. But do not confuse this expenditure for advertising that builds authentically new awareness. Give me some of that good, old-fashioned, idea-centric advertising and this industry will be back on track to differentiating itself from the OTAs.

Keep in mind that even though I use the term 'old-fashioned', I am not opposed to the use of new media. Just look at the recent craze over the ALS Ice Bucket Challenge. It's a simple-yet-brilliant proposition that's fun for others to watch online and keeps all participants accountable. If you have an elegant idea like this, new media can make you an overnight sensation. But know that, as with most social network campaigns, it's all too easy to be drowned in mediocrity. At least with paid advertising, you can 'bribe' consumers for a piece of their time. Any way you slice it, though, you must be bold if you want consumers to remember you.

Planning for Next Year?

Marketing is not just responding to TripAdvisor comments, keeping your website or social media up to date, and buying the usual collection of search terms in Google Adwords. To be sure, all are valuable tactics, deigned to keep your property at the forefront of guest inquiries and bookings. But in themselves, they are little more than loose trajectories, 'diddles' in the face of a continually changing guest-centric, information-rich, OTA-driven environment.

I like to turn to warfare for analogies, and a marketing campaign consists of many battles and skirmishes, all in the name of pushing towards some grand overall objective. Solid advertising starts with strategies that are designed to deliver this stated grand objective, and from those strategies a tactical, on-the-ground and minute-by-minute plan emerges. Without big ideas and the operational fortitude to fully integrate these programs into the fabric of your property's persona, chances are this coming year will be more of the same at best.

So, I challenge you (throwing down the gauntlet so to speak) to look at this year as the year that marketing makes a difference for your property. If your team members put their minds to it and you lead them through motivation and resource allocations, I am confident of your success.

Thinking of the Low Season

The period running from January through to Spring Break is traditionally a bane for hotels in the Northern Hemisphere – unpleasant weather, low occupancies, depressed ancillary capture and fewer events to drive group business. This nadir, this 'low season', is also a constant puzzle for marketers; many strive for ever-more creative tactics to stir up reservations, while others write it off entirely and pray that the high tides of summer will compensate.

Alas, coping with the commercial pits of winter is not a modern phenomenon, and it is something that hoteliers have had to contend with since the dawn of our industry. As an interesting aside, the early Greeks and Romans didn't even consider January and February worthy of being called months. They simply called this period the *intercalaris* – meaning the time between calendar years – a period to batten down and simply endure the cold. Life for them began in March – named for Mars, the god of war, and the start of the warring season – and ended in December – its root the Latin word for the number ten.

Before this becomes nothing but a history lecture, let me pose the salient question of the hour: Is the winter low season something we must all simply endure, or can we transform it into a profitable period? While sun destinations are flying high, the rest of us are scrambling. Even if you're reading this early in the New Year, there are still ways for you to drum up new business during this time – or at least a few things to consider for next year's plan.

Before I provide some thought towards developing opportunities for individual travelers, a few words on groups. By January, your sales team should have delivered a solid book of base group business. This not being the case, you may wish to consider remedial promotional support programs, though I suspect that it might be too late. However, it's still worth a try.

Now on to individual travelers. As an opening salvo to this exercise, put yourself in the customer's shoes. Even though the holiday season is meant to be a respite from the daily bustle, this is often not the reality, and many people are still vying for an actual break during the *intercalaris*. Specifically, consider the numerous industries where the holidays are some of the busiest days of the year – restaurants, hotels, retail and airlines, for example – and extended time off is out of the question. Furthermore, in our modern 24/7 workplace, taking a full week off over the holidays is a luxury that only a rare few can afford, with many offices instituting staggered employee vacations so that there's always coverage.

In summary, never underestimate a consumer's desire for a quick getaway during the winter months. All marketing promotions and tactical executions should play on people's emotional need to restore and to get a deserved break that was previously unobtainable.

Trigger words may include 'getaway', 'escape' and 'pampering'. Given that New Year's resolutions are big this time of year, you can even go the opposite route and focus packages on fitness, wellness and healthy eating options. Then if you want to spur some traffic for midweek, consider activities and events as a rallying cry – exciting prix fixe menus, outdoor sports activities, spa specials, cooking nights, wine & cheese socials, sponsored tastings, even arts and crafts. A few of these can have overlap with your groups business if designed properly. This should make for a good start.

A Very TV Christmas

The holidays are a season of family get-togethers, sumptuous feasts and, increasingly, binge-watching your favorite TV shows. Yes, it's a great time to cozy up in your sweats and get swept away in hours upon hours of DVR, Netflix, Hulu, HBO or Amazon Prime, all but forgetting the world outside exists until the inevitable return to work come January.

Binge-watching, streaming and cord cutting are trends that are here to stay. It's a new way of absorbing the medium, and today's viewers watch what they want, when they want it, with the ability to pause and resume at any point. We live in an era of media access, not media ownership, after all, and streaming videos of any kind is an incredibly easy task. Indeed, filmmakers have even adjusted the way they use heightened serialization tell stories to accommodate this behavioral progression.

But viewing habits mostly affect the home front; what do they have to do with hotels?

Streaming and binge-watching aren't just a holiday season phenomenon. They're a 365-day event. Hence, there is a demand for hotels fitted with big screens and the latest smart boxes that can facilitate said habits. These devices are a guestroom amenity worth advertising. Two hypothetical situations help articulate this point.

First, picture yourself as a road warrior salesperson. The combined stresses of airport travel, networking conferences, seminars and back-to-back meetings can leave you with little to no personal time beyond a half hour at the end of the evening to unwind before going to sleep. Wouldn't it be great to know that when you finally returned to your guestroom, you could remotely log in to your preferred on-demand streaming service, access your own account and pick up exactly where you left off as if you were at home?

Next, imagine you are planning a family vacation with the hubby and two energetic children. In this case, smart TVs that can recall the kids' streaming profiles and their favorite shows are especially handy for mollifying the youngsters in between planned activities. Furthermore, such an amenity can act as a brief distraction or bedtime accessory while the parents sneak off for a romantic dinner downstairs or for a couples' treatment at the spa. Knowing that the children will never be bored or, worse, annoying you while you are trying to enjoy your vacation is a non-negligible emotional driver.

While upgrading a property's in-room TV capabilities is hardly revolutionary – and there are many options for hoteliers to consider in this regard – hotels still aren't doing enough to promote these amenities. The extent of attention given to them is often limited to a short string of text buried somewhere in a long, bullet point list of all the guestroom features, written in 12-point font.

Instead, given how widespread the demand for streaming services is, your newfound installations of smart TVs that let guests breezily access exactly what they want should be described in full on the appropriate website pages and social channels. Make sure this is something you express at the tail end of any package or promotional e-blast wherever it's appropriate to do so. It's but one more way to sell your guestrooms, and something to think about while you laze about your house over the break.

What's in the Super Bowl?

Are you ready for 'The Big Game'? As you may already be aware, marketers are not allowed to use the term 'Super Bowl' – it's trademarked. The far more generic 'Big Game' title is all we're left with.

All cynicism aside, this is a huge sporting event...at least in North America. And oftentimes, the best part about it isn't the actual sportsmanship but the television advertisements! In fact, the ads have become such an attraction that the blogosphere erupts post-game with critiques, commentary and rankings of what each company presented. It's a sink or swim world; producing a great TV spot for a brand often results in a lot of new eyeballs and viral dissemination, whereas a bad commercial can turn a company into a temporary laughing stock.

Additionally, as the Super Bowl becomes more and more popular in terms of annual viewership, the ad buys are likewise increasing in price – we're taking millions upon millions of dollars for the rights to 30 seconds of airtime. These bids show no signs of leveling off either because of rudimentary supply and demand. In a world where there are thousands of cable channels, ever-shrinking Nielsen ratings and more cord-cutting consumers every day, the Super Bowl is one of the last shops in town where you can broadcast a message to a crowd that is guaranteed to be in the seven-digit range or higher.

Knowing the realities of this trend, the obvious question is: why aren't hotel chains advertising during this Big Game? There is a palpable lack of hotel advertisements, except for the stellar work from the OTAs, and it is about damn time that changed!

While only the biggest of big chains would have the resources to spend the millions necessary for airtime rights and video production worthy of the waves, the real 'meat' of Super Bowl advertisements has by now migrated to the digital world. A good TV concept is merely the core of an extensive pre-and post-game campaign propagated through website, social, PPC, retargeting and other electronic channels. Of course, this should also tie in to an onsite promotion that adds a tangible, physical aspect to the mix.

But this confluence of traditional and electronic – no matter the channel distribution – all hinges on great ideas. And who's to say that you or another team member can't have a flash of genius instead of such brilliance only existing in plush Madison Avenue corner suites.

As the Super Bowl approaches, brief your team on this as a project for next year with no expectations for budget or strategy – only brainstorming with the sky as the limit. Then on game day, rest your eyes during the actual playing time and make sure your tunnel vision is fully set once the commercials come on. This will prime you for what types of concepts work and what will inspire you for the months ahead. Hopefully one or two ideas will click, and then you'll have plenty of time to craft an excellent campaign ready for early February of the following year.

Quick Ideas for Valentine's Day

As soon as the calendar flips to February, many of us switch into high gear as we motor towards the finish line that is the 14th of the month. Normally, the planning for Valentine's Day is either the first marketing activity of the New Year or the foundation is laid sometime in the fourth quarter. But if the end of January is looming and you're only just getting underway with this project, don't despair! There are still many tasks you can complete in the days leading up to the main event.

Each year presents an exceptional opportunity. As such, my first recommendation is that you institute a two-night minimum stay for that weekend. If you do not sell out on the Saturday, well, let's just say it's given that you will sell out on Saturday. So, this policy will ensure that the Valentine's bounties extend to both Friday and Sunday nights.

Building on this, look to design a romance package that stresses bonuses rather than discounts. Instead of slashing your price to encourage sales, throw in a few more value-adds or vouchers – a spa or F&B component is always acceptable here. Another lucrative opportunity exists if you partner with local retailers. Shopping is routinely a favorite Valentine's weekend activity, and together you can easily work out a redemption system whereby if couples spend above a certain threshold at a store, their savings could be worth more than the cost of the actual package!

Next up, welcome gifts help set the mood and, assuming they're memorable and unique to your region, distinguish your property. Organized couple's activities can likewise heighten guest satisfaction. Whatever onsite amenities you intend to provide for your guests in this regard, be sure to mention them upfront in the package copy so that consumers know exactly how far their dollars will go.

Lastly, even if it's getting late in the game, themed events are always crowd-pleasers. For a start, consider a fashion show, live music or a cooking class. Get creative! For instance, the InterContinental Hong Kong now offers Preserved Floral Arrangement Classes, and

I'm sure once you put your heads together you can think up several other exciting alternatives.

I hope this helps, both for last-minute planners and those looking to add a few flourishes to their romantic weekend experiences. To finish, as diligent Valentine's preparations can take a long time, bookmark this article for next year so you have it on file when you get underway.

A Valentine's Postmortem

By the Monday morning that follows your romance-themed weekend, the aura of a hopefully bountiful Valentine's Day will have passed and, with a pound of chocolate-covered strawberries still lodged in your small intestine, it will be time to assess your successes and your shortcomings for this holiday boon. Importantly, such evaluations should be rather illuminating; they will be quite handy when planning next February's big day or any other major celebration of this nature throughout the year.

Typically, I start with a year-over-year packages sold comparison. This is followed by a detailed assessment of the big dinner, starting with year-over-year average dollars sold by table, and then drilling down to each dish to see which were most popular, beverages – primarily an analysis of the alcohol sold – and turns. Beyond this, I drill down to any specific experimentation that was done with the holiday, any associated metrics and any ensuing qualitative feedback. It also doesn't hurt to take a quick peek at TripAdvisor or other popular websites to see if there were any specific comments. That's it in its simplest form. Do you measure your results differently?

These sorts of rudimentary analyses will help you deliver a more satisfying (and hopefully lucrative!) Valentine's Day but my hope is that you can apply any accrued insights towards far greater purposes. Primarily, you should look to imbue a year-round romantic getaway package as well as your weddings business with the lessons learned from your February experiments. The apt question here is: How can you make every weekend just as special as Valentine's Day?

Obviously, most of this application must be considered on a property-by-property basis. One general suggestion I can make, which has seen substantial success in the past, is that you look to 'prix fixe' your package offerings. By this I mean that you should aim to hide the prices of individual line items inside one holistic fee, and then express all the promotion's features in elaborate detail.

Stray away from discounts – this should only be a last-minute tactic. Instead, focus on a superior price standpoint to elevate your brand with a glut of included features so that guests don't focus so much on the cost but on the benefits and the outstanding experience they will have. Making the package available only through direct contact with the property enhances margins through the obvious elimination of sales commissions. So, ask yourself how you would 'prix fixe' an ongoing package at your property and no doubt this will lead you in fruitful direction.

Officially on to Summer

Each year after Memorial Day, we find ourselves unofficially entering the summer travel season. Even though the technical start of summer falls more in line with the June solstice that describes our celestial positioning, the long weekend at the end of May serves as a better marker – the weather is amiable and that extra day off work helps justify a lengthy road trip.

But I'm not here to discuss Memorial Day. I'm here to talk about Memorial Day kicking off a whole season and a paradigm shift in how you do business. What do you have planned for the summer in terms of events, promotions, packages or new amenities? To simplify this a touch, what is your USP for this summer? What's that one cool thing that will linger in people's minds and get them talking?

The buzz word that applies here is glanceability, describing in an explicit portmanteau not only what a foremost goal should be for your property this season, but also the mindset of many consumers looking for a quick summer escape. Basically, if your property is 'glanceable' it means that there is some exceptional quality that draws the eye and makes people curious about what you're offering.

This is also often explained as the marketing equivalent of an elevator pitch, imagining that you only have the time in an elevator to make an impression on a stranger. I place this at around 10 seconds for actual, person-to-person meetings, although I have seen some sources go as high as 25. In the age of the internet of things and rapidly shrinking attention spans, though, I would optimistically put a digital elevator pitch between one to four seconds. That's right; if your hotel or resort doesn't raise consumers' blood within milliseconds, you've got problems!

If we are to think in terms of milliseconds, then it becomes clear that your pitch to prospective buyers should be visual, firstly, and any text should be brief and to the point. Moreover, unless you are talking serious slashes on your rates, and likely cutting into your margins, big numbers in flashing red won't work, as the modern consumer is wise to these tricks – they see them all the time and know what's a good deal.

What's important to remember with glanceability is that a person's logic centers – that is, higher brain functions – cannot respond within milliseconds to a stimulus. Hence, for something to be glanceable, it must appeal to one's emotions – the older, primordial parts of the brain. The phrase 'a picture is worth a thousand words' is a direct reflection of this, as images stir up thoughts in our heads long before our conscious interpretative nerve pathways have time to kick in.

As it turns out, your USP is your best shot at making your property glanceable because what's most unique about your abode is also what others cannot imitate, and therefore it's something consumers haven't seen before...or at least very often. Find that extraordinary quality, whatever it is, and express it through vivid photography or snappy headlines.

As for summer itself, start mapping out what to expect week-over-week and month-over-month. What events do you have booked? What are you doing to differentiate incoming leisure and business travelers? What are you doing that's special for the other long weekends or holidays that fall between the beginning of the season and Labor Day?

To end off, let me leave you with one broad idea I've introduced before time – the prix fixe vacation. We are all familiar with the concept of a prix fixe dinner. The psychology behind it is quite simple: give people a few choices within a preset selection so that they can express their individuality while not being overwhelmed by the multitude of true options.

We've seen this work on numerous occasions in restaurants, often attached to an easy-to-comprehend price tag to further reduce sales objections. A nice round figure combined with the guided nature of a prix fixe menu can make for an especially carefree experience that reduces the stress associated with decision making and enhanced dining overall.

Adapting this concept to a vacation or sightseeing itinerary might include a narrow selection of day trips that mix guided excursions, meals and transportation. Imagine a package where you offer a two-night stay with one complimentary 'day of adventure' including lunch and dinner as well as a selection of afternoon activities: guest's choice of touring local attractions, a winery or brewery tour, nature hike, guided shopping excursion, fishing trip, historical jaunt, surfing – essentially, whatever your area does best.

A model example of this I recently had a chance to explore further is the Fogo Island Inn which, due to its remote location off the coast of Newfoundland, cannot survive on a laissez faire, let-the-guests-do-whatever-they-want approach. Instead, the property embraces its natural location and has packaged together an assortment of day-long adventures including such esoteric jaunts as iceberg watching and orientations at local fisheries.

What other examples of prix fixe vacations or prix fixe adventures can you cite? Remember that it's all about maximizing the guest's journey while also minimizing travel anxiety and creating a rich experience that's unique to your setting.

Larry Mogelonsky

From Mayday to Labor Day

When you're heading into spring each year, you recognize that summer, and summer travel, is right around the corner. Although the official start of this sizzling season doesn't kick off until the end of the month, with the way global warming is going, the beginning of May is rapidly edging out that much-vaunted gap between too chilly and unbearably hot. Hence, if you begin with Mayday, that gives you four months of great weather until the summer vending machines close around Labor Day.

Note that this is coming from a North American perspective. If you live in the Southern Hemisphere, consider these ideas for when your summer creeps in around late October. And if you live in the tropics, where seasonal fluctuations are as palpable as the taste of rum in your next strawberry daiquiri, take what you can from this article and think kind thoughts for every hotelier suffering under the whims of the Earth's orbit.

For those of you in the north, as soon as the maypole's down, it's time to lacquer the deck chairs and lather on some sunscreen, and by that, I mean you had better get underway with the strategy and execution of your summer packages and promotions. If Memorial Day is looming and you haven't started this task, don't panic; the horns have blown but the ship hasn't sailed...yet.

When planning for summer travel and designing offers for incoming guests, undoubtedly you can look at year-over-year performance, and then make polishing adjustments to the previous round's iterations. If it isn't broke, why fix it, right? This is a solid strategy as it requires less effort to execute and you already know roughly how successful you are going to be.

But regurgitating past performances and expecting a repeat or better on revenues is a foolhardy attitude in today's travel world. More so than ever before, emphasis is being placed on unique experiences, both from the consumer as well as the corporate end. The trend is moving away from the safety of repetition and into the novel. The internet has opened people's eyes to a world filled with exceptional opportunities, so much so that no one wants to do the same thing twice because there are so many other experiences just around the corner.

If you haven't thought of this already, your task is to reflect upon your property and discern what it does best or what is does which is different from all other hotels or resorts in the area. In other words: what's your elevator pitch? Convince someone that they simply MUST come to your property in one sentence or less.

Once you have this in your head, apply it to your summer getaway or business travel packages. That is, what is your one great or exceptional feature, outside of monetary discounts, that will entice even the most fanciful consumers?

A related buzz word that I'm reminded of here is 'Hotelfie', which is a clever portmanteau of 'hotel' and 'selfie'. Once you've gotten over any initial millennial chagrin, it's important to ruminate on the importance of this word. Being part of the trending lexicon indicates that it is indeed popular for guests to take pictures of themselves at hotels. From there you can ask yourself: what makes your property picture-worthy? What unique features will compel a guest to put himself or herself in a photo with your property as the backdrop?

And aside from your pitch, you should make sure you are in the right elevator to begin with! That is, you should know your core markets, your prime demographics and your most enthused psychographics before you start talking.

Personally, I'm excited to see what bears fruit with each new summer season. It is a great time for experimentation, both in terms of new promotions and what crowds you attempt to please. Change is the new norm, and so you must institute at least one novel program to solidify your core or stretch your market appeal lest you are hopelessly underprepared for consumer behaviors for years to come.

Be a Mother to Your Team

Every May we celebrate the women who have cared for us, nurtured us, pampered us, nagged us, educated us, clothed us, fed us and smothered us all the way from infancy until well into adulthood. My own mother passed away over a decade ago, and since that time, I've played a supporting role for my two kids in their annual attempts to make my wife feel special for a day before reverting to their typical independent and apathetic millennial selves.

Mother's Day isn't what it used to be, though. To start and finish this subject matter, in my experience your mother would best be served with a big hug and appreciation on the other 364 days of the year in addition to a little something nice one Sunday in May. Yet, nowadays this day rolls around and we are bombarded by thousands of internet articles instructing us on the best ways to impress our moms, most methodologies involving some sort of, often sponsored, monetary purchase. In other words, it's been hijacked by the gods of capitalism.

Not that that's a bad thing. In fact, I'm a firm believer in a wholesome Mother's Day promotion for your hotel, often involving a nice prix fixe meal or a spa package. But taking on the perspective of the consumer, it's easy to see how this can all turn into an annoyance. It's the ugly side of 'white noise' all over again; if everyone's doing it – promoting their Mother's Day specials, that is – then it's a bombardment of many similar things all hitting the customer's eyeballs around the same time. This makes it harder for any individual entity to truly stand out.

With that said, I hope that the Mother's Day promotion you have designed is both traditional in structure and includes a few exceptional features that highlight your property and its area. If it's the Friday before, it's a tad late in the game to build and market a promotion for something two days away, so spend some time ruminating on what you are going to do for this year's Father's Day. For that, my only advice: think barbecue.

Instead of offering up a few tips and tricks to assist with your Mother's Day sales to customers, this time around I'd like to focus on the idea of being a 'mother' to your team. When you consider yourself in this light, what responsibilities might that role imply?

To start, being a 'mother' means to think of your staff as more than just a team, but a part of your hotel family. In this sense, Mother's Day becomes an opportunity to celebrate your hotel family and all the joy that it has brought. As mothers, you must love your employees (your children) even in some of their darker moments. Moreover, you should respect their desire to learn, grow and spread their wings, rewarding them with new challenges and responsibilities when they are ready. This holiday is an opportunity not only for pleasing guests, but to build team rapport and enthusiasm for the job.

And this affinity can be built through seemingly innocuous Mother's Day gestures that show you care. Think candies or chocolate for sweet sustenance, or flowers, which are always pleasant on the senses, inspiring creativity and elevating the mood. Make it a surprise for added effect. Purchase a few entertaining coffee books for the break room or a quality coffeemaker with espresso and cappuccino functionality. To take it a step further, arrange for a group wine tasting or a team movie night.

I'm just spit balling here, but the general idea here is to treat your team like you would a member of your family, or like you would your own mother. Because if you do, then they will return the favor by treating their jobs with the utmost professionalism for the other 364 days of the year.

Father's Day All Summer Long

As the third in the triune of hallmark holidays which also includes Valentine's Day and Mother's Day, Father's Day is easily the most subdued and the least elaborate.

Catering to its audience, most themed events or promotions are linked to popular summer activities and shared family experiences. These activities are especially fitting as the holiday is so close to the summer solstice, which means the most heat and the most sun for outdoor adventures. (It also means that technically the number of hours of daylight are in decline from here out, but don't let that depress you; we still have plenty of summer left to come.)

If you're reading about Father's Day two days beforehand, it's a tad late to start brainstorming ideas and putting promotions together from scratch, even for only a few last-minute sales. What you can do, however, is attempt to fully explore the question of 'What do Dads want?' and make that an undercurrent of any family-oriented packages up for grabs over July and August.

In this sense, think of Father's Day as a thought experiment where you are attempting to distill the essence of the holiday, then apply it to the rest of summer – and not just in the form of promotions but also in terms of F&B additions, poolside additions, equipment rentals and even potential room upgrades. So, what does the old man imagine as the perfect Father's Day?

As was alluded to above, this hallmark holiday should be one that maximizes both family fun and the enjoyment of summer. The first two archetypal thoughts pertain to sports and barbecue – all dads have a soft spot for one team game or, at the very least, some juicy, charred meat. Dwelling on these, do you have a summer BBQ menu as a part of the overall F&B program? Have you considered arranging for outdoor cooking classes? Moreover, are you hosting any sports-related events? What sports can be played onsite? How do you provide for league play or tournaments? Do you sell sportswear in the gift shop or rent equipment to accommodate spur-of-the-moment guests?

Next to mind, and most significant, is the all-encompassing term of 'shared family experiences'. These can be adventures both urban – sightseeing tours, museum trips, shopping excursions or lounging poolside – and rural – camping trips, exploring the countryside, water sports or nights around an open fire. What's key here is for you to make it an adventure for everyone involved, but one that comes with a prearranged itinerary – the family gets the rush of venturing into the unknown, without the stress of having to plan from scratch or jumble important details.

Of course, as I can personally attest, if the mother is happy then the father generally is, too. The summer is about relaxation and what better way to enjoy just that than with your loved one. To this end, extending the undertones of this holiday for all of summer should prudently include couples-oriented activities, something to do with the spa and perhaps a little romantic enabler sprinkled in here and there.

To conclude this scribbling, Father's Day is also a good time to look back at Mother's Day, Valentine's Day and any other occasionally celebrated hallmark holiday such as Children's Day, Siblings Day or Parents' Day. A reflection of sorts that should yield valuable insights for next year's events. What are your performance measurements? How can they be used to forecast for next year? Do you have any programs or aspects of a program that are in the trial run phase? If not, do you have any that you've considered but never had the time to implement?

Yes, as it's the summer solstice, daylight hours will be decreasing minute by minute with each passing day. But that also means we are one day closer to next year's holidays. Not to say that you should entrench yourself in planning right now, but you should start writing down rough ideas so you have a strong starting point when you commence activities of this sort sometime during the upcoming winter months.

Larry Mogelonsky

So Ends Summer, So Starts the Shoulder Season

The summer months will always be primetime for leisure vacations. But as we continue to break down the rules of traditional travel behaviors, the months straddling the summer on either end are rapidly becoming highly sought-after getaway blocks and not just stretches where only the businessperson ventures worth.

Heightened shoulder season travel makes sense, after all. Summer is peak season, which often means peak prices. As well, many of us in northern climates choose to stay home during the hotter months and enjoy the fruits of our backyards – gardening, barbecues, pool parties and so on. Specifically, for Canadians, many of us prefer the weekend cottage commute over top of an outright destination vacation.

But there's a key demographic shift that is helping this trend proliferate – the maturation of the baby boomers, myself included. As we age, we are accruing more disposable wealth via more senior job titles or pension dispersals in addition to more free time as we retire, downsize our workloads or 'empty the nests'. All this amounts to more time and money to devote to experiential travel as well as getaways that are far away from the kids.

So, right off the bat, when it comes to shoulder season, you must know your audience. If summer, spring break and the holiday season are for families, the shoulder seasons are for couples, be they seniors, retirees or even younger, childless pairs. As such, tailor your message to be more adult-oriented, with a sharp focus on mature attractions like museums and historical sites, shopping, sports, wellness and high-end dining.

Particularly as it concerns baby boomers, appeal to their desire for 'badge travel' instead of dedicated relaxation and restoration. Boomers have already been around the world and spent their fair share on material goods. What they seek now are unique experiences to check off their bucket lists. This is, of course, building on the de rigueur theme of 'authentically local'.

Ask yourself what badge your property offers? Is it an unsurpassed golf course or an utterly gorgeous ocean-facing vista?

Perhaps your restaurants are out-of-this-world and you complement this with truly outstanding staff. Or maybe you neighbor a prime destination for ecotourism and you offer packages for consumers to fully take advantage of this proximity.

Whatever it may be, distill what is most exceptional about your property, and then advertise it as a prestigious 'badge' that guests must attain rather than yet another property feature buried within a long list. Tell your narrative in such a way that you help the mature consumer picture himself or herself having a fully immersive 'event' at your hotel. Make your property stand out with a remarkable guest experience and watch the shoulder season months become some of your most successful times of year!

Embrace the Weird

In the past, I've talked about what you can do to create excitement around the mainstay holidays. For North Americans, these include Thanksgiving, Christmas, Valentine's Day, St. Patrick's Day, Father and Mother's Day, Easter, Memorial or Victoria Day, Independence or Canada Day, Labor Day and, yes, Halloween. I'd highly suggest you get a plan together for some or all of them.

But these common holidays raise a profound marketing question: if every hotel is working on some form of promotion or event for these abovementioned celebrations, how do you stand apart? It's like when you are at a Halloween party, having slaved for hours over your unique costume design only to discover that someone else is decked out with the exact same outfit. Aside from the candy, alcohol consumption and other debauchery, Halloween is all about individual expression. So, how would you feel if others were wearing similar costumes?

Thinking about this on a macro-scale, it's easy to see why perhaps your Christmas, Valentine's or Halloween promotions have fallen flat. It isn't that you aren't being creative or haven't put in enough effort; it's that too many other properties have also applied their resources to the task, diluting your returns. And the doom and gloom here is that there is almost nothing you can do – Christmas will always be Christmas and Halloween will continue to be the biggest costumed event of the year.

Again, I ask: how do you stand out? One way you can stir up some extra revenues is by embracing the weird or offbeat holidays that remain largely untouched by your comp set. Like everything, though, this is easier said than done, so here are a few tips to make sure you are selecting the correct eclectics for your hotel:

Think Local

What holidays or festivals do your local constituents already celebrate? Is there any way you can become a community leader by working with them and propagating their traditions and culture? This may just be the ticket to boosting your relationships with local vendors and suppliers to wondrous results in both cross-promotion and SEO.

Match Your Theme

International Talk Like a Pirate Day doesn't exactly mesh if you are an upscale boutique hotel in Midtown Manhattan, but it may well fit if you are a beachside Floridian or Dominican resort. Almost every day of the year is peppered with these bizarre or almost completely unknown celebrations. Search and scrutinize – you need only discover one or two that are the right match.

Find Your Food

Many of these pseudo-holidays are in fact food related, and so they present an opportunity for your chefs to excel. For instance, what if on National Ice Cream Day your culinary team decided to hand out free samples of house-made gelato in the lobby in a trio of exciting flavors (please, anything but the perfunctory chocolate, vanilla or strawberry). Likewise, there are days to honor coffee, beer, vegetarianism and, as any good Canuck will attest to, bacon.

Engineer the Fun

The key to any such holiday celebration is to put your full support behind it and get your team involved. Employees should be on the ground as wells as any participating guests. Let them take a few minutes out of their shift to come see all the excitement, sample what your chefs have crafted and socialize with one another in a relaxed environment. This will not only increase morale, it will heighten the sense of joy that all others experience.

Larry Mogelonsky

Gray is the New Green: The Marketing Gap

As someone active in the marketing and advertising world for almost 40 years, what I'm about to describe is not something I'm particularly proud of. Now that the millennials have officially surpassed the boomers in sheer numbers, it's become a trend to treat the latter group as a 'dying generation'. And from this has emerged the outlook that marketing slogans and campaigns attempting to appeal to boomers should focus on the motifs of retirement, aging and health.

While these three themes are on the back of most boomers' minds, they are hardly the foremost thoughts as we go about our days. Many of us are at the peaks of our careers, working to our wits' ends and still with a fervent passion to propel the world forward via whatever labor specialization or hobby we have perfected over the years. We boomers may be in decline numbers-wise, but we are not going down without a fight – our wallets and purses are our weapons!

If you look at most advertisements out there right now, there appears to be a binary split in what demographics are being targeted. On the one hand, ads are likely to portray young, attractive couples being active or the perfect family with two kids and parents in their forties. On the other are ads aimed at the elderly, which are quite morbid, with actors in their eighties or nineties often depicted as feeble and in need of assisted living.

Lest we forget, the graying of the boomers does not mean the death of the boomers. Where are the ads that appeal to people in between these two groups? What about those of us who are bald and saggy skinned yet still make it to the office by 9am every day? Something in the ad world is out of sync.

I'm not saying that there is a complete absence of promotional materials directed at the still-active boomer, but the ads I do see are seldom representative of where most boomers are in life. There is indeed a marketing gap between old and young insofar as the trend to interpret 'old' as 'geriatric' means that few campaigns target those of us who are still a few years away from an 8pm bedtime. Rather than leave this as a rant, however, it's best to interpret it as an opportunity for you and your organization to push ahead in your pursuit of boomers' wallets.

Yes, the millennials are a larger group by population, but nowhere near so when tabulated based on accumulated wealth. In that regard, boomers are still winning. Moreover, now that the kids have moved out and their college tuition payments are hopefully almost finished, we boomers are looking to take our excess cash and allocate it towards living life to the fullest with unique experiences to fill our days. Many prominent measurement agencies like Nielsen would have you believe that the primary focus of advertisement should be the 'prime' ages of 18 to 49, and yet I argue that this system is biased against new marketing prospects that fall outside of this range.

We boomers are ravenous consumers and retirement, when it happens, simply presents another chance to spend. Retirement means more travel time. When you realize that a trip might be your last to that location, splurging on a better room or a suite seems like a minor indulgence.

When designing your marketing materials for baby boomers, you must put yourself in the mindset of an active person between the ages of 55 and 75. This presents a tricky situation from the point of view of the hotel as no brand wants to appear old. As any marketer will tell you, it's a fine line to tread.

Think about who the boomers are. We are not frail, but strong in our wisdom and experience. We relish making hard business decisions and delight in a busy world. For most of us, the prospect of outright retirement at age 65 is now a pipedream, and so we look to be useful to society in more ways than just breathing and eating.

Larry Mogelonsky

Gray is the New Green: Old School Advertising

When was the last time you took a serious look at a traditional advertising campaign, by which I mean print (newspapers and magazines), broadcast (radio and television) and outdoor (billboards, bus shelters and posters)?

Given that we are well into the digital age, you may be under the belief that advertising has moved exclusively into the online domain, where automated programs such as Google Adwords, retargeting and SEO programs dominate. With traditional dissemination continuing to subside in perceived value year-over-year, many have come to rely solely on digital channels, which allow for smaller, ad hoc budgets and more direct monitoring. While electronic promotions' efficacy is not in dispute, the mass departure from traditional media has opened an opportunity for those who are game to re-enter the fold.

In other words, go where others are not to stand apart from the herd.

This Sunday, if you don't get your newspaper home-delivered, go to the local market and pick up a copy. Chances are you are not the only one who is still in the habit of spending a good portion of their Sunday morning glancing at the paper. We all know that newspaper ad revenue is declining due to decreasing readership. But if you're buying ad space for your hotel, you're purchasing eyeballs, not just trends.

Newspapers may be down, but they are hardly out! And if your target audience approximates that of the newspaper's circulation plan, why not consider it? I argue that many boomers have migrated away from printed materials, but many more have yet to do so.

For example, your property is in the northeastern part of the country. Your book of group business leaves definite midweek occupancy gaps – a perfect opportunity to fill with FITs. The ideal candidate guests are retired adults. After all, their kids have left the nest and those who are not snowbirds are looking for things to do. These just happen to be the same folks who are regularly perusing the newspaper. Promoting a getaway through traditional advertising should be a consideration.

Going 'old school' will take some getting used to. Concepts such as creative design, media buying, negotiation and placement are skills that will need to be dusted off. Chances are that your contemporary digital ad agency doesn't have the experience in this communications segment. You'll need to seek help from freelancers or specialists. But do not be deterred, as progress often comes from reinvention. And in this sense, the old school has become the new school!

But don't just run one ad and pass judgement on potentially thin results. Experience suggests that a typical frequency should be no less than three times in any single print media. Radio and television media buying is different than print but follows a similar strategic focus on reach and frequency.

The math suggests a three times frequency of a $5,000 ad will require an investment of about $16,500 once creative design is factored in. Say you have a two-night package at a promotional rate of $200, with a 75% contribution on accommodations. This means you'll have to book 55 packages to break even. If the publication's readership is 250,000, your breakeven conversion rate is well below 0.01%.

With those odds, a test program is clearly in order. However, there's also an intangibility factor at play – those people who interact with your ad but do not purchase. In the electronic space this is more easily measured in terms of reach or impressions, whereas in traditional mediums the statistics are not quite as exact. While it's always good for the ego to have a high conversion rate, never forget the advertising axiom pertaining to share of voice. By reinvigorating your old-school channels, you are competing for voice share on a whole other plane than most of your competitors.

Better to investigate your options now so that you can have the leg up by the time everyone else awakens to the renewed potential of traditional advertising.

Larry Mogelonsky

Gray is the New Green: The Luxury Boomer

I have written on this topic since August of last year, but as the grand horde of boomers among us continues to gradually work their way into retirement, this topic is once again worth addressing. Normally when we discuss retirement, we talk about the nuances of balancing a tighter budget with far fewer inbound monetary streams to buoy any excessive spending. In short, retirement at a macro level means less spending overall.

However, the baby boom presents a fascinating counterargument to this established demographic trend. That is, the boomers, at least in a North American sense, came into the world right at the zenith of American corporate hegemony, meaning that the salaries, stipends, bonuses and pensions accrued are greater on average than those doled out to members of the Greatest Generation or Gen X. In many cases, what we are left with is a retired boomer who – even after paying the full load of a son or daughter's college tuition and putting up the capital for said kid to move out of the basement – still has the dispensable funds for self-discovery.

This 'luxury boomer' or 'one-percenter' populace is rife with retired or semi-retired individuals in search of all the same brand qualities that appeal to wealthy Gen Xers or millennials. Moreover, their ample cash has afforded them the time and money to keep in touch with technology, meaning that said boomers are frequently proficient with smartphones, tablets, social media and any other popular tech. As well, you must consider the idea of an increased 'health span' relative to the rest of the population. That is, with surplus cash has come the ability to seek out healthier lifestyle options, meaning that overall wellness increases even as one ages.

The luxury boomer is an individual undergoing a renaissance of sorts with the vigor, means and desire for a bolder hotel experience. Such people are looking for self-discovery, which, if you recall your Maslow's Hierarchy of Needs, correlates to self-actualization phase at the top of the pyramid. Hence, I'd call boomer-appealing lifestyle brands 'self-actualization brands' as this term gives a better hint at what this demographic craves.

In fact, there are already quite a few brand entrants capitalizing on the notions of lifestyle and boutique hospitality with specific features and services to attract members of the luxury boomer class. Such titillating service features broadly pertain to personalization, surprise, flexibility and integrated activities.

The objective for luxury boomers is to create a sense of royalty. They are looking to bring home an experience — bragging rights so to speak. However, discussing this in a general sense won't give you a definitive clue as to what these one-percenters are after, so here are some specifics to get you started:

1. **Functional concierge:** adept at swiftly arranging for tickets, transportation, reservations or access any other trendy locale.

2. **Access to excellent food:** taste and smells are two senses that can also deliver exceptional experiences, so be sure to have great in-house food offerings as well as a handy mental rolodex of the newest Michelin-rated eateries or local joints with niche, esoteric or quintessential-to-a-certain-nationality cuisine.

3. **Private tours:** still wanting to see the most popular tourist attractions but wanting to do so in style and to the beat of their own drum.

4. **Late checkout and early check-in:** guests will appreciate your efforts to accommodate their idiosyncratic travel schedules, especially with concern to long transcontinental flights whereby one gets to the airport at 7pm and doesn't arrive at the hotel until 10am the following day (read: grumpy and in need of a clean bed).

5. **Free high speed internet:** no one likes to be nickeled and dimed, not even the wealthy.

6. **Welcome or departure gifts**: this falls under the purview of 'surprise' whereby you are exceeding expectations and creating another point of interaction with the brand.

7. **Shopping:** this activity can be enhanced through a designated shopping concierge, improving relationships

with local vendors, in-room samples, guidebooks or a host of other methods, all aimed at increasing the accessibility to local wares.

8. **Where everybody knows your name:** isn't it always nice to return to your hotel and find not only are the staff members friendly but they know a little bit about you and your purpose of travel?

Gray is the New Green: Appealing to the Go Go Generation

A recent newspaper articled dedicated to the financial requirements of retirees proposed a treatise on the matter with three key phases:

- The first was defined as **'Go Go'** where the individual, as if making up for lost time, was perpetually traveling to compensate for all those years raising a family and building a career.
- The middle phase was called **'Go Slow'** with said individual still traveling, but typically at a more reserved pace and on a localized basis.
- With a profound sense of melancholy, the last stage, the **'No Go'** travel era, characterized those who were restricted or unable to explore the globe, mainly for medical reasons.

For the hotelier, the 'Go Go' generation represents a significant business opportunity, and the best of these three late-life phases. These are potential guests who are literally itching to get out and discover new things. Free of kids and other serious obligations, you should consider these individuals as a primary leisure target audience. To put some better definition to the core of this demographic, think of them as:

- Typically, in their early sixties through mid-seventies
- Retired, obviously, but still active
- In good health for their age and attuned to the need for physical upkeep
- College educated yet seeking new knowledge and inspiration
- Both urban and suburban, but not typically rural
- Own a car and prepared to drive to a destination
- Adventurous, but not in an overly strenuous way
- More traditional in reading and viewing habits
- Will opt for a midweek leisure trip to avoid weekend crowds

- Will often travel with other Go Go couples
- Food and wine are key criteria as they tend to dine where they stay
- Familiar and responsive to promotional offers

Many hotels are missing the boat insofar as reaching out to this narrow slice of baby boomers. In a sales vernacular, these individuals are 'low hanging fruit'. In looking at leisure segment marketing, consider restricting your offers to midweek or low occupancy periods. In case you need to hold a blowtorch to your marketing team's finely coiffed hair, here are some ideas to package:

- Cooking demonstrations
- Local area antiquing (with a map developed)
- Wine tastings and/or winery tours
- Shopping, especially niche or off-the-beaten-path boutiques
- Book club activities or readings
- Outdoor activities
- History tours or guided excursions of local interest

Insofar as creating awareness for your promotions, consider adding some traditional media to the mix. Your marketing team may show reluctance as the KPIs for newspaper and radio are harder to measure over Google Adwords. But give it a try and see what you can deliver...you never know how successful this will be until you try!

Gray is the New Green: Technological Ageism

Ageism has always been a part of our social fabric, but whereas in the past it was standard to venerate the old for their experience and sagacity, nowadays the situation has been flipped somewhat due to the rapid proliferation of technology. With all the new devices, new media and new apps, it has become increasingly difficult for those who are proverbially 'set in their ways' and without young, sponge-like brains to keep up.

Much like how we abridge complex social stratifications into 'the have and the have-nots', we are likewise experiencing a generational movement about 'the techies and the tech-nots'. For those who were born into a world where the internet and social media were already ubiquitous aspects of our environment – circa 1985 and later – most digital interactions are readily intuitive. For instance, a tail-end millennial or post-millennial may not know how to code HTML, but give them an hour and they'll be able to source some great tutorial websites off Google to learn and write a few basic tricks. Infants these days know how to swipe an iPad even before they know how to talk for God's sake!

Although there are technology-literate boomers amongst us, when considering the entire population in the first world, the trend line shows a strong inverse relationship between age and electronic fluency. Even though I would like to subscribe myself to the minority of boomers who are 'with it', it still takes me far longer to grasp the same new concepts and developments that my juniors understand almost instantaneously. And therein lies an opportunity for you to more effectively target and service your elderly clientele.

Technological ageism presents itself in three main areas of guest interaction – sales channels, relationship channels and onsite. Boomers still respond to print advertisements, and they will dismiss expectations to use Twitter for guest service in favor of a physically talking to an actual staff member. Despite any technological differences amongst the generations, though, they still have a ton in common. Everyone is in search of new experiences and adventure, and we are looking to our chosen hospitality provider to treat us with the proper level of respect that dollars command.

Accounting for this technological ageism should nevertheless be a top consideration for all advertisements, hotel websites, social networks, on-property devices and staff training. Part of this 'respect' also means having empathy for those who are not digitally fluent, being patient with them and providing them with a few 'luddite' options.

To conclude, here are a few ways to better market to and satisfy those among us who are not necessarily up-to-snuff with all the latest technological advancements:

- Perform a boomer-specific user experience audit for your website (desktop, tablet and mobile), reviewing color selection, font size, navigational simplicity and other elements
- Recognize how elderly guests are most likely to find your hotel and book a room so that you can design the best possible sales funnels for both customer satisfaction and upselling
- Focus test the broad touch points of your advertising to determine if the appeal is on target
- Stay up-to-date with the latest research on what channels your target demographic use
- Understand the differences in how each generation provides feedback
- Refine your on-property experience so that it implies adventure and a sense of discovery without skewing too young
- Appeal specifically to boomers with onsite nuances that may go unappreciated by millennials
- Ensure that your staff are properly trained to good-naturedly explain how any in-room devices work – like, for example, setting up WiFi
- Many of those 'tech-nots' may be embarrassed to ask for help, so educate your team on how to attentively broach this topic

Gray is the New Green: Boomer Entitlement

With the premiere of latest Star Wars movie – possibly the most influential film series ever and one of the only franchises that pervades all living generations – it seems only appropriate that we discuss an issue related to both the young (millennials) and the old (boomers).

As a start, consider how bad a rap millennials have gotten from employers these days. They are often described as selfish, narcissistic, needy, lazy, tardy, prone to complaining, hedonistic and a slew of other negative attributors. The fashionable umbrella term for all this is 'entitlement'. Many of us in senior positions hold the perspective that millennial workers feel as if they are entitled to bypass the perfunctory, stripe-earning phase of their careers and that certain liberties apply to them because they are ostensibly fluent with modern technology.

The entitlement of the millennial workforce is a hot topic, but does it also work the other way around? That is to say, just because you are older, does that automatically bestow upon you certain privileges?

Many boomers would like to think so! But alas, age does not directly correlate with wisdom. When it comes to running a hotel, managing operations and adeptly marketing your inventory to the world, no one cares how old you are; they only care about how hard you work and whether you can get the job done.

Where I've seen this crop its ugly head the most is when discussions turn to modern customer behavior, specifically that of the younger demographics. To succinctly sum it up: the internet has changed the way everyone thinks about travel and many of us, especially those of us not born into this digital era, are struggling to grasp the full extent of this transformation, let alone keep up with it.

And therein lies an opportunity! Yes, the millennials will soon surpass the boomers in terms of total spending power, but if you've learned anything from this "Gray is the New Green" series, it's that the boomers will not go silently into the night. We will be a monetary force to be reckoned with for the next three decades by my estimate. This means that there will continue to be a lucrative market composed of those people who have failed to get with the tech savvy program and those who feel entitled to receive 'old school' hospitality service.

What exactly do I mean by 'old school'? People who don't give two shakes about being able to open their guestroom doors with their smartphones. Guests who want to converse with another human being upon arrival in the form of a smiling front desk clerk or bellhop. Customers whose first source of local knowledge, events and directions is the concierge and not an app or a social review website. Travelers who aren't concerned with the latest shiny toy but are more interested in being catered to by attentive staff members. Hotel visitors who want to read a printed newspaper and respect when it is delivered to their doorstep in the morning, instead of getting their news off a website on their tablets. And those of us who haven't bought in to the 'grab and go' foodservice culture, shunning it in favor of the traditional wait staff approach to dining.

This is also an important consideration when it comes to website design through what is now commonly referred to as UX or user experience. In terms of navigation and information access, what is intuitive to a millennial may not be the case for boomers. Having members of both tribes run quality assurance on your website is a worthwhile venture. Even more pronounced in this aspect is the mobile experience; many of us boomers aren't immediately copacetic to swiping left on a page to access the main navigation or that clicking the 'hamburger button' also performs this task. You may want to hire a sixty-something UX tester to audit your site to ensure that it's 'safe' for the mature crowd.

If you know that some boomers may feel entitled to having service their way, then this should inform what operational changes you make. You'll need one eye on the future to appease the millennials, but you cannot neglect the past or you will alienate the elderly. Of course, this all depends on your core market and whether you foresee that appealing to boomers will bear out or not. If you are in fact targeting those of us born between 1946 and 1965, do yourself a favor and appease their specific form of entitlement.

Gray is the New Green: Cross-Generational Travel

A while back, I wrote about cross-generational word of mouth, and about how ideas related to hospitality percolate up and down through the generations – daughters talking to mothers, granddads chatting with grandsons, uncles conversing with nieces and so on. The central observation was that we, as hoteliers and marketers, tend to compartmentalize our target demographics, oftentimes failing to see them as an interconnected web of nuclear families, extended families, workplace colleagues, neighbors and social circles of like-minded peers.

Thinking cross-generationally about word of mouth will help you design better promotional materials so that your message carries beyond the select few who hear it firsthand or who have had the pleasure of physically staying at your hotel. In the busy advertising world we find ourselves in, your messages need that staying power to outlast the constant distractions that plague our eyes and ears. But there's another aspect to cross-generational appeal, and that is the travel itself.

While we tend to generalize the business traveler as the independent road warrior or as a member of a large group of similarly aged corporate cogs, we also do the same for leisure. We think in terms of couples, parents with young kids, spa-pampering packages solely aimed at women, or a group of guys looking for a golf getaway. As such, we tend to neglect the rising flow of fully-grown, multi-generational families traveling together or reuniting at a predetermined locale.

And the reason for this trend's increase rests predominantly with the boomers. As they get older, they are accruing greater stores of free cash, especially once they become empty nesters. Meanwhile, the onset of retirement means more free time for travel. While journeying across the globe as mature or elderly couples consistently ranks high on every boomer's bucket list, we are also seeing members of this generation who want to splurge on their families by using a part of their disposable nest-eggs to bring the whole family together: young, old and all in-between.

Think a winter destination vacation at a Mexican resort with the grandparents flying in from Long Island, son, wife and young kids from Chicago, and daughter, husband and teenage kids from Seattle. This is but one arbitrary case of a multi-generational rendezvous on neutral ground. More commonly, such meet-ups are annual ventures over the holiday season, either down in the tropics or a preselected territory of mutual interest, or at the patriarch's or matriarch's seasonal abode, with nearby hotel accommodations often acting as bedroom overflow.

While there's not much you can do to control multi-generational travel to someone's personal domicile for a traditional turkey, roast ham and mashed potato dinner, you can control the cross-generational appeal and marketing message you disseminate to get families to consider your hotel in this manner. Essentially, you need to express that your property is compatible with a multitude of demographics, and that you deliver an exceptional experience for each divergent mindset.

Boomers want to feel young, millennials want to be treated like mature adults, and Gen Xers just want everybody to get along. While soft brands and independents have a modest advantage here insofar as it is easier for them to offer a bespoke experience, chain properties shouldn't despair. Any hotel can emphasize its unique qualities and how they apply to any given generation. It's just a matter of sitting your marketing team down and thinking holistically instead of fixating on only one or two target age groups.

Lifespan Versus Health Span

Another related topic worth addressing at this point is the current debate between lifespan and 'health span'. While the concept of lifespan or life expectancy is readily understood as how long the average person is alive – and indeed this number is increasing year-over-year in the Western World – health span looks at how long the average person is in good health.

Many statisticians have been quick to point out that lifespan is on the up largely because of advancements in medicine and technology that prolong an elderly person's later, enfeebled years – a time in which travel comes with its own set of difficulties, thus making it rare. Instead, health span would appear to be a better indicator of a population's overall vitality, as it incorporates such lifestyle choices as diet, exercise and cigarette usage. Ideally, you want lifespan to equal health span, but this is rarely the case.

Even though lifespan is much easier to measure than health span (life and death are binary, after all), we are finding that the latter is in fact increasing within the baby boomer population. When you put this trend through the marketing gauntlet, the pertinent question is: how can you target healthy boomers?

As our medical, dietary and fitness knowledge bases increase, more and more people are taking an active role to ensure that their health spans are as long as possible. Yes, the younger generations have a definitive leg up – for example, they know cigarettes are bad, they've been raised in a society where refined sugars are rightfully demonized, organic is king and there are carnivorous options beyond steroid-injected, grain-fed beef or poultry.

But older generations are catching up. Hotels that appeal to the health-conscious boomer's desire to live longer – in addition to a millennial's aspiration for clean eating and leading a regularly active life – will find a receptive audience.

Larry Mogelonsky

Gray is the New Green: Social Media Differences

Young people and old people use different social media platforms and behave differently online. Everyone knows this...or at least they should. And it has powerful implications for your digital marketing strategies.

It all started from the very onset of social networks, which were peer-to-peer outlets for early millennials while boomers were still completely in the dark. Facebook played a big role in changing this dynamic. What started as an interface for university students soon took on high school pupils, college alumni and then everyone else. As Mark Zuckerberg's character in *The Social Network* repeatedly drives home, Facebook was designed to be a 'cool' app. But what's cool about sharing a digital platform with your parents or grandparents for that matter? And so it came to pass that once us 'old farts' latched onto Facebook, the teenagers and twentysomethings migrated to newer, cooler social media like Instagram, Snapchat and, most recently, Periscope or Meerkat.

The moral of the story is that the advent of social media is still in its relative infancy, meaning that each platform's functions are ever-shifting and their user bases equally as mercurial. If you want to effectively target younger millennials – and in the next few years, teenage Gen Zers – with a promotion, would you have more success using Facebook Ads and the site's promoted posts functionality? Or would you be better off starting an Instagram or Snapchat channel with frequent updates, rich visual content and adeptly positioned captions?

As the title of this series is "Gray is the New Green", it's safe to assume that we are discussing best practices to reach boomers and Gen Xers on social media. Even though there is quite a lot of excitement surrounding the burgeoning, 'younger' channels like Snapchat or Meerkat and their marketing potential, such apps aren't accessible or widely adopted by crowds over the age of 30. Yes, millennials are the future when it comes to purchasing power, and you must patiently work to build a fan base in these demographics so that you can generate brand recognition and loyalty in the coming decades. But for the time being, boomers have the thickest wallets and they want to live large.

An incongruity in social network usage does not presuppose that boomers are luddites either. Many are tech laggards, but they've woken up to the imperative for adapting quickly to new apps or devices with universal relevance. My thought is that the 2008-2009 crash and the resultant focus on efficiencies ended with many boomers losing their jobs and unable to find new ones as their skill sets were replaced by robust new software and young workers fluent in its use. Undoubtedly this was also a stern wakeup call to all quadragenarians and older that they better accept this new reality or find themselves displaced.

Enough rambling and pontificating! If you are hoping to gain social influence amongst an older population set, your first stop should indeed be Facebook. It's a hub for news and events, with the opportunity for direct communications via comments or private messages. More importantly, while the young-ins have drifted over to the visual-centric platforms, this billion-user-plus social network has been wholly embraced by boomers.

For those of you who can only allocate minimal resources to social media, it is acceptable to treat your Facebook fan page as a copy of your hotel website's blog, events and promotions sections. This works because the average consumer is more likely to regularly log in to this social network than he or she is to check out any recent updates to your website. Furthermore, once users are logged on, they prefer to stay within that portal to get a snapshot of daily happenings, newsfeeds and pertinent information. (This same principle applies to LinkedIn, but that is more of a B2B communications tool, while our discussion here pertains to B2C strategies.)

The key here, unlike Twitter, is to limit your frequency to only the most titillating stories – the ones that are going to generate click-throughs back to your website. Whereas if you were going to target millennials with a Snapchat promotion, a good base frequency would be several photos shared per day, Facebook should only average around once, or twice maximum, per week.

Do any other social media apply? Pinterest, Tumbler, Yummly and any other hobby-focused sites are great if you have wares worth the effort of starting a curating a page on one of these niche platforms. In many ways, these catalogue-style social media sites can be likened to Instagram but with much heavier penetration with thirtysomethings and older. If you have a creative chef who is churning out masterpieces daily or if you are highly involved in the local art scene, these sites are a worthy avenue to showcase some of the more exceptional aspects of your hotel.

All this, though, presupposes a rather naïve question: Is social media even worth the trouble to reach people in elder demographics? The online channels are evolving so quickly, who is to say that Instagram and Snapchat won't also have widespread boomer adoption in five years' time? My bet, however, is that we have reached some sense of normalcy in social media. So, in a word, yes – social media is a viable path to reach the elder eyeballs, no matter how much macular degeneration or cataracts have set in.

The two-aforementioned photo-sharing apps are designed for exceedingly frequent usage, and time becomes quite fleeting when you're mid a career, raising a family and keeping up with mortgage annuities. Recurrent distractions during the day just aren't possible when real life hits. Hence, social media, all other forms of leisure, get left for moments in the day when extended breadths of time allow for a proper perusal of the site – roughly 15 minutes or longer during evenings, lunch breaks and the doldrums of quiet afternoons at the office.

I could go on for pages about appropriate social media protocols, but this seems like a good point to turn it over to you. What differences in social media usage have you observed between the different generations? What networks are best for whom? Or, when it comes to boomers and retirees, should hotels cling to traditional marketing tactics with only lip service given to these new age online platforms?

OPERATIONS

While The Savoy competes with many fine properties in London, its sense of arrival defines the ultimate in quality and proper, fastidious British service.

Photos copyright of the hotel and cannot be reproduced without its permission.

Larry Mogelonsky

A New Year Means a New Third Space

The modern hotel is not only a place for a good night's sleep; it's a place to see and be seen. Lobbies all over the world are being refitted to accommodate a renewed vigor for what is popularly known as 'The Third Space' or 'The Third Place', a public locale that serves a hybrid role somewhere between the home and the office.

The third space is one of productivity but also relaxation; one of quiet reflection but also socialization; one of sustenance but also libation. As the average workday moves away from a strict nine-to-five protocol, we are witnessing the rise of a labor force that thrives on this blending of the first and second spaces.

If you were to imagine a New Year's clock ticking down, undoubtedly a lobby remodeling or the modifying of another well-trafficked space to fit this new standard would be on many of your resolution lists. Rightfully so, as there is a powerful connection between the overall atmosphere of a property and guest satisfaction, which is crucial for achieving high TripAdvisor scores and a healthy number of return visits. But renovations of this magnitude are seldom cheap, quick or without widespread tinkering behind the scenes with things like budget, staffing and supply chain management.

As examples of two chains that, based on my own experience, have gotten it right, I refer you to W Hotels and the Library Hotel Collection. Each W Hotel location is considered 'the place to be' by young to middle-aged travelers. The attraction here comes from a convergence of many features including sleek design features, interactive spaces that are also visually stimulating, artful décor and comfortable, loungey furniture arrangements. Next, as a brand of only six boutique properties, Library Hotel Collection exists on the other side of the spectrum. Here, the concept of the living room is played to the extreme whereby the lobby area is transformed into a communal room with free WiFi, magazines, snacks and beverages, all available 24/7 – it's an irresistible congregation point that allows guests to intermingle.

Thinking of what these two leaders are doing right as well as considering many other properties that have something exceptional to offer in this regard (looking at you, Virgin Hotels Chicago), the essence of the third space can be distilled into three salient factors for which the upgrade costs are not blatantly prohibitive.

Your F&B must be great.

Meal time is conservation time, while meet-ups for coffee or cocktails are also a staple of our culture. An army of customers runs on its stomach after all, and you shouldn't give guests or locals a reason to venture elsewhere by being lousy in this arena. While a total menu overhaul can be quite daunting, for the third space angle, abide by the 'keep it simple' motto. It's better suited to today's fast-paced, grab-and-go lifestyle to have a simple, dozen-items-or-less menu – for both food as well as for drinks – than it is try to cater to every single person's specific, whimsical desires. A short menu will quicken consumer decision making, help reduce ingredient costs and streamline service delivery. Moreover, focusing on only a few items will ensure that each is exceptional.

Think café, not nightclub.

It's a common misconception when approaching the topic of third space redesigns to opt for mood lighting and a constant drumming of electronic lounge music as curated by a wannabe DJ off in one corner. The problem with this atmosphere is that when the tunes are too loud, it makes groups insular, and reducing the room's brightness prevents people from seeing their surroundings – both of which are inhibitors to communal conversations. Instead, such third spaces must be suitable for play as well as for work. Comfortable table settings with available power outlets and zippy WiFi are both tremendously important. A good litmus test is that patrons seated anywhere in the designated space should be able to hear the grinding of coffee beans from the barista counter – always a pleasant sound. While your décor may emulate that of a nightclub as a means of entertaining the eyes, it can't be so dark as to prevent reading and it must be congruent with the overall theme of the hotel.

Your team is as much the attraction as the place.

Think back on Rick's Café Americain in *Casablanca*. Yes, I realize that I've inculcated this example, but it still gets the point across. The source of all the hubbub is a stellar combination of an inviting host in the form of Humphrey Bogart, Sam on the piano and a well-oiled staff operating as efficiently as the Nazi army stationed just outside of town. Effervescent servers and the presence of managers on the floor both do wonders towards facilitating friendly banter, acting as the connective glue between disparate parties of guests and elevating the overall mood. Moreover, consider turning your chefs into celebrities by properly promoting them on the website and having them make the occasional front-of-house appearance.

When Your Property is in Sad Shape, What Should You Do?

Recently, I had an unfortunate experience while staying at a branded property that was clearly well past its best before date. Despite its prime location in its market and good promotional efforts, it was obvious that this chain outlet was not meeting any of the defined standards outlined by the corporate website.

I won't go into details, but let's just say that this economy-plus level hotel wasn't meeting some of the most basic criteria that characterize 'a good night's stay'. Being part of a group booking, it was apparent that I was not the only one who took notice of the property's blatant shortcomings. The grumblings passed along throughout the event sessions would have made for exceptionally shrill TripAdvisor commentary. The one saving grace was the staff – all were gracious and attentive, but it still wasn't enough.

Alas, we are all here to learn, not just to admonish those who might serve as cautionary tales in hotel dilapidation. As numerous external factors are poised to lure consumers away from the traditional ways of finding accommodations, our industry is shaky enough without these marginal operators. Part of running a flagged property is being true to that flag. Undoubtedly the higher-ups at the property in question know what's currently going on, but more importantly, what can they do and what should they do?

Standards are there for a reason.

Every brand has a standards manual. This outlines not only what is required – hard goods, amenities, colors and so on – but also maintenance levels that must be upheld. Think of these as 'bibles', whereby the scripture on each page represents the cumulative input of many experts in various operational areas who have, through many years of hard work, honed what the brand is today. The brand standards also relate to guest expectations – cheat on them and you are cheating your guests! Knowing this simple relationship, the most obvious path to revitalization is to follow the brand standards manual.

Compliance management should not be an adversarial relationship.

If you're reading this and you have responsibility for a property or group, compliance management should be considered fundamental. You cannot allow any member of your portfolio to fail. Remember, your brand's viability is only as good as your weakest link. Travel to all your properties regularly, inspecting and anticipating areas of improvement. Share results openly with owners and operators to get everyone on the same wavelength. Reinforce the critical nature of product delivery as the basis for success. These should be congenial conversations, with everyone working together to restore problematic areas of operations. My advice is to always keep the guest at the forefront of your thoughts – when everyone is focused on improving the overall guest experience, it keeps everyone banded together towards a common goal.

Operators have responsibility, too.

If you're the operator, consider brand standards as the minimum requirement – the base from which each property leaps and soars. Understand these requirements and factor reserve allocations for future maintenance needs into your operating costs. Study your TripAdvisor and OTA reviews to ensure that you've not missed anything. And once you've met the brand's criteria, formulate your own plan of attack to boost guest satisfaction scores by adding nuances so that your property stands apart from the comp set. It's these unique touches that will bring character to your hotel that guests will remember beyond the sense of normalcy proffered by the brand standards.

Passing the buck or selling to avoid renovation.

I've heard many times about those who want to sell rather than renovate. Usually these decisions are strictly done on a financial or cash flow basis. But don't hide behind a flag. Savvy brands are making it much harder to get away with the for-sale sign as a reason for not renovating. Understand that you have an obligation to maintain; you're under contract so to speak. Try selling your property without a flag – I'm skeptical that it will be worth as much.

So, You've Hired an Intern, Now What?

Interns are far more than just temporary recruits brought aboard to finish all the menial jobs piling up around the office. In many cases, there are laws preventing this kind of treatment – ones stipulating that interns must complete 'meaningful labor'.

Recently, I was approached by an eager hotelier looking to get the most of her shiny new summer intern fresh from a premier university. This hotelier was seeking a road map to help direct her own efforts in guiding the intern on a path that was, as inscribed in the requirement cited above, meaningful. After some deliberation, I gave her eight questions to aid in her treatment of this intern. Given that summer is upon us, these are seven that I will share with you as well.

Do you have an overall plan for the intern?
In other words, what do you hope the intern will learn during his or her short time with you? I say 'overall' because this is meant to be answered in a brief and quite broad sense, acting as a logline of sorts that you can come back to whenever things veer off course. Obviously, a large part of this will come from the interns themselves, in terms of what they have previously agreed to do for you and what they hope to accomplish.

Do you have a clear orientation program?
In other words, how are you introducing the intern to the intricacies of your organization? For starters, you might consider having one member of each department agree to show said intern each respective area of operations for a few hours. Interns should also spend a night or two as guests so they gain a different perspective on how the property functions.

Who is supervising the intern?
Whether it's one designated employee or shift-work, you cannot leave an intern unsupervised until they know the ropes. And knowing the ropes won't come before the completion of an orientation

program. In most cases, it won't even come before the summer is over and done. When the intern is ready for autonomous labor, start them off with specific tasks that they have already been trained to handle.

What can they write for you?

Writing in all its various forms is under the purview of 'meaningful'. So get your interns working on reports that will not only improve their own writing skills but also serve to aid aspects of your operations. For instance, have them scout the local competition and prepare a comparative analysis. Or, have them review your website in relation to others with the hope of pointing out opportunities for improvement. A rate analysis is another worthy project, looking at specific time frames with comparisons and recommendations.

Can you help you with TripAdvisor?

Have your intern audit your property's TripAdvisor business page. Then, train them in how to properly respond to good and bad reviews.

What can they do to help you plan promotions?

Young minds are full of creative ideas, while interns' rookie outsider statuses ensure that they will provide some insights your managers have likely been conditioned to not even consider. Have your interns review past promotions so that they understand what is operationally feasible, and then connect them with your marketing and reservations teams so they can learn how best to sell your property.

Do you have a departure gift ready?

It doesn't have to be expensive, but just like the nature of their work, the gift should also be meaningful. Always end relationships on a good note as you never know when you will meet again!

A Healthy Team Means Healthy Profits

There is now undeniable evidence linking one's eating habits and fitness routine with one's intelligence and drive for success. While there still is a genetic component at work – that is, some people may be naturally more adept in some areas – and some are more motivated to work than others, the bottom line is that the healthier you are, the more of your potential you will realize.

That is a concept that everyone can get behind – hard work and devotion to a set goal will almost always trump innate talent. So, if you dedicate yourself to living a healthier lifestyle with more omega-3 fats, a bountiful portion of green vegetables at every meal and less refined sugar, you will see a difference, both in your waistline and in your aptitude.

In this modern era, where health is so much the focus of our everyday lives, it makes fiscal sense for organizations to improve the wellness of their employees so that the company can actualize the greatest part of their potential. After all, a healthy team means faster learners, fewer sick days and more efficiency across the board. As a bonus, a culture of wellness rubs off on guests, too, leading to positive guest attribution.

I am not suggesting a draconian mandate be installed in this regard, but rather simple and subtle nudges to promote a healthier corporate culture. Here are five for you to consider:

Lead by example.
Actions speak louder than words. Don't talk about making a change, just do it! If you initiate a change in your diet or your fitness routine without trying to force it on others, people will come to admire you for your perseverance, especially when they see the results for themselves, and will want to follow your lead.

Reduce unhealthy temptations.
It's all too easy to indulge when such options are readily available. Whether it's the treats that a colleague has graciously brought into the staff kitchen or the dessert items at the end of the cafeteria lineup,

unhealthy temptations are everywhere, so much so that abstinence can become overwhelming. A good adage to remember here is: Out of sight, out of mind. For example, did you know that you are much more likely to eat the foods at the front of a kitchen cabinet than at the back? Therefore, simply moving the junk to the back of the cabinet will reduce its consumption.

Moreover, if someone brings in candies or other insulin-spiking foods, don't leave them out on the counter. Employers can have even more profound influences here by way of their food purchases – less processed food, more fruits and vegetables and going organic are all good options. Your property's employee cafeteria is a good place to start.

Piecemeal education.
Giving someone a 400-page book on nutrition can be daunting, especially for the uninitiated – a brief article or tip passed around every day can be a more effective reinforcement tool. And the best part is, you don't even need to come up with these on your own; there are dozens of resources already available on the web.

Standing desks.
Some suggest that sitting is the new smoking, or so they say. It's an unnatural body position that can reduce flexibility, increase chances of heart disease and lead to severe back pain. Standing desks eliminate many of these problems. Additionally, many reports suggest that standing can burn over 50% more calories per hour than sitting – compound that over a year's time, and then see what happens!

Public declarations.
We all avoid public embarrassment and we all hate it when we fail a group or team. Hence, if you openly declare to your friends or colleagues that you are embarking on a dietary quest, they will hold you accountable should you lapse. In this sense, your desire for improved health is no longer a private concern but a communal one, with every person you've told acting as a control

mechanism to keep you on the right path. This can play out in many different forms in the office environment, from a physical or digital progress board to monthly meetings and roundtable discussions. Caution here: be mindful of employee rights and any actions that discriminate against non-participants. Remember, you can set an example, but ultimately, we are employers and should respect all employees' rights.

Unsung Heroes of Hospitality: Rooms Division Director

When one thinks of senior hotel management, the first thought is usually of the general manager. Yet, within the typical executive committee, the rooms division director – and positions with equivalent names – is the one who serves as the 'people's leader'.

Celebrating its 90th anniversary, the Boca Raton Resort & Club is physically split into two distinct locations. The Resort incorporates the original structure and several expansions, as well as the conference center, marina, six pools, spa, 12 restaurants, retail, tennis academy and courts, and two golf courses. The Club is a much newer structure, completed in 2009 and situated about half a mile away along the Atlantic Ocean with its own management complex of facilities, management team and staff.

I've stayed several times at this property in both the Club and the Resort. Each on their own is impressive, but together, they form one of America's very special destinations.

Recently, I had an opportunity to sit down with Jamaal Simington, Rooms Division Director of the Waldorf Astoria Boca Raton Resort to learn more about the position and its responsibilities. The idea of a sit down was a little awkward for Jamaal; after meeting him, I suspect that he's continuously on the move.

Let's start with bit of background on your career to-date.

I've been at the Resort for the past year. Prior to this terrific assignment, I worked at the Boston Park Plaza as the director of guest experience, and before that at The Westin Snowmass Resort as their complex director of rooms and property service culture trainer. Of course, there were several other fantastic property assignments.

Tell me a little bit about the role of rooms division director at the Boca Raton Resort.

I am responsible for front desk, bell services, housekeeping, laundry, valet, guest services, concierge, guest transportation and experience. Each of these departments has a team leader who forms part of my management team. In effect, I manage the people assets of the Resort, excluding F&B, with a total staff complement of about 250 persons.

And whom do you report to?
In addition to myself, other members of the executive team for the property such as our F&B beverage director, executive chef, director of catering and convention services, facilities director and revenue director report to the general manager.

What is your typical day like?
Well, I'm rarely found in my office. My focus is on the guest, and the best way to learn is to be in the center of the action – in the lobby, front office area, front drive or housekeeping. Many of the staff are starting to think that I must be 'cloned' as I can easily put several miles on my Fitbit attending meetings, talking to team members or greeting guests. This is a large property, with the Resort alone comprising some 350+ acres as well as 1,047 rooms and suites in multiple buildings. Thank goodness for our cell phones, as I could not imagine this job prior to this technology.

Do you differentiate between guests, say, someone who has come in through an OTA booking versus someone who booked direct or through a travel agent?
Anyone who arrives at the Resort wants to be treated as a VIP. After all, we are certainly not inexpensive! Our welcome process is well-refined. It certainly helps that all guests must first pass through a welcome gate. Thus, we know who the guest is before they make their way to our front door. Yet, even the highest-level VIP and the first-time visitor will receive the same Floridian welcome. To do this, we have a valet staff of 30 who work in tandem with our bell staff and front desk to speed guests through the arrival process. To see this on a late Friday afternoon – our peak check-in time – is like watching a symphony orchestra. It is impressive, particularly given

our short distance from the front doors to the reception counter – probably no more than 40 feet.

And if there's a problem?

No one is perfect; no team flawless. After all, we're only human. Given the number of interactions to successfully check a guest in and move them through to their room, it is incredible to me that our success rate approaches 100%. Yet, there are often challenges, be it a late checkout that renders a designated room not ready, an engineering concern or just a simple reservations error. That is why we empower our team to find the best solution, often without further layers of management involvement. Through this, we are not only providing better hospitality, but also training our frontline staff to be better at their positions and move up to managerial functions.

Just how do you manage all of this and retain any sense of sanity?

Simply put: delegation and teamwork. I've long since recognized two things. First, the sum often exceeds the whole of the parts – put two or three great people together and they will forge a result that is more than one could anticipate for each operating individually. And, second, you cannot 'push a chain' – you need to set an example, provide encouragement and give responsibilities to everyone. Sanity comes with confidence that your team members are being given the latitude to get their work done, and seeing them step to up the plate!

What advice do you have for those wishing to pursue a career in hospitality?

Our business is not about technology, but rather it is all about people. You have to totally immerse yourself in this amazing profession and learn to focus on nurturing your team. The Resort's success clearly demonstrates that you simply cannot do it all yourself. You have to, literally, roll up your sleeves and get your hands dirty in order to immerse yourself in providing unparalleled guest experiences. In doing so, you will enrich the lives of your guests and your team as well as your own well-being.

Unsung Heroes of Hospitality: Reservationist

With so much attention these days on digital sales channels, we sometimes forget the power of a good salesperson, specifically a reservationist. To learn some more about this crucial position, I sought out Jodi Tower, a Senior Reservation Sales Agent for FRHI Hotels & Resorts. For those unfamiliar with FRHI, it is a Toronto-based hotel management company that supervises the Fairmont, Raffles and Swissôtel brands with over 110 properties in 32 countries. In the time since this interview was completed, FRHI has become part of the Accor brand family.

With experience in human resources and marketing, Jodi works out of FRHI's Global Reservation Center (GRC) in Moncton, New Brunswick, Canada with 300 other some odd specialists who deal primarily with inbound telephone calls but also handle all loyalty program services and technical support issues. The GRC offers services in English, French, Spanish and Arabic, 24/7.

What makes for a great reservationist?
A great reservation sales agent needs to have exceptional listening skills to anticipate what the guests' needs are before they know what they want. This is complemented by superior product knowledge, which gives us credibility, establishing a trusting relationship and enabling relevant recommendations to be made to the guest. Because we do not actually see the guest – limiting the two-way communication process – listening with your 'third ear' helps our guests realize how valued they are to our company.

What is the training regimen?
After the initial three-week training period, ongoing support is provided on a daily basis by sales leadership, reservation sales agents (in the form of peer-to-peer mentoring) and customer service teams. Additionally, we have a quality monitoring team that reviews our calls. Feedback from these four groups ensures that we have the tools and knowledge to be successful in our role. A cardinal rule to follow is that today's guests want the straight facts, and they

want to deal with sales professionals who are service-orientated and concerned about meeting their needs.

How do you learn about the properties?

We have an internal website that contains all the pertinent information required to close the sale on a call. This is supplemented by each hotel region coming to the center on an annual basis to present what is new and exciting at their property and destination. It keeps the passion alive for us. Another component that we participate in is S.I.T.E. trips (Selling It Through Education). This program enables us to travel as a group of 10-15 agents at a time out into the field to visit various regions. Once there, the hotels provide us with tours of the hotel and city as well as an authentically local activity such as a ride on the London Eye or zip lining in Whistler.

When listening to a customer, what are the clues that they are interested in your suggestions?

Tone plays a big factor as this helps in determining the guest's interest. I also need to listen for pauses and understand the silences as this might mean a customer is contemplating, is not interested, wasn't listening or doesn't understand the offer. Asking a clarifying question at this point brings us back and allows me to move forward. Being engaged reinforces the relationship and trust that is developed on the call. A person can sense interest during the process.

Do you have a favorite period to sell?

Christmas is my favorite because many of our properties create such a magical holiday season atmosphere that I love sharing with customers. From the Plaza Hotel with their specially selected designer Christmas tree in the lobby to the Fairmont San Francisco and the larger-than-life gingerbread house complete with a computer to send a letter to Santa. All our hotels embrace the season with something special.

What kind of promotion are you most passionate about?

My favorite promotion ties in with my favorite period – Christmas in November at Fairmont Jasper Park Lodge. They have been running this promotion for so long – over 20 years – that our clientele has passed from mother and daughter to grandmother and granddaughter!

What is worst experience on a call?

The worst experience I face is when I cannot provide the guest with what they are looking for. I really and truly become disappointed.

What do you recommend that managers looking for reservationists do to find the best and keep them as part of the team?

Creating an engaging and fun work environment that welcomes a competitive spirit, collaboration and creativity is important. Managers need to lead through clear expectations and by example. Here at the GRC, we are encouraged to bring our individual talents to the table and use them to reach our common goals.

Could a hotel GM survive a full shift at the reservation center?

Certainly, with the proper training and talents they could. At the same time, I have had the opportunity to have general managers and vice presidents listen to my sales calls and they seem to approach this activity from a totally different perspective. Based on my personal experience, they tend to think about the hotel operations processes. Some may find it difficult as I completely focus on selling and setting the stage for a positive guest experience at whatever hotel the guest is visiting. I must say that they are always in awe with the amount of information I sift through and the level of multitasking that takes place...all while carrying on a natural conversation with the guest!

Larry Mogelonsky

The Suite Life

I've been spoiled. Each year, I stay in about 50 different hotels, and often, I am upgraded to their suite products. With a nod to all those hoteliers who have graciously provided this bonus, I say thank you. Attempting to learn from these experiences, I ask: What makes a suite special? And, if properly differentiated, how can you fashion your suites as a truly differentiated product set?

First, let's define a suite. Whereas many hoteliers may consider it as just a larger guestroom, a true suite has a door that physically separates the sleeping quarters from the living and dining area. Note, many hoteliers try to define a larger room as a mini-suite, but without the true separation this does not meet the actual criteria.

In effect, a suite provides the guest with both private and public spaces, making it ideal for many lodging circumstances where a standard room would be awkward, informal or undesirable. Many of the larger suites or multi-bedroom units may also have an additional powder room and mini-kitchen.

Furthermore, some hotels are suite-only, such as the Embassy Suites brand. However, for most properties there is usually a mix of these tiers. I have rarely heard of a hotelier who is happy with this ratio, and in my experience the overall demand for suites is outstripping that of regular rooms, although this may differ depending upon local and competitive circumstances. The reasons why suites are gaining in demand are numerous. Here are a few:

- **Rising affluence:** Those who can afford it are opting for more space and a suite delivers a loftier guestroom experience.
- **Families traveling with a child:** No need for two adjoining rooms; the child can sleep on the comfortable sofa bed in the living room.
- **Older guests:** Those of retirement age spend more time in their guestrooms, especially with the draw of being able to enjoy in-room meals.

- **One of the couple snores:** Don't laugh! A serious snoring problem by one half of the couple makes life miserable for the other – you need a getaway!
- **Conducting business in the hotel:** As an example, you can't conduct a professional interview while sitting at the side of a bed.

It's more than just physical size and rate, though. There are many opportunities for you to improve your guests' suite experience. Setting aside capital cost items such as larger TVs, improved drapes and carpeting, polished floors and enhanced lighting, here are some more ideas for consideration:

- Free WiFi or free access to the higher tier of internet bandwidth
- Upgraded bathroom amenities such as better name brand toiletries
- Extended amenity kit to include razor, shaving cream, toothbrush, toothpaste, comb, mouthwash and other basics
- Thicker bathrobes, perhaps with a different monogram
- Fresh flowers in the bathroom and at bedside
- Complimentary bottled water
- Turndown service
- Additional channels on the in-room TV service
- Extended check in and checkout hours
- Priority seating in the dining room or priority room service
- Additional newspapers
- Complimentary city magazines
- Upgraded beds, linens and pillows
- Restaurant and spa discounts
- Free use of fitness facilities and perhaps the use of a fitness trainer
- Preferred golf tee times
- Limousine airport pick up and return
- In-room refrigerator
- Concierge services
- Personal welcome letter and welcome amenities

Once you have built your suite product, promote its unique points of difference. First, sell your staff and, in particular, your reservations team. Make mention of your suites in social media. Create a persona to make it special by, for instance, giving each suite a unique name. Ensure the suites lead your accommodations listing on your website to differentiate your property from those who typically start with their 'basic' offerings. Extensive use of photography will add to the 'reasons why' to buy. Don't forget to elaborate on the amenity additions within your online booking engine.

Pricing your suites is a matter of market factors. For a start, look at the square footage and proportion of the suite to a standard room. There are no set rules here. Many other factors may indicate even higher premiums, such as oceanfront settings. Simply put: instead of giving away your suites each night as complimentary upgrades, learn how to sell your best product.

Bathrooms as a Make or Break Experience Redux

In an article from an earlier book, I expanded on how important the bathroom is for the overall guestroom experience. It's such a personal, private space that any minor annoyances are especially hard to forgive because of their heightened impact on one's emotional state.

You simply need to browse through TripAdvisor or other third-party review site comments to see how vital it is to provide for a superior washroom experience. Before diving into a whole new batch of grievances, let's recap what was already covered:

- Bathroom not properly cleaned
- Not enough towels, floor mats or hand towels
- Not enough hygiene products
- Mold, rust, grime or other forms of deterioration
- Poor lighting
- Small mirrors
- Cramped countertops
- Perplexing showerheads and controls

With those already explained, or hopefully offering an explanation that should be straightforward from the bullet points, let's move on to several more that have cropped up over the last few months.

1. **A towel too far.** Bridging the grievance gap between having too few washcloths or floor mats is the annoyance of having to walk across cold tiles to reach the towel rack. Apart from the minor aggravation of getting chilly after escaping the confines of the hot shower is the major concern over slipping on a wet floor. Even the thought of this danger is enough to cause distress.

2. **Soaked toilet paper.** You want towels to be within arms' length of the shower door, but you do not want tissues or

toilet paper rolls to be within splash distance when the shower or bathtub is in use.

3. **Who bathes anymore?** Speaking of bathtubs, who uses tubs anymore? Traditionally speaking, a bathtub is a necessary component of any domicile, but these times they are a-changin'. Especially regarding business and younger leisure travelers, the bathtub apparatus is rarely in use relative to its shower counterpart. Unless you are catering to avid bathers, why have a bathtub at all? Dedicated or rain showers are much more comfortable for standing and will augment the cleansing experience for most of your guests.

4. **Anticipate airport snafus.** Given how much trouble it is to bring toiletries through airports these days, it's all too easy for a guest to forget one or two essential items. Instead of stocking only the perfunctory shampoos, conditioners and soaps, why not supply other small disposables like toothpaste, dental floss, mouthwash, hair gel, nail polish remover or lip balm. You might even take this a step further and provide a small sample of your own branded fragrances with cologne and perfume options so both sexes can sample.

5. **Accessorize!** Outside of any extra disposables you provision, you might also want to consider offering the 'hardware'. Start with a shaving kit, scissors and nail clippers, then move beyond blow-dryers and into fancy brushes, straightening irons or electric razors.

6. **Private means private.** In the previous article, I talked about difficult doors – ones that are a struggle to close or a struggle to keep closed. You must remember that bathrooms are the most private of all spaces and they should be respected as such. There shouldn't be any windows or other semi-opaque opening onto the bedroom. Moreover, the door should be thick enough to partially block sounds, both those attempting to enter the bathroom and those trying to escape – think fans or any other flourishes of air.

The bathroom is a very tricky area to deal with because there is so little physical space to work with that everything must be placed in the precise position for it all to come together as a single pleasurable experience. You're probably already doing most of this at least at a satisfactory level, but use these tips in combination with whatever crops up on your online guest reviews to decide where you can improve.

Ten Pet Peeves of Hotel Fitness Centers

With the desire for healthy eating, exercise and all-round wellness on the rise, creating an environment conducive for guests at your hotel's fitness facilities is paramount. As a road warrior staying at some 50 different properties annually, I've had the opportunity to experience a wide variety of these amenities.

I don't contend to be an expert on fitness equipment – this likely requires a PhD in bio-mechanics – but it is nevertheless easy to spot where some hotels are excelling in this regard compared to others. On this basis, here is my top ten list of pet peeves with hotel fitness centers.

1. **Not being open when I want to exercise.** I am an early riser. A fitness center that is not open is like candy in a window of a closed store. You drool, but cannot get satisfaction. A 7am opening is way too late; 5 or 6am is better. As for wrapping up for the day, 11pm or midnight works best.

2. **Stale air and poor ventilation.** The worst experience was a fitness center which seemed to be crammed between the hot tub and the laundry. If the humidity is such that you cannot breathe, how can you be realistically capable of working out and unleashing pounds of sweat? Furthermore, there's nothing as unappetizing as sucking in another person's unrestrained body odor or cheap spray deodorant because the ventilation systems aren't flowing adequately.

3. **Equipment that does not work properly.** Frustrating but true, the more sophisticated the equipment, the more complex the programming and the higher the repair requirements. Most modern cardio bikes and treadmills come with built in plugs for mobile devices as well as televisions – ensure that these function perfectly. Also, clean and lubricate weighted and cable machines so the resistance is fluid.

4. **Too much equipment.** It seems that many operators think they can cram in as much as the space will fit and thereby improve their fitness centers' overall usage. In doing so, space allocated for stretching and free body exercises is typically eliminated – you can forget about performing routines with a partner. You must find a balance; as any good fitness freak will tell you, flexibility movements are easily as important as resistance training.

5. **Rust.** Oxidizing metals look great on rooftops but anything that rusts has no place in your fitness center. It reflects poor maintenance and poor ventilation. This is particularly noticeable on cheap free weights.

6. **Cheap or thin towels**. Towels should be thick so that only one is needed to absorb all the sweat produced during the average one or two-hour workout. Moreover, these should be comprised of a material soft enough to rub over one's face without agitation.

7. **Clocks everywhere.** Yes, clocks are great for keeping track of time, especially during interval training. But nowadays, everyone brings their mobile devices with them to the gym for this task. Why do you still need to have clocks on every wall?

8. **Anything but perfect cleanliness.** I'm not just talking about a wipe down at the end of the day, but consummate spot checking. Many people rudely don't return dumbbells to their proper resting place and having to trawl the gym floor to locate a matching pair shouldn't be a part of any guest's workout. Additionally, that giant sweat imprint on the mats doesn't exactly say "Lay down here, please."

9. **Roaming staff and trainers.** Oftentimes, it's easy for all the gym staff to perform their basic duties then cluster in some remote corner out of direct eye contact with members. Think of the gym as you would a restaurant; staff members should constantly be on patrol: for cleaning spot checks, to occasionally offer exercise tips and, most importantly, to make themselves available for conversation with guests.

10. **Surcharges for use.** This is a non-starter, as is the same for any drip pricing tactic. Just like charging $4.99 for a bottle of water, hotels should be encouraging fitness rather than throwing up barriers to usage. It comes to the guest's experience – any constraints you set up lessen a visitor's overall degree of exposure to your property and thereby decrease the impression you can make.

Eight Tips to Improve Your Fitness Facilities

Wellness is all the rage these days, and that isn't bound to change anytime in the next decade. We are increasingly becoming a health-conscious society and, with comfortable guestrooms, spas, restaurants and fitness facilities, hotels are primed to capitalize on this movement.

It's the latter of these operations that is the focus here. Spas and wellness go hand-in-hand, and your F&B department likewise has numerous options in this regard including organics, local sourcing, gluten-free and calorie counts. A property's gym and any other associated sports facilities are often neglected, which represents a real guest experience opportunity. Here are some of the ideas that you can consider:

1. **Great trainers.** Just as your staff is the lifeblood of the hotel, your trainers form the core of your fitness operations. They must be attentive, knowledgeable and highly personable. They should make themselves available to everyone, not just those who have an appointment. They should remember names, past conversations and any concerns people have had.

2. **Make the gym social.** Yes, trainers take a large role in this by talking to people and connecting guests with one another. But it's also a matter of arranging the space so that it encourages interactions. Think TVs, lounge areas with comfortable seating and a juice bar.

3. **Sports training.** The three most common – and therefore expected – forms of gym usage are weight loss, building muscle and toning. Designing a sports-specific program or two will differentiate your fitness product. Plus, these are typically fun and highly interactive. Obviously, the options you offer are dependent on what specific facilities you have – whether they include tennis courts, pools or running tracks – but there are still quite a few sports that can be covered on the gym floor.

4. **Complex, superior machines.** Just as hotels establish a strong sense of place with unique lobby and guestroom designs, so too can you elicit a similar feeling for your gymnasium by installing intricate and eye-catching machinery. Chest presses and lateral pulldowns are in every club around the world (boring!), but how many have spacious TRX setups or a FreeMotion Dual Cable Cross? There are also many new fascinating machines on the market nowadays; take for instance the recently patented Isophit from Striation 6, a physiotherapy studio here in Toronto, which is an adjustable bench solely for isometric workouts.

5. **Differentiated towel service.** Close your eyes and imagine your average gym towel: square, reasonably sized, off-white in color and probably not that soft on the skin. Given this is the expectation, there are several options to exceed. Firstly, any fabric destined to touch a guest's skin should be the pinnacle of soft. You can also make an impression by choosing a color or colors for your towels to match those of your brand. Lastly, consider scenting them, for instance, with a zesty lemon smell.

6. **Fact of the day.** Make your fitness room more interactive by posting helpful tips throughout. These can range from pictures outlining how to use multi-purpose machines to brief dietary pamphlets by the reception or juice bar. These tidbits will heighten the space's interactivity – if they aren't totally overwhelming in their length.

7. **Start the day strong.** Many of us only have less than an hour in the wee hours of the morning allotted for a workout. Not only should your fitness room be open at this time to appease the early risers, 5:30-6:00am preferably, but it should be as lively a space as it is later on in the day after everyone's had their first coffee. This will elevate the moods of those guests exercising and thus heighten the overall experience.

8. **Cleanliness.** A dirty gym may be 99% as functional as a spotless one, but it doesn't inspire people to perform at their best. Yes, staff should be constantly roving the floors to tidy weights and remove garbage, but cleanliness goes beyond this. It involves hygienic aesthetics such as pleasant aromas to mask sweat and metallic odors, appealing music outside of the latest Top 40 pop singles and perhaps a few grander upgrades like small fountains at the entranceway.

Larry Mogelonsky

Hotel Exterior Restorations to Enhance Sense of Place

Hotel architecture is one of the more intricate and creative aspects of our industry. Even though most of us will never have any input in the design of a new property from the ground up – leave that to the accredited architects – there are still numerous opportunities to leave your mark on a hotel via smaller-scale refurbishment projects – necessary tasks to keep up with the times.

Guestrooms need reconfiguration and new furniture purchases to better accommodate the modern, tech-centric business traveler. Lobby spaces require alterations to enhance their 'third space' hybrid functionality. Restaurants that feel dated should be renovated as should their menus. Bathrooms are constantly audited. And all other soft elements must go through the necessary cycle at least once a decade.

An aspect of architecture and design that is often neglected, though, pertains to that of a hotel's exterior and how you populate these spaces to create dramatic points of interest and to generate a distinct sense of place. To borrow a term from the real estate field, what we are discussing here is 'curb appeal' – that gut reaction your guests feel when they first lay eyes upon your property, even before they enter the lobby or interact with a staff member.

The primary reason for establishing a strong sense of place even before guests physically enter the hotel is to tap into their emotions and build positive sentiments right from the start. A grand art deco facade and carport primes visitors to believe that they are in for a luxurious, sophisticated experience. Postmodern materials and angles at the entranceway cue guests to anticipate other hip and novel design features throughout their stay. Clean exteriors assure guests that the interiors are likewise hygienic. Eclectic sculptures build anticipation for more curious attractions in the lobby and corridors.

As you can see, there are many ways to enhance curb appeal and exterior sense of place. As many of these upgrades will break the bank, my bet is that you have neither the disposable cash nor the authorization to initiate such a sweeping overhaul. Hence, we must get creative with our solutions, and below are a few general suggestions to help you find something that works.

Façade Facelifts

As a former professional engineer, I can say with hypothesis-tested certainty that once a hotel is built, it takes more than a pretty penny to enhance or modify a building's outward architecture. That said, we are all guilty of judging a book by its cover, even if this only happens subconsciously. Ergo, there comes a time when power-washing the concrete, repointing the masonry or pargeting the brickwork mortar simply won't do, and a full-scale facelift is needed to fashion a remarkable sense of place and build anticipation.

Structural modifications are the costliest suggestion here, both in terms of money spent and construction time, but they also have the greatest impact. This is not something done on an ad hoc basis; it can take years of planning to execute a change of this magnitude. Two general observations are that we are moving towards more 'open design' with a plethora of glass for better natural light and that builders are actively incorporating more recycled materials.

Beyond this, consult an architect near you, keeping in the back of your mind that fashion cannot trump function. That is, you should strike a balance between creating an impressive entranceway and one that can handle the traffic at peak periods without bottlenecks or convoluted routes to the main lobby floor. I've visited quite a few properties where the designers remained entirely 'off leash', resulting in some spectacular frontage that functions perfectly... except when arriving guests need directions to find the front desk, an issue that's doubly troubling during the dinner rush or large events.

Art and Sculptures

When chosen prudently, fine art can act as a focal point for an exterior location or as a divider for multi-use. It can breathe new life into a space as well as drawing the eyes away from the less savory aspects of your façade. We are moving in descending order from most to least expensive, and it's easy to see why outdoor space can run up a tab. Not only are sizeable pieces costly to produce – often requiring dozens of hours in labor – but they must be made from materials capable of surviving the four seasons.

Additionally, I stress that art affords you the chance to build ties with the community. Thinking beyond inbound links and paltry media coverage, art can be utilized to enrich the local, authentic experience. Two examples help demonstrate this hidden advantage. First up is Ojai Valley Inn & Spa, nestled in a tranquil Californian valley. Ever the local champion, the resort has bought so many pieces from the region's artist enclave and the indigenous Chumash tribe that they could create their very own Art Walk around the property's 220 acres. Second is the Hotel Berlin, Berlin, a modern conference-centric hotel that has impeccably married itself to its hometown by purchasing a large piece of the Berlin Wall and displaying it next to the entranceway along with some descriptive labeling.

Water

Fountains or waterfalls incorporated into outdoor sculptures, expensive as they are, hit our senses on a primal level. The sight of flowing, clean water has always been a form of revitalization. The sounds of gently sloshing liquid can also calm us. Occasionally a slight mist will coat your face, simultaneously shooting you with a rush of cold and refreshing your skin. Water vapor even has a satisfying smell to it. The point here is that water acts upon far more than just your eyeballs, and even though its applications are uncommon, it is nonetheless a tactic towards differentiation.

Lighting and Color

As any photographer will tell you, lighting is everything. Would Las Vegas be iconic without its millions of lights? How would the art deco properties along Ocean Drive in Miami look at night without a little shine? Chandeliers enchant when they're suspended over ballrooms. Christmas trees twinkle through the falling snow and warm our hearts. The pink hue of fluorescent bulbs is palpably distinct from the emblazoned white of LEDs or the warmth of yellow incandescence. Even the now ubiquitous rows of flat screen televisions in sports bars can nudge us to feel a certain way about a space.

In short, when you change the lighting, you change the game all together. This is doubly true when the sun dips below the horizon. Moreover, as light is only as good as the surfaces it reflects off, any discussion along these lines must also take into consideration the color of the paint used on the walls and all other surface materials.

Flora and Fauna

Tall grasses, trees and shrubs can hide unsightly parts of a building's façade, divide large areas into multi-use spaces or add texture and color. Particularly if you are thinking about flowers or herbs, fragrances also become a factor as they work on a subliminal level to elevate guests' moods. And even though we are primarily discussing plants, this section is titled 'Flora and Fauna' because the careful selection of such life can attract members of the animal kingdom, both attractive (birds with vibrant plumage) and aggravating (wasps and mosquitoes).

Plant life from your own regional ecosystem also affords you the opportunity to better establish your property as a purveyor of the much-vaunted local authentic experience. But all this can come with a hefty cost, namely in water requirements and seasonal upkeep. This is in addition, of course, to the preliminary costs of perennial garden purchases and all associated landscape designer or consultant fees. In many instances, striving for local can be even more of a budget killer if the sought-after species are rare or endangered.

Outdoor Third Place

The concept of the 'third place' – used interchangeably with 'third space' – isn't anything new, but it's gained momentum recently with the rise of the hybrid traveler – those who orient leisure vacations around business trips. Along these lines, modern hotel guests desire flexibility in their experiences and in their accommodations. They want to decide on their own daily routines, mix and match client meetings with personal time, and pick where they dine via online research. As it concerns your property, travelers increasingly seek a combination of dedicated work space with a more social environment.

But when considering a third-place approach, hoteliers and designers think mostly about remodeling the lobby floor or an interior area already established as a lounge or business facility. Multi-use spaces that integrate a bar or café atmosphere, grab-and-go foodservices and the desire for business communications via informal meetings, casual group work or mobile-enabled coordination (WiFi) are all in high demand, and there's no reason why these qualities must be exclusive to the indoors.

Creative space segmentation is essential, with attention given to ensure that furniture is comfortable, functional and durable. In many cases, your first thought may be to recruit an F&B franchise to adjoin your hotel, and there is nothing wrong with that so long as there is brand congruence and their signage doesn't diminish your own.

Conclusion

Building the ideal exterior hotel space requires a push for that elusive 'wow' factor and a pull for functionality without breaking the bank in the process. You must strike a memorable first impression while also taking into consideration the theme of the interior, the target consumer demographics, durability and whether the design will stand the test of time. With many aspects that are often at odds with one another, it begs the question: Why bother?

If you don't have the budget, you don't have the budget, plain and simple. But if it's possible to set aside some yearly cash flow for a capital expenditure of this nature, it is something to consider. Try a combination of the six broad tactics explored above.

It's all in the pursuit of first impressions, after all, which are especially powerful emotion influencers. From the moment a guest lays eyes on your property, they are already forming ideas about your hotel, their expectations and what they will tell their friends. An architecturally significant and well-trafficked entrance speaks volumes and sets the tone for an excellent guest experience. Well worth the expensive if you ask me!

Five-Star Housekeeping for Five-Star Properties

Having just completed an exhaustive Pacific hotel tour, my report to hoteliers is this: No matter what your brand or luxury status, housekeeping remains a prickly beast and a constant challenge. Seventeen nights on the road in luxury hotels and one would think that the results are all coming up like daisies. Well, I wish I could report perfection but alas this is not so!

In all five properties that I surveyed, housekeeping errors topped the list. Where others see shortcomings, however, I see opportunities for growth.

While my analysis certainly is not comprehensive, it is interesting to report that not one of my accommodations scored perfect in this regard, this despite being, I suspect, VIP-ed along the way. What is particularly surprising is that these properties are all purported to be in the five-star range, yet still suffered similar flaws. While the errors noted were minor, at the rack rates being charged, there is cause for concern.

Here is the list of errors identified. While most are trivial, the results tend to tarnish an otherwise stellar performance. I have intentionally not mentioned the names of the hotels. Is your property guilty of similar infractions?

1. **Missing dressing gowns.** After use, they are not replaced. A call to guest services relieved the problem quickly, but why should a five-star customer have to ring downstairs to fix the issue?
2. **Improperly made beds.** Not just corners that don't meet specification, but sheets folded incorrectly so that the bed had to be remade. Do you conduct quality control checks and test for this?
3. **Where's the soap?** One small bar of soap in a bathroom that has a separate tub, sink and shower is clearly a stocking error. This was not rectified on subsequent days, which possibly suggests a cost savings measure of ill conception.

4. **Two shower gels, no shampoo.** It's an easy mistake to make when the bottles all look the same. Who does this amenity package design in any event? And why are the products identical in color too?

5. **Odd servicing times.** In one property, housekeepers arrived between 4-5pm every day, which is quite an inconvenience when you are trying to get ready for dinner. By the third day, you would think that they would have recorded our – that is, the guest's – schedule and adjusted service times accordingly.

6. **Sinks that do not drain properly.** A common challenge, but a good housekeeper will test and identify the problem, then issue a repair order to maintenance before the guest has to call and complain.

7. **Showerheads that spray in odd ways.** Rain-style heads are so much in vogue these days. That doesn't they are exempt from upkeep and inspection, though. The narrow channels that create the rain effect are subject to calcification, causing strange diversions of water flow. Whether it falls into the hands of maintenance or housekeeping to fix, this is nonetheless another minor annoyance reminding the guest that all is not perfect.

8. **Sometimes we have turndown service; other times maybe not.** There appeared to be some challenges in timing turndown service. Not one of the properties got it right every time, especially odd given that we were not in the room from 7pm onwards.

I might add, cleanliness was exceptional, so the core work is accomplished. However, it appears that a checklist of sorts represents a clear opportunity. Remember, I am being very fussy here, but so too are your guests! Why spoil their stay through minor errors that are easily remedied? Challenge your executive housekeeper to find solutions that respect your housekeeping team and reward perfection.

Your Quarterly Performance Audit is Here

March, as a month, indicates, at least for North Americans, the denouement of winter and the traditional low season for non-business and non-tropical travel. Many of us also have our taxes to file around this time of year. And then, of course, Spring Break is upon us, and once the snows give way to soggy grass, it's hard not to start yearning for summer.

Alongside north-easterners craving for warmer pastures often comes a returned sense of planning and goals, both personal and organizational. For the former, many of you may be looking to shed a few pounds in time for beach season or even begin the undertaking of a lifelong milestone like running a marathon. Use this last example as a metaphor for any corporate goals you might have: a marathon is comprised of many, many sprints and you can't simply wake up in late June and train for a competition the following week.

The point I'm trying to make is that good planning takes time. Therefore, mid-March is ideal for a performance review, coupled with a public holiday so you don't forget.

Key to any good planning, though, is knowing in what direction to head. Hence, melding several established concepts together, I present to you the Quarterly Performance Audit, designed to be a straightforward questionnaire to keep you on track through the summer, autumn and all the way to next March.

As this is a quarterly appraisal, there are four essential areas to check. Limiting ourselves to four is intentional, as it keeps any produced report brief – one or two pages' tops. This brevity ensures that it is read by decision makers and that there is a readily palpable call to action.

First up is the **asset**. That is, you will want to lens your property through the owners' perspective and assess how the asset has changed in value versus previous quarters or years. Moreover, this entails a surface-level evaluation of the competition and any new entrants that have emerged since your last audit. How do you compare? Are you keeping up with trends or are you falling behind on renovations?

Next comes **human resources**. That is, answering the question as to whether employees like working at your company. Is it a happy office environment? And, as someone who might want to get honest outside feedback, do people like working with you personally?

The third aspect relates to **guest performance**. Nowadays, this often starts by recruiting a social media aggregate software service to review the power of your online presence, digital word of mouth (word of mouse) and what the consensus is amongst your electronic commentators. Key here is to look for recurring problems and any websites where managers could take a more active role in placating reviewers. Guest performance also means doing your own hands-on assessments of essential service features like housekeeping, F&B, front desk, concierge, valet and security. Look for small, uncomplicated ways to improve, not grand overarching changes that are too daunting for the short run.

Fourth and last relates back to **finances**. Yes, looking at a property as an asset is mainly the concern of the owners, but the brand and management have slightly different goals. They might want to know more in depth about ADR, RevPAR, occupancy and where the key costs are. Again, similar to what you might recommend as part of your guest performance audit, seek out simple corrections that you can implement promptly upon their approval.

And just as you should be perusing the remarks left by guests about your hotel, I now ask you for comments on this proposed system. Anything you would add? Is one of the four areas mentioned not as important as it may seem?

Too Many Cooks in the Hotel Kitchen

You've undoubtedly heard the phrase 'Took Many Cooks in the Kitchen' before, used to describe a situation where instead of a leader bestowing a project, product or company with a singular, unified vision, a mission gets watered down to something safe, bland and often incomprehensible. We know this 'design by committee' exists – as it is written into every HR textbook this side of World War II – but we seldom consider it for our own organization.

Moreover, when was the last time you were in a hotel kitchen? During peak hours, it's a battleground – chefs and washers hustling to and fro; the endless clanging of metal and china dishes; open flames and sizzling pans; servers yelling at cooks and vice versa – and not exactly a comfortable setting where there's room to go against the person in charge. When there are customers to be served, you buckle down and complete the task as best you can based upon the vision of the executive chef.

Using this as a prelude, you should give this topic some thought to see how it applies to your own surroundings. With owners, asset managers, general managers, executive committees, management companies, brand affiliations, brand managers, soft brands, hard brands and a host of other stakeholders or company mandates all vying for a chance to steer the ship that we call a hotel, it's all too easy to lose sight of that frisson of vision which will bring something truly exceptional to a property.

I am in no way espousing a complete excision of internally crowdsourced ideas or forming a committee to handle a creative project. At best, there should be a system in place to evaluate which tasks should be decided by an individual versus a group. In a general sense, such a scheme would entail a greater reliance on visionary and bold leadership, but beyond this the criteria would be especially tricky to formulate as they would depend upon the preexisting makeup of an organization's specific corporate structure.

I think we all know inherently when an idea has succumbed to groupthink – you simply don't feel it. This is something I learned from my early days in the advertising world; you can discuss marketing in terms of selling features and benefits all you want, but in the end if you can't make a prospective consumer emotionally connect with your brand then you will fail. As an exercise, look at a piece of advertising and record your gut reaction. If you are in tune with your own emotions, it should be self-evident whether a billboard, magazine spread or television commercial was led by a clear vision or over-boiled to the point where all the flavor has been leached out.

A too many cooks approach to marketing naturally dictates that you 'play it safe' and try to give 'something to everyone'. But when you try to appeal to everyone, you end up emotionally appealing to no one. You'd be better off aggressively pursuing a narrowcast group and pique their specific interests. In this sense, your 'foot in the door' doesn't reach the entire block, but your close ratio increases, which can be a big cost saver.

As a preventative or treatment for any form of operational groupthink – whether it be in marketing, amenities or even a total hotel redesign – the first step should be to clearly define parameters for how to balance short-term and long-term strategies as well as boundaries for each high-ranking position. For instance, a GM may focus on occupancy and ADR for upwards of two to four months ahead of time, often in collaboration with a brand manager, whereas the asset manager or owner has set goals to achieve at every five-year interval. This gets even more complicated when you consider that the asset and the brand may have completely different objectives regardless of timeframe.

Yes, a compromise is essential for these sorts of business relationships to work, but there nevertheless needs to be a grand vision to add as the soul of the property – one that weighs the scales from the point of view of the asset, the brand, the individual property and the management company. It's not an easy task to balance this soul with short-term and long-term objectives – especially in a highly turbulent hospitality landscape – but I have no doubt that with enough hard work you will prevail!

Hotels Need Intrapreneurs

For many, Labor Day is a time of geographical and mental change. Summer holidays are over and it's time to get into that 'back to school' mode – or 'back to work' mode for that matter. This means a gung-ho attitude towards getting jobs done and far less ducking out for a two-hour alfresco lunch. Early September is a great time to harness that sense of refreshed ambition and put it to good use for your property by finding and nurturing your intrapreneurs.

Firstly, a definition is in order. As the name suggests, intrapreneurs carry with them the spirit of entrepreneurship, only they are acting within a larger corporation instead of on their own accord. They are the employees with a certain degree of autonomy to lead new projects and those empowered to break routine to find novel ways to advance the organization's goals.

The prime traits for an intrapreneur are twofold: a diehard passion for the business and an unorthodox approach to corporate structuring. They love their work – in this case, hospitality – and they don't necessarily play by the rules. Often, they flounder when thrown into the meat grinder like everyone else.

How do you go about finding these individuals? Simple: follow the passion. You aren't going to uncover an intrapreneur within a person who views his or her work as 'a job', only those who are career-bound. Verifying this with a direct question to an employee is a good start. Look for those individuals who truly love hospitality and are ceaselessly curious about its operations. Often, you'll find that the persons who are the most disagreeable or objectionable during meetings are the ones with the most zeal; they act this way because they care. In contrast, the team members who just nod their heads at every suggestion are afraid, apathetic, sycophantic or lacking in knowledge to form a counterargument – none are good qualities for senior management.

Beyond passion, the two other characteristics which help are a strong work ethic and a semblance of creative intellect. The former trait – hardworking – should be a direct outcome from an enthusiasm for one's chosen career. The latter – creativity – is a little harder to pin down, but if you consider someone's inventive thrust to be in part attributed to abstract integration of disparate ideas, then having your employees read the trades will certainly help. You never know where the next big thing will come from, so best to soak in as much knowledge as possible about the industry, then let the eureka moments flow.

Once you've found people who have the gumption to lead projects or make unorthodox suggestions, it's time to cultivate their positive energy. Intrapreneurs, like entrepreneurs, naturally operate on their own schedules. Stifle that and you'll have one more unmotivated employee on your hands or, worse, a two weeks' notice on your desk.

Luckily, nurturing begins with a simple conversation. Ask motivated employees about how they'd improve your business, what aspects of hotel operations they observe to be antiquated and any interesting ideas they feel would enrich the guest experience. From there, empower them with small tasks, but also with the explicit opportunity for escalation – both in the magnitude of responsibility as well as in compensation.

Mentoring is also essential as no one gets it right the first time. So, once the last glimmer of summer has come to pass with this Labor Day weekend, start by finding the young along with the veterans who are keen to grow your business, and then give them a chance to become organizational leaders under your diligent tutelage.

FOOD & BEVERAGE

The modern, eclectic design and artwork of the Raffles Le Royal Monceau in Paris contrasts with its historic architecture to create a uniquely memorable venue.

Photos copyright of the hotel and cannot be reproduced without its permission.

Develop Your Food Stories

Food is by far one of the best ways to differentiate your property and make a lasting impression with guests. Why? For one, eating involves a range of senses – taste, smell, sight, touch and, if you count the hustle-bustle of a lively ambiance, sound. It's this activation of so many senses that primes our emotions and signals our memory centers to start taking notes. Plus, there's the emotional transference effect – good times at a restaurant reflect kindly on the parent property.

Next, there are so many ways to stand out and deliver a unique experience in a much cheaper capacity than, say, renovating the lobby or refurnishing the guestrooms. You can accomplish this through unique cuisine or beverage choices, exceptional presentation, chic décor or the creation of a highly social atmosphere. It's this last point that can also help you generate cross-traffic with the actual hotel; making your lobby bar or restaurant the town's hotspot will in turn bestow your guestrooms with an aura of popularity and allow you to command a slightly elevated ADR.

For these reasons, upgrading your F&B experience should be a top priority. And to clarify, you should aim to develop the overall narrative told by your dining experience. What I mean by this is that it isn't just the food, but everything leading up and surrounding the meal, so much so that the sum is greater than all the parts.

If you think about what makes a story great, then that should be your starting point for figuring out the best way to your boost F&B program. Good stories have specificity, variety and theme. Here are some tips to help elucidate what you can do:

1. **Pictures.** Taking photos of one's meal isn't solely reserved for foodies. There's a little gourmand in every one of us. Pictures help jog the memory long after the fact and they are a starting point for sharing with friends, whether in person or online. To get your food noticed online and start a conversation – a task far easier with visual stimulation than just text – you need to have creative presentation

both in layout and ingredients used. My advice? Lots of color. But think beyond food; is your restaurant décor photo-friendly? Is the lighting conducive for taking snapshots of those assembled? Do you have any fun knickknacks on the table? Anything else worthy of a photograph?

2. **Ingredient selection.** Each component of a meal tells a certain portion of the overall story, and it's important that you express the detail surrounding each part. For instance, if you are serving steak on the menu, where exactly did that beef come from and why did you select that cut? Have you partnered with any local, regional or certified organic farms worth mentioning? Along these lines, you might also consider substituting ordinary ingredients with similar but far more esoteric fare – obscure mushroom varieties or replacing lettuce with kohlrabi, for instance. How about cheeses? There are so many eclectic varieties outside of cheddar and mozzarella to get the mind thinking, even if it's only for a split second. If you serve pasta, what stands out more: having a server walk around offering freshly shaved parmesan or another lesser known firm cheese like pecorino or manchego?

3. **Menu as storybook.** Many restaurants treat menus as a means to an end – that is, displaying what's offered in clear lettering and that's all. But what if the menu was something more? What if the meal options were exhibited in more of an infographic arrangement? In this sense, you could have the actual menu items as bolded slug lines with a short paragraph below outlining why the chef chose this dish as well as any unique aspects of the preparation – with thematically appropriate images placed artfully throughout, of course.

4. **Staff as storytellers.** I can't stress enough how important it is to have knowledgeable and expressive servers and managers. After all, what is a story if there's no one articulate enough to convey the proper timbre and gravitas to an audience? You need to hire charismatic individuals, but

part of this can come from 'menu confidence' via proper training. The question to end all questions in this regard occurs when a patron asks, "What you do recommend?" This can be a tremendous launch pad for your frontline staffers to demonstrate the true value of your restaurant's dining experience and fill in the blanks wherever they may be.

These four broad suggestions barely touch the surface as to what you can do. The key is that you create talking points and unique differentiators so that your dining experience is not exactly like any other place around. My final suggestion is that you get out there and learn from the world. Visit restaurants of all cuisine types and price ranges, and observe what makes each exceptional – or not exceptional, which is a valuable exercise. Learn from everywhere and I guarantee good things will come.

Ten Considerations for a Restaurant Redo

While subcontracting your F&B operations to experts is always a viable option, many operators continue to stick to their guns and keep their restaurants firmly within arm's reach. Let's assume that you are in such a situation and are content with your margins, your online reviews, your staff's performance and your chef. *"Ola kala!"* as they say on a Greek island paradise near you, "Everything is fine."

But 'fine' is hardly a substitute for perfect, and unless you are constantly attempting to improve your operations, you run the risk of instilling complacency and a tired brand perception. "The only constant is change," as they also say everywhere except for in those picturesque Greek archipelagos where change isn't necessary.

With new restaurants opening daily with fresh menus and ideations sourced from across the world, your job as a manager and restaurateur is only getting harder. And part of my job is to scour the world in search of contemporary successes, and then report back to you on ways in which you might improve. In the past few months, I've traveled to Australia, Hawaii, Texas, California, Florida, across Canada and to New York City, dining out for all meals. Here are ten of the better takeaways for you to consider.

1. **A restaurant doesn't have to focus on one specialty.** Yes, it's easier to market, but blending two very different yet established styles in one venue can work if you give both the attention they deserve. The one example that captured the best of both worlds was a steakhouse with sushi for appetizers and several fish fillet entrées.

2. **Reinventing house wines.** Why not create custom blends at recognized vineyards, curated uniquely for your restaurant? Partner with serious wineries and price your bottles appropriately – no bottom-of-the-barrel jug wines – to provide a beverage experience unique to your property.

3. **Mix and match appetizers.** Often couples or groups want to share taste experiences as it adds to the

conversation. This is especially true for starter or tapas-style menus. Using a 'three place' and 'four place' serving dish, offer the customers an opportunity to select multiple appetizers at a combined price.

4. **Appetizer samples with beverages.** Imagine that every cocktail served in the bar had an accompanying appetizer that was specifically matched to the drink. This creates a playful companion service while adding to margins. You might also consider a tiny portion accompaniment as an amuse bouche to introduce an element of surprise.

5. **The case for tacos.** I've been smitten by some of the best tacos ever created on the face of the earth, and this trend is not exclusive to the American Southwest. Literally, any meat, vegetable and sauce mixture your chef can create can be supported within a soft taco shell. Use your imagination and have some fun. Tacos can be apportioned for starters or mains – they're adaptable!

6. **Tea time done right.** Sorry, but few of us outside of the Commonwealth elite know how to serve tea properly, the traditional British way. It's time to take tea seriously: teapots unique to each tea blend, teacups with saucers and very hot water. Local sourcing isn't always possible, but nevertheless be on the lookout for small-batch suppliers.

7. **The days of 'supersizing' are over.** Smaller portions and unique preparations are the future. Even something as simple as a burger and fries has been right-sized. The key is higher quality ingredients; patrons will feel full from smaller portions because the ingredients have higher concentrations of nutrients. Local sourcing naturally implies quality, as most forms of storage or processing reduce nutrient concentrations.

8. **Heat has no bounds.** Hot sauces, spicy accompaniments and custom chipotle items are appearing everywhere. A chili infusion seems to be the standard for many new menu elements, even if it's a subtle kick muddled by yogurt or aioli.

Sriracha is the new hot sauce; harissa is the new Sriracha. Any way you put it, the days of bland food are over.

9. **Breakfasts are no longer boring.** Throw out your standard continental breakfast menu. Yes, many people will seek normalcy to kick off their days, but the world is slowly awakening to a more adventurous morning. Think regional specialties and unique approaches to staples like eggs benny and artisanal breads. Find your chefs the freedom they need to innovate.

10. **Buffets for foodies.** The words 'buffet' and 'foodie' are rarely used in the same sentence, unless of course you are dealing with a foodie subculture devoted to the former. Consider the new trend of high-end buffets which are more in the ways of samplers with everything you would expect at a chef's table – not inexpensive, obviously, but still an outstanding way to break from the pack.

With these ten suggestions, it's time to challenge your team. Encourage them to go to new restaurants on a regular basis. Learn what you can and don't be afraid to make it happen.

Larry Mogelonsky

It's Not Just for Breakfast Anymore

In 2015, McDonald's posted an impressive 5.7% annual growth, largely due to a simple change in its operations. The food giant started offering its mouth-watering Egg McMuffin sandwich on a 24/7 basis instead of ending its availability at 11am. Great news for the shareholders and McMuffin fans!

In a similar fashion, my company's 'executive cafeteria' is a delicatessen located within our Toronto office building called the Pickle Barrel. Here, breakfast is on the menu at lunch as well as dinner. When I inquired with the general manager, he told me that breakfasts are the third best-selling item category behind traditional deli sandwiches and salads. What is more remarkable about this data is that the Pickle Barrel opens every day at 9am, well past the typical breakfast rush hour.

Lastly, I've been known to frequent Las Vegas casino restaurants and order breakfast at times that would not be considered traditional for this type of fare. Breakfast is always on the menu on The Strip, which is a definite relief for bacon-and-eggs fellows like me.

Non-scientific in my sample base, I reviewed the collection of menus acquired from hotels I've experienced over the past two years. In this analysis, I eliminated those properties with menus designed exclusively for breakfast hours. And the results: only three out of 47 properties made mention of the availability of breakfast outside of morning hours. Interestingly, another six had some form of breakfast available on their late-night menus but didn't list these dishes for lunch or dinner.

So, what's the lesson from McDonald's, The Pickle Barrel and all this menu perusal? Give your customers what they want. And they want breakfast all day long!

Remember the 1993 movie *Falling Down*? In it, the star, Michael Douglas, goes into a quick-serve restaurant and attempts to order breakfast at 11:35am, a few minutes after the morning menu has ended. What follows is a famous line where he asks, "Have you ever heard the expression: The customer is always right?" and the manager's response is, "That's not our policy here." If you have not seen this sequence recently, got to YouTube, as it is quite provocative

Now, think about your customers at lunch hour. They may not be explicitly asking for breakfast but you're not offering it either! What is wrong with listing an all-day breakfast menu item? Consider traditional continental-style bacon and eggs or huevos rancheros for those in search of a tad more color on their plates. You can even style the dish differently at lunch via plating or other garnishes.

This is not going to require much additional kitchen preparation or training, so have fun. And above all, give your customers what they want!

How Limited-Service Properties Can Effectively Source Local Foods

Like many of you, I have fond childhood memories of idyllic trips from to farm country where my family would stop at roadside stands during harvest time to buy some produce. Nowadays, I rekindle these summertime outings with frequent visits to urban farmers' markets. What these experiences have in common is that they are both all about fresh fruits and vegetables with unrivaled flavor, seasonal variations and a far deeper trust as you exchange money directly with the farmer.

Now apply this sense of nostalgia to your hotel and you arrive at one of the fundamental rationales for the local food or locavore movement. Spend a few minutes with any chef and he or she will quickly tell you that the success of any dish is based upon the ingredients used. If fresher results in a better taste as well as better visual appeal and nutritional value, then locavore is the way to go.

The past decade has seen local foods go from niche to mainstream and even to a guest expectation. Indeed, I've visited many restaurants where the menu proudly lists the names of the farms or producers whose ingredients were utilized, often accompanied by a map showing their respective locations in relation to the property. This identification process provides not only a badge of authenticity for the restaurant, it boosts guest satisfaction and offers great social media fodder.

This is a trend that's here to stay. But why does regionally sourced have to be limited to Michelin-starred restaurants and other haute cuisine establishments? While there is a greater expectation for local foods at fine dining eateries, nothing should prevent a limited-service or smaller independent property from jumping on the locavore bandwagon. And the sooner you do so, the sooner you will reap the rewards!

Assess Your Needs and Start Small

With few exceptions, North America has a bounty of outstanding farms producing just about everything that can be grown outside of an equatorial climate, often with many smaller operations located within easy reach of your property. Take a drive in pretty much any direction and you're bound to find a few. Better yet, make it a company outing!

Rather than set out on a magical mystery tour in search of the perfect farm partner, start with an assessment of your F&B program and the logical integration of local product. If you operate a free-breakfast-only establishment, you're somewhat restricted insofar as what you can introduce. For dedicated, rigidly structured restaurants like this, you have to test the waters. Consider an independent baker for your baked goods, introduce some craft jams or jellies or seasonally source fruit from a close-by orchard.

If you have a full-service restaurant, your opportunities for local input are endless. I recommend a strategic approach, though. Start with an examination of available suppliers. Don't go 'cold turkey' with a goal of 100% locally sourced menus overnight. Sourcing in this manner is not the same as calling a wholesaler. Some items might not be available in the quantities and timing you require. Still others may create a form of sticker shock given their higher prices, especially regarding organic foods.

Strategic local sourcing means identifying suppliers, testing product quality, optimizing delivery performance and accepting a wider range of product variances. It also requires heightened communications between your chef and suppliers, both in terms of greater frequency with each individual supplier and a larger number of suppliers to deal with.

Again, start small. Think one or two local items such as fruit and vegetables, bread and pastries, or condiments and jams or jellies. Then, after completing your initial strategic assessment, include chocolate and confectionaries, tea or coffee producers, spices and specialty items – packaged brands that guests can discuss onsite or bring home with them as part of a trinket souvenir.

At the entry level, with a few exceptions, shy away from meat, poultry and dairy products. There may also be some restrictions within your master franchise agreement that preclude you from considering these, not to mention agricultural inspection requirements as well as storage and handling. With anything consumed, product safety is paramount; any supplier that you feel does not deliver in this category is not partnership material.

Next, recognize that going local may lead to cost increases, largely due to the loss of economies of scale. It may seem odd, but a head of lettuce packed and air-freighted from South America is often cheaper than the same lettuce delivered from a farm 30 minutes away. Profitability is vital after all, but some lenience must be accommodated in lieu of the marketing and community-building benefits that local foods will accrue.

Wine and Beer

Read any industry beverage magazine and you'll quickly discover that 'craft culture' has widespread appeal. Not only do local wines and beers provide a sense of exclusivity to your venue, but chances are that you can build better margins in the process because customers are willing to pay a premium for recognized quality and regional authenticity. Depending upon supplier relationships and what's allowed by law, your menu program can be easily extended into promotional activities that might include winery or brewery tours as well as discount coupons and home-ship programs.

One lucrative strategy is to claim 'only local products served' status. While there are always some guests who are diehard Budweiser drinkers, this move is nevertheless exciting, provocative and bound to attract a good crowd. As a softer alternative, position yourself as a 'local wine and craft beer headquarters'. Either way, for maximum exposure, make sure to lead your beverage menu with these specialty items. And if you are a tad shaky in your knowledge of these products, I am confident that you'll find many volunteers ready to assist you in tasting your selections!

Communications is Key to Success

In any locally oriented program, the adage to remember is 'to tell is to sell'.

Begin with your own team members. Familiarize them with your programs, recipes, products and overarching goals. Use maps to show them the actual location of each supplier. Then personalize the expression by, for example, exclaiming, "We get our apples from Joe Black's orchard located in Beanstown, just 42 miles from here."

Next, give your team the opportunity to taste everything so they can sell from experience. Have your chef explain the differences in how he or she prepares each dish. Have your bartender extol the virtues and unique taste sensations of the selected wines and beers. Create a small cheat sheet that gives line staff bullet points to jog their memory. Remember, your success will be based upon their ability to sell these products, and selling starts with telling the story.

With B2B communications as the foundation of awareness within the restaurant itself, consumers must also be made aware of your commitment in going local outside of this space. Depending on your budget and marketing parameters, your approach should include guestroom sell sheets, tent cards, website displays and lobby posters. Local newspapers and community television networks are always interested in supporting programs of this nature. Lastly, social media is perfect for continual dissemination.

Hug a Farmer

The farming, wine and brewing communities are small. Word will spread that you are local-friendly. You may soon discover that suppliers are approaching you! They may even have more than a few good suggestions to help you take full advantage of what's around. In any case, your neighbors are to be cherished, and as a hotel you should strive to leverage your local sourcing endeavors to become a community leader.

It's a mutually beneficial relationship – as your success increases due to your locavore embrace, so too does that of your suppliers. Even though local sourcing is not feasible in all instances or as easy as calling a wholesaler to execute your entire shopping list, it nonetheless offers substantial rewards in the form of community pride and better product offerings overall.

Larry Mogelonsky

Five-Step Recipe for F&B Success

Fairmont Le Chateau Frontenac in Quebec City is not just the most iconic property in this provincial capital city, but also all of Canada. To be the executive chef of this property is more than just a position – it is to be the flag-bearer for the cuisine of the hotel, city, region and in fact the entire Quebecois population. This is no small order! Add to this the task of realigning the entire F&B for this 611-room property as part of a recent $75 million renovation.

Enter Executive Chef Baptiste Peupion, determined to reclaim the property's leadership in the F&B arena. As Chef Peupion explains, "The property was resting on laurels established many, many years ago. The good news was that there were no sacred cows and no one who would feel put out by reorganizing the entire F&B concept."

The work was so extensive that someone visiting the property prior to the renovation would not recognize any of the new outlets or locations. The lower level occasion restaurant was converted into a dining space for groups and meeting rooms. The main floor dining room, bar and outdoor spaces were completely gutted and replaced with a three-part combination of deluxe restaurant-bar-bistro. Total budget for this project probably exceeded the cost of building an entire 100-room, limited-service property!

You get what you pay for, and armed with a completely new dining room and kitchen, Chef Peupion has instituted a remarkable five point fundamental approach to cuisine – one that is easily replicated within your F&B outlets. In a nutshell, his fundamentals are:

1. **Simplicity.** Follow the basics. Your guests should be able to easily understand what you are serving and what the ingredients are.
2. **Essentials.** All the core selections should be available to the guest. The guest should make the selection, not the chef.
3. **Originality.** Just because you are delivering, say, a beef steak, it does not mean it should be boring. Use your creativity to deliver a memorable experience with interesting

sides that delight the senses and compliment the flavor of the meat.

4. **Passion.** Every member of your team should share your passion for food and taste experiences. If they are not committed, they have no place in your kitchen. Delivering exceptional dishes is a total team effort.

5. **Fun and pleasure.** Food is fun; eating should be pleasurable. Heck, it better be given that we do it so often. Keep this in mind in all that you do.

Chef Peupion, together with Restaurant Chef Stéphane Modat, has worked to conceive a menu for the signature restaurant, Champlain, that not only capitalizes upon local suppliers, but also brings taste sensations that fit the five point fundamental program.

Our conversation moved beyond the chefs' 'pleasure dome' to the broader issue of being a restaurateur within the hotel setting. As Chef Peupion remarked, the origin of hotels and inns started with the food experience – a filling meal to soothe the stomach of a weary traveler. Then, as hoteliers focused more upon profitability, F&B became less important, even to the extent that many hotels franchised or sub-contracted their restaurants. Now, as the differences between hotel properties are narrowing, hoteliers are once again realizing that a memorable stay can start in the kitchen.

Both Chef Peupion and Chef Modat are under forty – young for senior chefs. It's exciting to know that they work in a great hotel and have already achieved this level of success. And as every astute hotelier knows, you should make F&B a top priority: EVERYONE EATS!

Larry Mogelonsky

What Is Modern American Cuisine?

The United States of America: 50 states, East Coast, West Coast, Heartland, over 320 million people and a heck of a lot going on everywhere. On the food front, you have clam chowder in New England, burritos in the Southwest, fried chicken in the South, deep dish pizza in Chicago and myriad other regional offerings. How are we supposed to summarize the culinary habits of this gigantic nation under the banner of 'Modern American Cuisine' let alone 'American Cuisine' when there is so much diversity?

In the 1950s, 1960s, 1970s and 1980s, before the rise of craft enterprises and our present food revolution, perhaps we could have written about the homogeneity of American cuisine: doughnuts, hamburgers, apple pie, thick-cut steaks, mac'n'cheese, corndogs, peanut butter and jelly sandwiches, bland coffee or whatever else was sold at the quintessential roadside diners. While these dishes could all easily fit within the description of 'Classic American', the modifier of 'Modern American' is more synonymous with ingenuity and international cultural fusions than with anything traditional.

The Unites States is, after all, a nation of immigrants, and one that has always survived on its entrepreneurial gumption, so it makes sense to ascribe these attributes to the country's 21st century food creations. Only in America will you readily find avocado on pizza – the doughy pie first brought over by the throngs of Italian migrants around the turn of the century while avocados were adopted as a major source of umami flavor from our Mesoamerican neighbors. Only in America will Asian staples like sriracha and kimchi become wildly popular burger toppings; the word 'hamburger' is itself borrowed from Germany, following the millions of people from the fatherland who crossed the pond prior to World War I. Only in America...I think you get the idea.

However, in many ways describing your restaurant's cuisine as 'American' is utterly meaningless, especially when your restaurant is situated in one of the 50 states. The fact remains that the USA is such a diverse and constantly changing nation that this identifier doesn't help form an image in a consumer's mind of what type or genre of food is crafted at a locale. These preformed images are important to be aware of because they establish what a customer will come to expect from their forthcoming dining experience. And if you have any marketing wherewithal at all, you know that expectations are everything. Using the term 'Californian' works, as would 'Floridian' or 'Midwestern' or 'Kentuckian'. But 'American'? No.

Whereas an eatery described as 'Modern Spanish' might readily circumscribe consumer expectations of an exquisitely vivid tapas menu, 'Modern American' isn't nearly as specific. It can mean creative burger combinations, counterintuitive pizza toppings, cosmopolitan taco permutations or even a new way of preparing a prime rib roast. When it comes to building customer expectations, 'Modern American' is hardly precise terminology, and therefore it should be avoided unless you know exactly how to use it. There are exceptions, of course, like, say, an American restaurant in Moscow that only serves the perfunctory burgers, fries, milkshakes and fruit pies – in this case, using this modifier does in fact help set the bar. But wait, such a place already exists – it's called McDonald's.

My point with all this is that we are largely misusing or under-representing the potential inscribed by the 'Modern American' or 'New American' monikers. Whereas McDonald's, Burger King and other fast casual outlets might embody 'Classic American' cuisine with burgers and hot dogs reigning supreme, and while some chains like Checkers still offer the archetypal 1950s drive-in experience, Modern American strives for bolder flavor combinations and incorporates food concepts on a global scale.

Along these lines, must a restaurant in this category have to serve a conventionally dressed hamburger with lettuce, pickles, onions, bacon and processed cheese? Ditto for pizza, wings, meat entrées, Caesar salads, grilled cheese sandwiches and so on. Why not surprise guests by offering a waygu beef patty (a Japanese cattle breed) with agave-glazed (a Mexican plant) pork belly and spicy piri piri sauce (an African chili cultivar) on a hemp seed bun? That's three continents in a single bite. Hungry yet?

Essentially, deploying the 'Modern American' qualifier should carry with it the tacit marketing message of, "We are innovators.

We are tinkering with your taste buds." Like the Gilded Age and the great advancements made during that time to electrify our society, in the great food revolution we are currently experiencing I encourage you to take an Edisonian approach to your cuisine. The core of Modern American fare is the process of trial and error, repeated and scrutinized until you craft something that is truly remarkable.

Many forward-thinking chefs are already hard at work towards this goal, striving to achieve their own American Food Dream. Regrettably, following the time-tested paradigm that scarcity often fuels the best innovation, this contemporary evolution is widely taking place outside of hotel properties and is currently in the hands of food truck operators, first-time restaurant owners and anyone else with a culinary vision but nominal monetary safety net.

My hope for you, as a hotelier, is to recognize this opportunity and to make your F&B offerings a vaunted amenity on par with or surpassing all other operations. Harness the safety net afforded to your restaurants by being part of a larger entity to drive creativity. Challenge your executive chefs to run wild with their grand ideas. From well before the Gilded Age and right up until the start of the modern era, the hotel was the epicenter for the best cuisine available in any given city or region. Now is the time for the hospitality industry to regain its former glory, and embracing the full potential of the 'Modern American' banner may just be the rallying cry you need for F&B success.

Fast Food Restaurants Are Where Food Trends Go to Die

One sunny Saturday afternoon, I find myself walking about through downtown Toronto, my home city, and I pass by an A&W, a popular Canadian fast food restaurant, proudly flaunting its newest menu item: sriracha burgers. I stop, scratching my head, troubled by this discovery.

For those of you still strictly in the meat and potatoes camp, sriracha is a fiery Thai chili sauce that has only recently become a table name, largely due to the highly adept marketing and distribution tactics of a Huy Fong Foods, Los Angeles-based producer. I've known about sriracha's unique taste for well over a decade as it's been a pervasive condiment offering at the numerous hole-in-the-wall Thai restaurants scattered through Toronto's highly multicultural city center. Within the past five years or so, however, inventive chefs at hip restaurants and the proprietors of food trucks have embraced the sauce as a novel way to spice up their menus. Now it appears sriracha has wholly crossed over into mainstream appeal.

This is troubling, for me, because when fast casual and fast food eateries adopt a cuisine trend such as sriracha, that trend loses its novelty, thereby threatening the individuality of other 'more elegant' establishments.

As a proud Canadian with a keen eye on culinary developments, there are two other recent examples that immediately come to mind: poutine and maple bacon.

Poutine – French fries and cheese curds lathered in hot gravy – is traditionally associated with the French-speaking province of Quebec, and indeed, it is still hard to find authentic poutine anywhere else. Sometime within the past three years, though, McDonald's started offering the dish at locations throughout the country with, frankly, subpar quality levels. Additionally, there are now several franchises dedicated entirely to selling and serving this cuisine. The poutine market is 'saturated', and any new poutine-related launches would be hard-pressed to elicit any reaction but an eye roll.

Maple and bacon are a tad easier to understand. Long considered an archetypal Canadian food, maple syrup and bacon have been added at gourmet restaurants to infuse a given dish with a sweet-umami blast. And then the trend started to creep into the lower tier, popping up like sriracha at popular fast food burger franchises and as a purchasable item at just about every grocery store in the country. The problem was that as maple bacon usage became ubiquitous, quality suffered – cheaper cuts of meat and blander syrup flavoring to name two. As a result, perceptions of this food have forever been altered, and not necessarily for the better.

These are but three cases that I've observed as a Torontonian. Undoubtedly you'll be able to apply your own region-specific examples.

The message here is that if you want to continue to excite and delight with your F&B offerings, you have to stay ahead of the adoption curve. Sriracha is no longer a 'bold new flavor'. The trend is done; move on. Why bother adding poutine to the menu when it's already available at your five closest competitors?

Of course, there is something to be said about the classics and staying true to form with their execution. If you have outstanding ingredient quality and superior cooking methods then offering poutine or a maple bacon burger won't count against you. But they certainly won't make for a good marketing push either.

To be unique in the world of F&B, you have to be just that – unique! If a fast food chain with over 800 locations is now marketing sriracha to its customers, how would it benefit your restaurant to follow suit? Would you honestly consider your outlet's poutine creation to be exceptional when the French fry dish is also available at every McDonald's for a hundred kilometers in all directions?

As hoteliers, it's our job to be food leaders, entrepreneurs and inventors. The challenge for your executive chef and culinary team is to be aware of when a food craze is petering out, and then adjust accordingly. It's a perpetual game of cat and mouse to stay ahead of the curve, but that's also part of the fun!

The Year of the Pulse

In 2016, the General Assembly of the United Nations proudly declared it be the 'International Year of Pulses'. Before your mind wonders onto thoughts of electromagnetism, impending solar flares and what not, know that a pulse is simply another, more encompassing term for a bean. And the timing couldn't be better to bring these powerhouse foods back into the limelight.

As the saying goes, beans are good for your heart – the more you eat them, the more you...like them! And this is without-a-doubt true. Beans, lentils, peas and chickpeas are all fibrous carbohydrates with lower glycemic indexes than wheat or rice, and many species are packed with antioxidants. The fiber and oligosaccharides in pulses are also good for culturing healthy gut bacteria that stave off colon cancer, boost nutrient absorption and offer a host of other positive effects. It's also been found that one's diet connects with how a person looks and feels, with beans and the good microflora they encourage helping to positively influence aging and mood.

With the mounting stigma against artificial flavors and ingredients, pulses represent both a natural thickener and 'umami' additive as well as a vegetarian and vegan protein alternative. Yes, they can be ground up into powders, but they can be likewise be readily incorporated into soups or vegetable mashes. Beans also come in a rainbow of colors, allowing chefs to create dishes that are as pleasing and vibrant to the eyes as they are to the stomach.

In short, beans are excellent. This 'year of pulses' trend is part of a larger movement of going back to ancient grains and superfoods that are now scientifically proven to enhance your health. For this reason alone, hotels should look to become leaders in bean-dominant cuisine so that they can thereby become advocates for healthier lifestyles.

It amazes me that beans aren't more commonplace in the traditional Western diet. Undoubtedly if you make this a mandate, your chefs will already have a thousand different ways to bring pulses to the forefront of a menu. And for inspiration, organize a culinary tour of a few of the many cultures for which beans have been a staple for millennia both in terms of simple street food and fine dining – Indian, Lebanese and Ethiopian are three of my favorites.

Lastly, if your restaurant has answered the UN's call, be sure to advertise your involvement through social and other digital media so that your fans can come appreciate your efforts in leading the charge for healthier diets.

Predicting Next Year's Food Trends from Fall Fairs

Gourmet burgers are so 2013. Tacos? I thought they peaked a while back. What's next year's hot dish going to be? When will our current bacon craze go belly up? (Pun intended.) Important to us hoteliers, if we have a vague semblance of where food trends are headed, then we can plan menus accordingly and harness the 'hype' surrounding on-the-up cuisines for an extra marketing boost.

The Ex, short for the Canadian National Exhibition, is Toronto's (my hometown's) annual carnival event and provincial fair, held during the tail end of August at Exhibition Place near the city center. It also happens to be a massive gathering for food trucks and countless other avant-garde culinary pioneers. Having long since considered the rickety mechanical rides and games as juvenile, I'm one of thousands who visits The Ex solely to try several esoteric snacks.

Joining the throng in the convention-sized Food Building where deep-fried Mars bars, blooming onions and other treats you shouldn't tell your doctor about are all but perfunctory, I find myself each year on the hunt for the newest, wildest creations. Last year I sampled chocolate bar-stuffed pastries, cocoa-infused fried chicken with chocolate-infused ketchup (surprisingly tasty!) and peanut butter sriracha rolls. The year before that was enfeebled by an *E. coli* breakout traced back to a vendor selling cronut burgers.

Most of these crazy creations are one-and-done; you try them once and for whatever reason you aren't drawn to them again — their appeal is sheer novelty. However, these foods are predictive in a lot of ways of what will soon reach the chic downtown restaurants as gourmet menu offerings, appearing at various chain eateries sometime down the road. For this reason alone, annual fairs like The Ex or any other food-oriented symposiums are worth perusing.

Go by yourself or with your family, give someone on your culinary staff a good measure from the petty cash fund to write a report, or make it a fun team outing. You can take a broad approach, looking for general trends like adding bacon to nearly everything or the over-smattering of chocolate on traditional comfort foods. Alternatively, hunt down one or two unique meals that stand a good chance of working with your current inventory and making an impact on your menu.

It's an exercise in staying slightly ahead of the times and in finding a food item that will get people talking about your restaurant. After all, F&B is a relatively inexpensive way to experiment when compared to other operations.

Although novelty generates headlines and draws in the crowds, the key here is to find foods that are both inventive and tasty enough to warrant repeat visits. Seek out fare that is familiar with only one or two mildly eccentric additions. For instance, red velvet pancakes work because they taste like their ordinary fluffy counterparts but are scarlet in color instead of yellowish-brown. Deep-fried mac and cheese is another winner as the savory, creamy flavors of the pasta are gastronomically compatible with the salty goodness of boiling batter. Éclair hot dogs on the other hand? Sorry, but cheap meat and refined sugar just aren't meant for each other in that way.

The best litmus test is to try each of these for yourself, and then get a few other trusted opinions. Dig deep – there may be admirable elements in a certain snack that are hamstrung through detrimental combinations. If this is the case, look to extract what works and brainstorm as to how they might be applied elsewhere.

Lastly, food research is a consummate process. My journey to The Ex only happens once a year. However, that doesn't mean I'm not out on the town for the other 50 weeks actively trying new restaurants in search of other creative new cuisines – ones which may or may not draw their inspiration from gluttonous food fairs such as The Ex.

While the food at The Ex may be a story of year-over-year one-upmanship, there are always ingenious chefs about to unveil the next big thing at a restaurant near you. With this, my concluding point is this: To have an adventurous F&B menu that guests will remember, you must first be adventurous with your own palate. And if you don't succeed, then try, try again!

Halloween Cuisine

My interest in Halloween-centric foods piqued early this year, when I visited the annual late summer exhibition in my hometown of Toronto and one of the latest oddities was a bloomin' candy apple. Inspired by the fairground staple that is the deep-fried bloomin' onion, this super sweet cavity culprit brought me back to my early childhood when candied apples were still handed out to trick or treaters by loving parents in the neighborhood. Yes, I'm that old.

When you think of Halloween cuisine, besides the syrup-dipped fruit, you'll likely conjure up images of cookies, chocolates and other confectionaries, all decorated to fit the spooky theme. And getting the basics of this theme right isn't hard either – crack out the orange food coloring, layer it over some black or brown treats, add in marshmallows, lather on one iteration of sugar or another and then shape it all into something readily identifiable like a ghost, a spider or a vampire bat.

But again, that's only the basic level, and the sky's the limit for what you and your chefs can do to, say, spruce up the F&B presentation at an All Hallows Eve party. Remember that we eat with our eyes as much as we do our palates and nostrils – a strikingly creative interpretation of cuisine helps to craft a unique dining experience.

Think cakes, cupcakes or cookies adorned with icing in the shape of spider webs or gnarled ghoul hands. Candies pressed in the form of one scary creature or another. Classic ice cream flavors specially colored and packed with toppings to imitate any manner of witches' brew or zombie brain confit. Going the healthy route, you could try throwing in some pepitas – otherwise known as pumpkin seeds – to complement any main or salad. Or, as presentation is everything, you could hollow out the flesh of any member of the gourd or squash family and use the thick hush as a bowl for soups or stews.

"Those are great ideas, Larry. But Halloween is tomorrow. It's a tad late to put these into action for the annual party we throw in the ballroom."

True, if it's already late October, then it's a little late to start planning a party. In an earlier book, I published an article entitled "Embrace the Weird," which used our titular festival as a launch pad to discuss marketing opportunities for other B-list holidays peppering the calendar. Along these lines, it is now a good time to use Halloween cuisine as a base camp for what you can do to differentiate your F&B presentation for other upcoming festivities – Thanksgiving, Christmas, New Year's Eve, Valentine's Day and Easter, to name the five that are top of my mind.

In most cases, the base ingredients or dishes are already set, and your main goal will be to find some exceptionally creative way to express those ingredients. Take Thanksgiving for example. Whereas Halloween is all about sugar, Thanksgiving is time for the savory and the sumptuous: turkey, gravy, stuffing, mash and pumpkin pie. If every hotel under the sun is offering a classic holiday dinner with these five elements, even if your turkeys are cooked to perfection and your ingredient quality is top notch, it will be difficult to stand apart from the pack. While there's nothing wrong with a classic meal like this, it is still 'just a turkey dinner'.

Instead of a turkey sandwich, why not offer a turkey crepe with chopped turkey bacon? I've even seen Belgian waffles with turkey stuffing on top. Instead of roasted parsnips, try candying them with a pinch of Indian spices. Regular mash can be replaced with sweet potato mash. Or, as Paleo dieting is all the rage these days, offer a faux mash made from puréed cauliflower with grated Parmesan and truffle shavings for an umami punch.

The possibilities for each festivity are endless, and it always comes down to the ingenuity of your chefs and the freedom they are afforded to be adventurous. As I continue to stress, be different and be exceptional in every aspect of your operations if you want to succeed. Food just happens to be one of the relatively inexpensive routes to this end, and thus I encourage you to explore what's possible. Happy Halloween!

Using Ingredients Native to Your Region to Market Your Restaurant

A decade ago, the locavore movement was still an emerging trend, saved mostly for niche artisanal shops and ultra-posh restaurants with four-digit price tags. Heck, even the portmanteau 'locavore' was seldom understood or recognized by readers. Now, though, if your restaurant isn't sourcing locally in at least some capacity, you might as well lump yourself into the fast-casual dining category. The times, they are a-changin'...and they're a-changin' fast!

Furthermore, local ingredient sourcing is no longer perceived as a value-add – it's become an expectation for guests of all ages and dispositions. And we've done this to ourselves, after all. With restaurants the world over using some iteration of 'Locally Sourced' as part of their marketing efforts to usurp the competition, consumers have become numb to the terminology. In other words, basic locavore tactics by themselves no longer impress guests enough to generate that vital word of mouth, nor are they a clear point of differentiation.

Before you misinterpret me, know that I'm not advocating for you to abandon the practice of local sourcing. It's a noble pursuit and one that all restaurants should aspire to have in place. Rather, it's time we beef up your locavore crusade so that you can continue to wow guests and give them an exceptional dining experience that they will remember long after the meal is complete. With this as a goal, let's discuss implementing an 'indigenous' F&B program.

Defining Indigenous Foods

If you want to take your locavore efforts to the next level, consider infusing the menu with flora and fauna that are indigenous to the area – that is, foods that were naturally thriving in the local ecosystem before the intervention of humankind. Also called 'Forest to Table' as a comparative term to 'Farm to Table', I prefer the label 'indigenous' because many of us don't live in or near woodland regions. I suppose if you ran a seafood joint, the term 'Ocean to Table' would be an easy substitute, and along those lines 'Field to Table' and 'Sand to Table' might also apply. As delivering an 'authentic local guest experience' is all the rage these days, what is more authentically local than the species that have dwelled and evolved in the region for eons?

To successfully craft cuisine that fits this profile, a serious upgrade to your food knowledge is essential, as you have five millennia of agricultural terraforming to contend with. Take tomatoes for instance. A staple to the culinary traditions of numerous Old World cultures, don't forget that they didn't exist outside of Mesoamerica prior to the arrival of Hernán Cortés and the start of the Columbian Exchange. In fact, the Italian for tomato – *pomodoro* – translates back to English as 'golden apple', alluding to the marketing verbiage that Renaissance merchants used to sell these erstwhile exotic, little red (and often yellow) fruits.

The same goes for corn, potatoes, sweet potatoes, zucchini, squash, bell peppers, chilis, cashews, peanuts and numerous others – all of which were domesticated by Central and South American peoples prior to the arrival of the conquistadors. Likewise, most domesticated animals, and countless other vegetables and fruits for that matter, originate in the Old World, thus disqualifying them from indigenous status for any eatery in the Americas. Furthermore, the 'Old World' denotes Europe, Africa and all of Asia – a blanket term, in other words. This means that, for example, unless your property is situated within the Fertile Crescent, you'd be making a very bold claim by saying that your bread or pasta is indigenous.

As you might have already guessed, designing an entire menu of indigenous foods, no matter your locale, would be more restrictive than working with a paleo raw vegan dietary regimen. Hence, this is not what I recommend. Instead, consider indigenous foods as featured and seasonal selections. For starters, think native fish species, local fowl, big game, regional herbs, indigenous berries or wild mushrooms (though please consult a mycologist as many wild fungi are poisonous), using such ingredients either as the centerpiece or as a conspicuous infusion to another entrée. And then, as a more audacious extension of this concept, put a single dish on the menu that is exclusively indigenous. At the very least, it'll certainly make for a good talking point to enhance the dining experience, regardless of whether it is ordered or not.

Selling Indigenous Foods

Indigenous eating isn't for everyone. They are hard to consistently source. They might not be within budget to attain. As mostly undomesticated species, they may be difficult to prepare. Consumers may not be accustomed to their flavor profiles and find them displeasing. Some may be too intimidated to order the item off the menu. And others may even take offense at the use of the word 'indigenous' (another reason why 'Forest to Table' is in the mix).

However, we now find ourselves in an era of rapid food evolution, and with the awakening of adventurous palates the world over, all of them ready to try new cuisines as a vehicle for entertainment, braggadocio, self-discovery or personal expression. The locavore movement is in vogue right now and your efforts to this end won't go unnoticed, especially if you have a unique angle to highlight.

What I stress is that you weave your indigenous ingredients into your overall property or restaurant narrative, whether this is expressed via a blurb on the menu, a javascripted popup on the website or additional training for your servers so that they can communicate this point of differentiation directly, this last method preferable if you plan to use this tactic for daily specials. For example, you might use a local fowl on the menu as a point of entry to describe aspects of the region's history, touching on interesting factoids about native species, what the environment looked like prior to the arrival of European settlement, any fascinating cultural traditions that existed before the bleaching of modern consumerism and so on. It's not meant to be a college lecture, so keep it short and make it fun.

Another alternative to consider is to go native with your cuisine presentation. There aren't too many options in this camp, but that doesn't mean they can't make an impact. For instance, local might pertain to serving a butternut squash soup in a locally produced mason jar, whereas indigenous would mean presenting charcuterie on a board made from a tree distinct to a nearby ecosystem.

Indigenous Versus Invasive

While indigenous food sourcing is on the rise, many restaurateurs are headed the opposite direction. Instead of targeting the species native to the region for consumption, they are going after those that have been artificially introduced and are running amok due to a lack of natural predators. While not directly falling under the banner of 'authentically' local, the rationale behind this movement is sound: by training consumers to select and eat invasive species, we are protecting our ecosystems from irreversible damage and allowing indigenous species to thrive.

This is not to say that supporting indigenous eating makes you an environmental persona non grata. Often is the case where by supporting native pedigrees – especially endangered ones – you are preventing them from being pushed out by more economically viable species. Two notable examples here include the heirloom Chopee okra, native to South Carolina but rapidly being usurped by its African mainstay, and amaranth, indigenous to Mexico but being pushed out in favor of other more common grains.

Invasive ingredients aren't without problems of their own either. While ruminating on invasive eating, I'm constantly reminded of my zany Australian relatives who insisted that I shoot all rabbits on sight – a pest on the continent and certainly a viable candidate for this locavore sub-trend once they figure out their vaccination issues. If only the Aussies could find a way to neutralize the toxins in cane toads then they'd be good as gold. Hitting a little closer to home, I once had zebra mussels and I can politely tell you that there's a reason why they aren't a sought-after dish at the neighborhood seafood shack, or at least it isn't an entrée you'd want to consume without a generous dose of aioli. Ditto for Asian carp – hard to debone, harder still on the palate.

Even with these drawbacks, through trial and error as well as a little bravado from the executive chef, you will find something that works. And the marketing bonus will come via the fact that you are helping the local environment, not just the local economy as most other locavore adopters are currently doing.

Conclusion
Whether you go with indigenous or invasive, the underlying message is that you need to innovate your F&B offerings to continue to draw the big crowds. These are exciting times for culinary evolution and for the hospitality industry to become true leaders in this regard. Be bold with your cuisine and the marketing, the buzz, the word of mouth and the revenues will follow.

Larry Mogelonsky

Room to Brew: The Future of In-Room Coffee

My morning coffee is a perpetual delight in my life, warming my insides, prickling my nose with its soothing aroma and sparking my brain for the day ahead. It's a simple pleasure, a momentary respite and a ritual I do not take lightly. I bet many of you are in the same boat! All subtle addictions aside, coffee is an essential part of many people's lives and as such it merits your attention – both at home and at work.

In this case, let's assume your place of work is a hotel or related to a hospitality setting in some manner or another. But that doesn't mean that the home coffee experience is not applicable – quite the opposite in fact. We want our guests to 'feel at home', and any actions we can take to better emulate a person's image of the ideal daily caffeine ritual will be greatly appreciated.

I ask you to give your own honest opinion as a traveler and not as a hotelier proud of his or her place of work: Do you like in-room coffee? Do you get the same sense of solace and rejuvenation from a hotel cup as you do at home? Does anyone for that matter? Coffeemakers in guestrooms are all but mandatory design elements, but many properties only pay them lip service. Therefore, whatever you can do to augment this micro-experience will do wonders towards guest satisfactions because it will come as unexpected.

It's critical that you reassess your caffeinated endeavors at this juncture because our collective appreciation of these beverages continues to climb through the roof. Call it the 'Starbuckification' of coffee, as ever since this chain broke out in the 90s, we've all come to respect and crave a superior quality brew. This is coming, of course, from a North American perspective; many parts of Europe, Africa and Asia have upheld a high caliber of coffee-making for many decades or centuries prior to this company's worldwide expansion. Regardless of any oldfangled customs, nowadays Starbucks and its ilk represent somewhat of a gold standard for coffee excellence; if you can't match what they are doing then you're failing to impress guests in this regard.

Another important note on diction: I am talking about improving the overall 'coffee experience' and not just the actual coffeemaker. In this sense, we are talking a bit broader, encompassing in-room possibilities as well as anything pertaining to the 'club lounge' or 'social station' model. While augmenting in both areas will see results, you need only devote your energies to just one of the pair – as long as it's to the point where it becomes a feature worthy of praise.

As it stands right now, most in-room coffeemakers aren't total eyesores, but they aren't doing the room any favors either. Their designs often don't match the room's theme or color tones, nor are the most common accessories – such as plastic wrappings, cardboard sleeves and Styrofoam cups – very appetizing either, especially for our inner germaphobes. Chic, new and easy-to-use models like those offered by Nespresso or Keurig present a viable option for upgrading your in-room coffee selections. Apart from a few drawbacks such as restocking issues, these single-cup brewing machines provide guests with a variety of delicious flavors beyond stock packets of ground beans, thus adding to the perceived value. Moreover, you can investigate other niche coffee apparatuses like a French press or a cold brew system – anything to differentiate your services and leave an impression with guests.

The other main area to explore pertains to tea. If you aren't a tea drinker, give it a shot; those three letters will change your life! Green, white, black, oolong, herbal and all in-between – there are so many different types of tea for you to choose from above the normal offerings you see on menus everywhere else. With tea, you must also take into account the wide range of accompanying fragrances, which contribute to the extraordinary nature of each individual experience. Yes, give guests one or two familiar options so they don't feel completely blindsided, but then go for a few esoteric varieties to heighten the sense of surprise and interactivity – unfamiliar or exotic tea bag labels can spur guests' curiosity by prompting them to read. All the better if your hotel already has its own private label or has partnered with a company that does just that.

Jumping over to the other side of the fence is the break room or social station concept. Often 24-hours in operation, these are perpetually restocked common areas where guests can procure their choice of caffeinated beverages in addition to other food items like fresh croissants, specialty pastries or sweet and savory cookies. Although a topic for a whole other discussion, let's just say that such companion treats have a tremendous compounding effect on one's coffee experience, and they represent a great boon for differentiating a hotel's petit dejeuner.

The obvious shortcoming of favoring lounge concepts over in-room coffee is that guests have to journey beyond their own rooms in order to take advantage of these complimentary treats. Despite this inconvenience, there are far too many advantages to this system for me to side with any in-room partisans, so much so that one could easily see how in-room hotel coffeemakers will become extinct within a matter of years.

First, by catering to everyone at once, it allows you to source a more complex coffee or espresso machine, delivering a far better brew for nothing more than the cost of regular maintenance and intimidating a few tenderfoot guests. Next, this lounge style encourages a social environment, which is oh-so-important to today's grab-and-go, millennial-centric culture – heaven forbid you don't offer free WiFi at these locations. Third, with well-placed signage, such stations can become highly educational (who doesn't want to learn about what they put in their bodies?), transforming a quick coffee break into an interactive mixology event.

Last and importantly, because you can offer fresh food in conjunction with coffee or tea, it's an excellent opportunity to showcase local produce and to theme your F&B presentation in line with a few of your brand's exceptional qualities. For a property in the United Kingdom, you better have an impressive spread of English teas, biscuits, shortbreads and scones. Or, if orange is the dominant color of your brand, why not theme your coffee breaks accordingly with orange pekoe tea, fresh citrus fruits and chocolate-tangerine-infused confections? Many cultures and countries have their own takes on how to best prepare these amazing beans and leaves and the onus is on you to embrace the authenticity of your surroundings.

With points made both for and against, which side do you fall on? Is in-room coffee a thing of the past or is the proliferation of these social stations just a temporary phenomenon?

Larry Mogelonsky

Hosting a Chefs' Competition

Recently, I was invited up to the BMO (Bank of Montreal) Institute for Learning (IFL) in the suburbs of my hometown of Toronto. The purpose of my visit was to guest judge the regional IACC Copper Skillet Competition for Ontario, whereby chefs operating in conference centers were given all the same ingredients and only two skillets to complete dishes in less than 45 minutes.

As one of two evaluators alongside Rose Reisman, we marked each chef's creation based on taste, presentation and applicability to a banqueting or catering scenario. This year's contest included:

- Luc McCabe from the NAV Centre in Cornwall, Ontario
- Rebecca Lynore Marett and Alvin Guilas from the IFL in Scarborough, Ontario
- Alexsandra Lalonde and Barrington Graham from St. Andrew's Club & Conference Centre in downtown Toronto, Ontario
- James Van Hagen and Kent Phillips from the Ivey Spencer Leadership Centre in London, Ontario

To sum it up, the food delivered by all seven competing chefs was utterly fantastic. For the three chosen mains, the Cornish hen was succulent – hard to do with only a skillet and a limited timeframe – the pork tenderloin was well-spiced and the fishiness of the trout was balanced with lemon, herbs and just the right amount of butter. While each chef worked frantically to get their plates ready, they were all humble, enthusiastic and thoroughly knowledgeable about their cuisine after the show.

Last year only had five participants, and so the organizers could keep the competition behind closed doors within the confines of IFL's kitchen. However, this year, with seven contestants, that was no longer possible. Instead, tables were assembled along a central corridor in the building's atrium with all guests free to walk around and watch the chefs in action. I told the organizers this after the event was over and I'll repeat it now: Hosting this competition out in the open was an outstanding idea.

Yes, it raised a few minor safety issues as you had passersby coming close to hot pans, open flames and sharp knives, but the positives far outweigh any such drawbacks. Observing professional chefs in action isn't something we're privy to every day, which makes this contest both exceptional and highly memorable. By letting people witness the event, the organizers got them talking, both in person and via social media as noted by the dozens of smartphones cameras whipped out to document the occasion. Lastly, it was quite interactive as onlookers were invited to sample the cuisine and to ask questions.

While the Copper Skillet Competition comes but once a year to Ontario (with many other regional and international iterations), I pose the question to you: Why can't your hotel host a public cooking show or competition?

We all know that cooking shows are popular these days, and your own culinary event can piggyback on this contemporary craze. At its most basic level, you could host a contest only between the chefs working at one property. More challenging will be to bring participants together from multiple locations – either those operating at the behest of a specific management company or a given brand (either soft branded, association or chain). Of course, there are logistical challenges – safety concerns, spacing, electrical access and so on – but the returns are too great to ignore.

Not only will these types of events highlight a hotel or conference center's prestige as a culinary destination, they will also inspire all chefs to continue to hone their craft in the kitchen. Much like how other industries have trade shows for the exchange of ideas, so too do gourmets need to occasionally rendezvous to exhibit their culinary creativity. Then think of your guests. Such a competition is memorable and interactive – both incredible attributes to heighten guest satisfaction and build a loyal customer base.

Larry Mogelonsky

Cinemagraphs: The Future of Menus

For our purposes as hoteliers, cinemagraphs are essentially a form of animated GIF with a short, repetitive action to give the appearance of continuous movement. With smartphone cameras getting better and better with each year's iteration, in addition to improved animated GIF software features, cinemagraphs are no longer exclusive to the professionals. On the other end of the spectrum, tablets are becoming cheaper and more widespread, and both desktop and mobile browsers are now far more accommodating to such embedded moving pictures. In short, technological advancements will soon enable cinemagraphs to replace all digital photography.

All after, with a picture worth a thousand words, a video is worth a thousand pictures. Cinemagraphs and videos are thus a marketer's best friend, and you'd be wise to understand their applications before the competition does, and before they lose their early adopter luster. So, how can you use cinemagraphs to sell your property and its amenities?

The most pronounced application is for your website and the digital photography housed therein. For each landing page where pictures are prominently featured – either as embedded features within a text-centric element or as part of a slider – still images can be replaced by cinemagraphs to add some texture to the page. Whether the topic of the page is the hotel lobby, F&B, spa or area attractions, working in a slight movement will captivate the eyes and subtly hint at the mystique of your property.

Nowhere is this more apparent than for a restaurant menu. In the short-term, you can spice up an F&B page with cinemagraphs of a cup of coffee accented by billowing vapor, a thick steak with jus bubbling from its edges against a white plate or a slice of cheesecake with molten chocolate snaking along a rivulet towards the apex. These are three examples of well-focused still shots where repetitive motion gives the sense of freshness and thereby increases the perceived value of each dish. Next, consider the long-term and how the widening prevalence of tablets will soon enable many eateries to forgo paper altogether. Imagine building an app for your restaurant's menu where every item was accompanied by a cinemagraph.

The notion of heightened perceived value through video applies in less direct ways to every other aspect of your operations. Think lobby waterfalls, flowers in a vase wavering in a slight breeze, cyclical ripples in a picture of the hotel pool, blades of grass vacillating against a stunning mountain vista from the tee-off on the golf course or steam dancing upwards against the backdrop of the wooden sidewalls of a sauna room.

You simply find the recurring movement in everyday objects, and then capture it with a suitable camera. So, next time you are due for a photography update, ask about cinemagraphs and what you might do to keep up with this budding trend.

Larry Mogelonsky

Putting on the Ritz in the Kitchen

When you think of upscale dining at hotel brands such as St. Regis, Four Seasons or Ritz Carlton, do you think about wearing formal or semiformal attire? For most, tradition dictates that a five-star hotel naturally comes with an uber-luxury restaurant accompaniment. This dining establishment would typically feature high priced menu items, often themed, and an expansive wine selection. Service would always be exemplary. In all, every detail would lend itself to an incredible and often unforgettable dining experience (with prices to boot!).

The exceedingly casual lifestyle of locations like South Florida challenge this 'fancy dining' proposition. In these places, while there is no shortage of dining options, one would be hard-pressed to find anyone wearing a jacket or formal dress, except perhaps at a life cycle function such as a wedding.

Take for example The Ritz Carlton in Sarasota, Florida, a stunning, 266-room luxury property. When opened in 2001, it featured a traditional dining establishment. Catering primarily to in-house guests, the restaurant's pricing rendered it essentially 'special occasion only.'

To improve overall revenue, management embarked on a bold vision, repositioning the venue under a new name: Jack Dusty. According to Chef de Cuisine Caleb Taylor, the plan was to create an environment that was locally focused, fun and welcoming. He notes, "Despite the widespread availability of exceptional locavore products, it was nevertheless difficult to find anyone focusing on this trend."

He continues, "With this as a base, we set out to build a menu with each food item priced one or two dollars below the equivalent in our competitive set. In this way, local diners would immediately recognize value. Thus, our goal was to deliver fresh food, expertly prepared, value priced and all in our incredibly luxurious environment." That was the first step.

Next was to create a memorable and 'fun' experience. Consistent with the Jack Dusty theme, the Ritz Carlton team designed menus with courier-esque fonts that look like they were produced on a manual typewriter with old-style wood-block illustrations. The menu is presented on a clipboard, adding to the casual vibe.

Food presentation is simple, with settings and dishes casual and not a white tablecloth in sight. Even bread is made in house, baked and served from a tin can.

As an exciting ending to the meal, the dessert menu is printed on a pseudo-treasure map of Florida, the paper extensively beaten then rolled into a glass bottle for tabletop distribution. Menu items are anything but orthodox and always have an interesting twist. Did you ever think that you would see s'mores and whoopee pies on a Ritz Carlton menu?

Results have been impressive, with overall restaurant volume up over 50%. Locals now represent over 60% of total traffic – in all, a remarkable transformation. Significantly, attracting more community members to the Jack Dusty concept has had a halo effect on other product offerings at the hotel.

So, if a Ritz Carlton can totally change their food offering like this, why can't you? Examine your restaurant operation. Are you truly happy with the performance? Do your price points appeal to the local market? Or, to be more precise, is your restaurant's atmosphere appealing to people in the neighborhood?

Change is an attitude. Jack Dusty's brilliance is in the creativity and the execution. The Ritz Carlton recognized the challenges in the marketplace and stuck to a plan that delivers for the target audience. Applause to them. Now it's your turn!

Four Success Traits for Your Next Executive Chef

Do you remember the times when the top restaurants in most cities happened to be in the best downtown hotels? This was the era of the carving station serving chateaubriand for two, Caesar salad with dressing made by the waiter tableside and flambéed desserts.

Today, however, this isn't a guarantee. Excellent restaurants can be found nearly anywhere, and even though hotel restaurants in the luxury segment have matured significantly, they are nevertheless engaged in a perpetual war for culinary dominance with just about every other upscale purveyor in the area.

As every brand sharpens their accommodations, amenities and service levels, restaurants become key differentiators. There's a fundamental logic to this. Food consumption is core to our existence, forging permanent memories. And even if you somehow forget the décor or the size of the suite you recently stayed at, chances are a great meal will still be top-of-mind.

From a social media standpoint, nothing is as 'tweetable' or 'likeable on Facebook' as a photo of a just-served dinner entrée or dessert in its full regalia. The quantity of these photos is a significant multiple greater than the number snapped of guestrooms or even views from the hotel window. I'll even wager that a property's overall TripAdvisor rating can be reduced or enhanced based upon guests' experiences at the in-house restaurant.

Four Characteristics that Make the Executive Chef

At the core of any restaurant operation is the executive chef. He or she is the spark plug that generates those 'wow' dishes that create lasting images and memories for your guests. As the restaurant experience continues to evolve, so too does the role of executive chef. Your exec's responsibilities in the front of the house are as important as those in the kitchen. So, what skills should you look for during the selection of this most critical position?

1. **It's all about the food.** The is the most obvious: Can your chef deliver a menu that sets your property apart and

can it be done within the context of your property's strategic operating plan? It used to be that the GM could interview a prospective chef in the kitchen, as if the ability to wield a knife and manage heat was sufficient. This is a fundamental skill, but nowadays it's insufficient as a hiring criterion.

2. **It's about balance and teamwork.** No matter how high profile the chef, he is but one person amongst a team working in this department. Your chef has to respect the contribution of others and partner effectively with your F&B director. Lone wolf chefs rarely last long and tend to leave an incredible mess in their wake.

3. **Personality.** Being executive chef is no longer just about being a chef. Larger than life, your chef's capabilities transcend the kitchen, dining room and even the property. Your exec has to be as comfortable in the front of the house with guests as he or she is in the back of house with the staff. He has to be able to work with your PR team, share recipes, pose for photos and, ultimately, be accessible.

4. **Your chef must generate social sparks.** Social sparks are those items that are worthy of sharing. Now more than ever, chefs should be a part of the social fabric of your organization. In other words, your chef should be an outgoing activist, embracing your social media programs and sharing his or her behind the scenes approach to making the restaurant a true business differentiator. Your chef must be as comfortable with his smartphone as he is with your back-of-house technology.

In Vino Veritas Section Introduction

Lest you forget that F&B amounts to more than just creative or trending culinary additions to your menu, the 'beverage' side of the equation represents half of a restaurant's quest to satisfy each and every patron, and it often generates well over half of an outlet's profits. As alcohol is a high-margin product, healthy drink sales can be make-or-break for an F&B operation.

It is with this impetus that I've written extensively on various topics related to how you can boost your restaurant revenues through the sale of wine, beer and spirits. Just as the modern customer yearns for a more authentic experience with each meal that's ordered, these same individuals also crave more exclusive beverages to complement their food. Thus, not only are beverages a worthy profit-maker, but they can also enhance dining satisfaction which in turn can boost overall sentiments for the hotel.

The world of alcohol is endlessly diverse with each country and each region within each country passionately crafting their own unique specialties, generation after generation. With global supply chains and access to niche producers from all corners of the globe, alcoholic beverages are now less a matter of having some form of immediate lubrication for your meal or a source of inebriation and more a journey of cultural discovery, giving you a glimpse into a land's proud traditions and heritage.

While contemporary terms like 'small batch' or 'craft producer' touch upon this point, they do not fully express how pleasurable it can be to sample different products and deepen your understanding of this complex industry. It is up to you as the avid hotelier and bold marketer to give your wine and spirit offerings the same respect as you would your regular food menu. Stay true to the theme and brand of your restaurant, but always strive to provide guests with a beverage experience that they cannot find anywhere else.

In Vino Veritas: Should You Have Your Own Private Wine Label?

Private labeling of wine at restaurants, clubs or hotel properties can be incredibly lucrative, but it also comes with its own set of challenges and caveats. Operators all over the world are already engaged in this 'curated wines' practice, and so to answer the titular question: A resounding yes! You should have your own branded wine – one red and one white for a start, and with no premium options. Just make sure you understand what you are getting into as it is far from a catch-all solution.

Let's start with the positives. Private labeling gives you complete control from a pricing perspective, allowing you to avoid comparison shopping on the menu because it's a product that's unique to only you. That and your margins will be better.

Second and even more significant are its effects towards brand reinforcement. Private labeling means putting your property's name on one more touch point with the consumer, especially one that is connected to a sense beyond mere sight – taste, smell and touch if they pick the bottle up. This brand reinforcement can be further amplified by offering your private label as a gratis, in-room amenity or for client gifting. Dovetailing this are the opportunities to expand your brand presence via social media whenever someone takes a picture of your label.

The biggest red flag, aside from staining a white cloth in red wine and tying it around a stick, is that private labeling, if done properly, will cannibalize sales away from other bottles on the list. Then there's the potential that such a venture will tarnish your reputation given that the most common perception of private labels is that they're table wines or low-end stock.

While examples certainly exist at the high end, it will take a lot to change people's minds, especially if you are operating in the haute cuisine or luxury space. I'd recommend that you position your private label not as the lowest retail option but somewhere around the top of the bottom quartile of your wine list so that it appeals to neophytes as well as to more sophisticated drinkers in need of a quick and palatable glass or two.

This is a very broad introduction to the subject of private label, and if you are at least intrigued, reach out to local wineries and vineyards to see if a partner is possible. And as an extension, consider that this doesn't have to pertain only to wine, particularly if your hotel isn't located in or near a growing region. How about in-house private label cheeses? Ditto for breads, snacks, chocolates, confectionaries or whatever else best suites your brand.

In Vino Veritas: A Wine List Time Capsule

A friend's cookbook gift unearthed a remarkable bonus – a 50-year old wine list from a luxury Caribbean resort, The Dorado Beach Resort in Puerto Rico. Half a century ago, I was not even of legal drinking age, nor had I any inkling of the varieties of wine available for purchase. At the time, my parent's wine habits consisted of 'red' or 'white', while the Californian wine industry was basically a volume business of jug wines at low prices. Drinking fine wine was clearly a fringe experience reserved for the finest restaurants and aristocratic palates. Oh, how times have changed!

How did they sell wine half a century ago? As a 'primary source' for historical research, this wine list gives us some strong evidence. First, there is a detailed description about each of the types of wines with grapes and growing regions. Rarely have I seen such a voluminous text inclusion on any modern wine list.

Next, within each wine type and region, bottles are sorted in price order with key features identified. Many half bottles are available as well, far more than what would be currently offered. The products available include only two American vintages, while all the remaining offerings are from France and Germany, underscoring how wine production has evolved since then. Lastly and tying into this second point, there is a final section entitled 'Some of the Rarest Wines in the World' with an introductory paragraph that makes them feel more like circus oddities than exquisite drinking experiences.

Today, North American tastes for wine have been well educated, and the array of available product options has expanded exponentially. A typical wine list at a four or five-star property will run many pages, potentially intimidating the novice drinker but also intriguing for those who are interested in exploring the many facets of this miraculous liquid.

What is most interesting about the old wine list is the pricing. The lowest prices for full bottles are the two rosés, both at $3.60. The most expensive was a Chateau Margaux 1929 for $35. But, you could have saved money and bought the 1964 vintage for only $18. Interestingly, the ratio of most expensive to cheapest is roughly 10:1.

One can't help but note the significant rise in pricing at the ultra-high-end; we are probably at a range-price ratio of nearly 1000:1 by now. Just examine your latest wine list. If your lowest offering is, say, $35, what do you offer for $175 or $350? Like everything in life, the best continues to be sought out with vigorous demand and the scarce are only becoming scarcer. Some things change for the better, though. Just consider the shock of not having Californian wines readily available for stocking, at least for a North American property.

Moreover, reflecting on the past can help us predict the future. As wine awareness increases, more and more previously taboo regions will become acceptable for consumption. Ask people what they thought of Californian wines in 1966 and they might scrunch their noses. Nowadays, they lick their lips.

In the past two decades, we have seen a similar growth and acceptance of Argentine, Australian, Chilean, New Zealand and South African wines. What will the next 20 years bring us? Oregon now makes Pinot Noirs that rival Napa in all but prestige and price. The Finger Lakes are experimenting with Baco Noir to elevate that varietal above jug status. I hear that Lebanon and Northern Israel are bringing viticultural decadence back to the Levant, a region where wine has been exalted for over six millennia. A little birdie told me that even Mexico has a small but burgeoning wine culture. And Eastern European nations like Hungary, Romania, Georgia and Bulgaria are finally emerging from their communist doldrums to globally export some truly delightful bottles.

Lastly, what can we extrapolate about wine prices in the coming decades? If the past 50 years have been any indication, expect the high-end to only go higher. And this makes sense as worldwide appreciation increases – an effect most pronounced by the recent proliferation of Chinese demand for fine wines. What will happen when wine reaches similar levels of popularity in India, another country of over a billion souls? That 1000:1 ratio might reach 10000:1 by the time my tongue gives out.

In conclusion, the world of wine is only getting larger and more elaborate. If you plan to use this beverage as a means for more restaurant revenues and increased guest satisfaction, you best stay on top of the trends, as you never know where the next big thing will come from.

Larry Mogelonsky

In Vino Veritas: 100-Point Wines

What's in a number? More specifically, what does '100' mean on a rating scale? Typically, something that reaches triple digits like this is equivalent to a perfect score – the best there is.

When it comes to wine, numbers are important. Those who are aficionados understand ratings issued by Wine Spectator, Robert Parker, Wine Advocate and so on. New entrants are also coming onto the scene to guide beginner oenophiles on their quest for grape enlightenment – try playing around with the mobile app 'Vivino'.

Each of these well-known resources ranks vintages every year based upon their staffs' finely tuned and trained palates. The rating scales used tend to be logarithmic in design, whereby an 88-scoring drop – while quite acceptable for the average person – is the equivalent of a Chateau Plonk for the calibrated tongue. When a wine is ranked 100, it is not just a good wine; it is one of the very best in the world. And if you think about the tens of thousands of vineyards and the multiple varieties sold by each winery, it is incredible to think that a 100 rating is annually bestowed on a handful of bottles at most. In fact, a 100 wine is so rare that even to drink one is a very special occasion – perhaps one should wear a tuxedo or evening gown for the occasion.

Given their rarity, few hotel restaurants offer 100-rated bottles on their wine list. If they do, fewer places still have more than one or two, and in very limited quantity. On top of all that, with prices soaring into the high triple and quadruple (and quintuple!) figures, there are only a morsel of consumers willing to fork over the necessary cash for such an indulgence. In this sense, a restaurant's 100-rated wines are not really for drinking, but instead a source of cachet to propel the wine list into the limelight.

Hence, while drinking 100-point wines is on my bucket list in perpetuity, I don't actively seek them out on a regular basis as I'd be broke within a matter of weeks. Instead, I use the presence of said bottles as a barometer for the rest of the cellar. A respectable collection of 100-pointers indicates a commendable selection of everything else.

When you extrapolate from this inductive reasoning, it's easy to see how a well-curated wine list can serve as an alternative promotional vehicle for an establishment; be renowned for your cuisine as well as your wine. Moreover, when a restaurant (in a hotel to boot) has a vast store of 100-rated bottles, not just a handful, it greatly augments the wine's marketing power to the point where the cellar becomes an attraction in its own right.

A recent trip to Crystal Springs Resort in Hamburg, New Jersey, just outside of New York City, and its Restaurant Latour, a Wine Spectator Grand Award Winner for many years, provided a firsthand experience with one of the finest cellars on the continent. Here, wine is not just a computerized bin number – there are close to 135,000 bottles in stock – but a true passion. Here you will find over 200 different 100's, and they are all for sale with more than one of each available. The cellar itself is built like a museum; a true *cave à vin*, it is designed to be visited.

I lucked out in that my own tour was directed by Robby Younes, Vice President of Hospitality & Lodging as well as the hotel's wine director (parallel positions). Robby holds a sommelier certification, as well as membership in Les Chevaliers du Grand Vin and a Masters of Wine certification. Charismatic to the core and effusive about all things food and wine, Robby knows the cellar blindfolded. On this basement level, which is ostensibly far larger than my whole house, we meandered our way through tight, cold, stone-walled corridors, ambling between viewing windows for each of two dozen featured French chateaus, Super Tuscans, rare Californians, Rioja gems and so much more. And when we finally sat down for a meal, the wine list was presented in the form of two-inch-thick binders (one for red, one for white).

This isn't just wine appreciation on steroids; it's oenophile heaven, with an injection of Captain America's super soldier serum. And in rural New Jersey no less! The strategy here is that Crystal Springs Resort has clearly levered its world-class wine cellar as a prime differentiator. In its competitive market for meetings and groups business, the hotel's wine list serves as a core asset to draw this segment and other corporate social events.

As Robby elaborated, the wine isn't merely an adjunct to the restaurant; at this level, it acts as its own hotel amenity whereby guests can tour the cellar at their own convenience, independent of whether they are about to dine or not. With a valuation at over $25 million, the property's *cave à vin* is virtually unforgettable, which plays a significant role in both repeat visits and positive word of mouth.

As has been iterated in several of these 'In Vino Veritas' articles, it's all about creating as unique and authentic an experience as possible. While reaching the echelon of Crystal Springs Resort in this regard may be a tad out of reach, there are still many opportunities for you to excel on the wine front. Be the best you can at local wines, focusing on one vineyard or even one specialty (for example, ice wines). By getting involved and creating something exceptional, you will add to your property and your sales.

In Vino Veritas: Focus on Terroir

There are many aspects of viticulture that distinguish two bottles of wine from one another. The layman will focus on the grape varietal, the vintage and the country of origin – including that region's established growing practices – as the three primary factors. They seldom direct their attention to the combination of specific geography and geology as well as the resultant microclimates which help endow each region's soil with unique properties that are ultimately expressed in the grapes.

The word that best describes this topographical consideration is terroir, and it makes for a good talking point with patrons.

Many people won't be familiar with or have even heard of the word, so it's up to your wait staff, if prompted, to educate guests in as simple a manner as possible. Who doesn't like to learn something new after all?

Terroir will flesh out a bottle's story in an entertaining way and thereby enrich the overall dining experience. And that's what we are talking about here. By knowing one or two facts about each wine's unique backstory, servers will have one more angle to not only enhance liquor sales, but also to deepen the rapport with patrons.

For instance, suppose a guest is undecided between two bottles of red – the first is an outstanding, reasonably expensive Californian pinot noir and the second is the cheapest one on the menu. Obviously, you should push for the upsell, both for monetary gain but, more importantly, because you know that this customer will enjoy the former selection. The question is: How do you go about convincing this patron to dish out the extra cash?

The most apparent route is to explain the benefits of choosing the Californian pinot through a narrative. A brief description like this might touch on the unique flavor of this varietal, the vintage if it is noteworthy, perhaps a couple specific aspects of the winemaker's growing practices and (as it's in the title of the article!) the wine's terroir. To this end, you might describe how the vineyard is located along the leeward slope of a sierra which makes the microclimate just a touch drier, better concentrating the sugars in the grapes.

Discussions of terroir can incorporate proximity to mountain ranges like this along with closeness to rivers, headwaters, valleys, dormant or extinct volcanoes, mineral deposits, old growth forests or strong ocean currents. Terroir is a blanket term for nearly everything that has or will affect the soil in which the grape roots will feed.

It isn't vital that your team know every characteristic of a bottle's terroir, but one or two interesting or exceptional aspects will go a long way towards enriching the stories used to sell more wine and boost the positive sentiments that consumers have for your restaurants.

In Vino Veritas: Aging Barrels

When discussing wine and what differentiates one bottle from another, the three most common topics are grape varietal, place of origin (country, appellation, terroir) and vintage year. From a sales perspective, having confidence in your knowledge of these three will go a long way towards developing a 'wine story' to woo and sell to patrons. Just in case those three can't seal the deal, aging barrels represent a fourth element you can add to this conversation. Fermenting in barrels is also done, but that's a separate topic from aging.

After all, aging wine in wood barrels can drastically alter the taste profile and often make the beverage unrecognizable when compared to its un-aged counterpart. Discussing a label in terms of its unique aging process is a great way to deepen the guest-staff rapport, especially given that the effect of barreling isn't common knowledge. Such a chat may or may not lead directly to increased liquor sales on the spot, but it will most certainly augment the overall dining experience. Hence, everyone in the F&B game should know a bit about how wine is aged.

At its most fundamental level, the only three materials for barreling you need to know are stainless steel, American oak and French oak. Stainless steel is the simplest, imparting minimal flavor and allowing the liquid to stew in its chemicals. The other two, however, are slightly porous, allowing for slow evaporation (concentration of flavor and aroma profiles) and oxygenation (softening the taste of the tannins). Oak is unique in this porous-yet-watertight characteristic, making it the ideal wood for years-long wine maturation.

Next of importance is how much the coopers 'toast' the barrels — that is, how much they burn or char the insides. This is done to help shape the wood but more so to impart flavor to the wine as the reactive liquid slowly chews away at its inner lining over months or years and incorporates chemicals from the oak into its flavor profile. A good barrel can withstand about three years of leaching from wine before it becomes inert.

Of course, the flavors of toasted American and French oak differ greatly, with the former considered to impart bolder, more intense flavors and the latter often likened to sweeter tasting notes. Think butter, caramel, cinnamon and vanilla additions for whites and coffee, smoke and spice for reds. As barrels can impart stronger flavors, this becomes an issue when dealing with patrons who prefer mellow, sweeter wines. In these cases, a steel cask sauvignon blanc is better than a two-year, American oak chardonnay, while a pinot noir would obviously be preferable to a Bordeaux aged in French oak.

As someone who has long understood the wooden aging process and its effects, the use of American oak, French oak or steel is second nature. However, if your palate is underdeveloped, the best way to learn to distinguish these discrepancies is to complete a vertical tasting of the same wine matured under the three different conditions. And in terms of conveying this knowledge to the customer, it may be best to give your servers a quick elevator pitch on how aging barrels can let a freshly fermented wine evolve into something else entirely.

In Vino Veritas: Choose Your Wine Glass Wisely

"You have chosen...wisely," is what the immortal knight says to Indiana Jones after he drinks from the Holy Grail – an unassuming wooden cup hidden among a swath of poisonous chalices and jeweled goblets.

I'm reminded of this scene at the climax of *The Last Crusade* whenever I make a decision as to how best to pair a chosen wine with its appropriate glassware. Not that it is a blatant faux pas to mismatch wine and glass (at least not in my circle of friends), but proper etiquette should be followed wherever possible. Not only do shape and size affect aroma and flavor via a series of complex molecular interactions, but they offer a strong visual demarcation to augment the overall drinking experience.

Just Google any listing of wine glass styles and it's apparent that there are quite a few more types of glasses than you might have stocked at your restaurant. You might only carry white and red glasses with flutes for champagne, in which case it would serve you well to source perhaps one or two more types so that different wine orders are given a palpably different treatment.

Think of it as the wine's garnish. Imagine a couple dining out – one orders a zinfandel while the other gets a cabernet sauvignon. If you present both in the same glassware, there will be little insofar as visible demarcation as both varietals' purple-red colorations are practically indistinguishable to the layperson. Now pour the zinfandel in standard red and the cabernet sauvignon in a large Bordeaux wine glass – a drastically augmented and more complex drinking experience for both patrons. These effects would be even more pronounced for, say, a guest with a gewürztraminer in an Alsace glass sitting opposite someone with white wine in a wide Chardonnay glass.

From one quick internet search on the many types of glassware, it's easy to go overboard to the point where you are confusing your servers. Expand as you see fit; the main takeaway here is that when it comes to wine, beer, cocktails, coffee, tea or even milkshakes, we drink with our eyes as much as we do our mouths.

Presentation matters; it influences perceived value as well as what you can charge.

Lastly, there has been a recent change towards the more casual 'tumbler' style of glasses. These are appropriate for a bistro-style affair and you might wish to consider them for after hours or in a more informal setting. But they should not be utilized for fine dining or with expensive wine.

In Vino Veritas: Biodynamic Wines

One topic that has been much discussed is organic wines and how they can be leveraged to enhance alcohol sales through their health and wellness appeal. Whether or not it's January – the month of dietary pledges and austere new regimens – the time is ripe (pun intended!) to talk a little about biodynamic wines and their prospects as another weapon in your F&B arsenal.

Essentially, this is organic taken to the nth level with soil, plant and livestock health all considered ecologically interlinked. And the numbers reflect the obscurity of this model, as there are only some 450 wine producers worldwide following biodynamic practices.

It all revolves around what is best for the health of the soil, especially during the off-months when the grapevines are hibernating. Key principles include diverse crop rotations, a lack of herbicides or pesticides, the use of cover crops and the cultivation of green manures to enrich mineral content and soil carbon dioxide levels. There's also a spiritual undercurrent to biodynamic agriculture whereby certain protocols dictate that ground quartz be dispersed over the terrain and stuffed animal horns be buried under the earth.

While appealing to a customer's desire for sustainable practices is a good angle, its effects will be muted because a vineyard's overall health is not a primary reason to buy wine. The leading question is: Does the wine taste good? And the answer for biodynamic labels is increasingly affirmative in this regard, both from blind taste tests and from my own personal experiences.

In the end, though, writing in the word 'biodynamic' next to a bottle on the wine list is nothing more than a conversation starter and a modifier to induce more sales. As the latter point is quite straightforward, it's the former that interests me more. If a patron asks what is implied by biodynamic, this is a green light for the server or bartender to launch into a concise story and, importantly, to build rapport with said guest.

Meal satisfaction is more than just the food on the plate – it's the furnishings, the sounds, the service, the crowds and the personal relationships formed with staff. A running current throughout this

'In Vino Veritas' series has been to educate your team and make sure that they are passionate about wine – so that they can boost alcohol sales, but also so that they can add another dimension to the dining experience. And given the correlation between how a guest feels about their meal and their overall satisfaction with the hotel, it goes without saying that augmenting the dining experience should be a consummate goal.

In Vino Veritas: Returning to NorCal

NorCal, short for Northern California, produces ostensibly the best wines in North America. Ever since Chateau Montelena's chardonnay beat out the longstanding French incumbents in a blind taste test in Paris in 1976 (the lighthearted 2008 film *Bottle Shock* portrays these events), Napa Valley and Californian wines have been on an upward spiral of fame, flavor and price. Nowadays, the very mention of the word 'Napa' is synonymous with quality.

In geo-political terms, NorCal is traditionally defined as stretching from Monterrey County north to the Oregon border. But when it comes to wine, we are primarily talking Napa and Sonoma Valleys, and to a lesser extend Mendocino and Lake Counties. This distinguishes it from the Central Coast AVA, which encompasses all vineyards from below the Bay Area to just north of Santa Barbara.

My purpose in writing about NorCal is not to give a concise background on the region, its core varietals, and some of the more remarkable labels I've experienced like Grgich Hills, Heitz Cellars, Stags Leap and (once-in-a-lifetime) Screaming Eagle. If you are looking for a quick tour of the finest wines produced, I recommend wine-searcher.com, which reveals that 44 of the 50 most expensive bottles in the United States come from Napa County (the rest come from Sonoma County and just one from the Ojai region).

Rather, with its leading reputation and often-exorbitant prices, sourcing product from this region can be a hassle for any property that isn't ultra-high-end. How can you tell what's good and what's only perceived as good because of the Napa appellation? How can you stock bottles that are both explosively tasty and quintessentially Californian, but also cost accessible? Lastly, how do you convince guests that the steep bottle price is worth the purchase?

In other words, when approaching NorCal wines, you need a strategy. At the bare minimum, recruit a prudent wine merchant with experience in the region. Let him or her do the initial leg work and make recommendations based upon your unique situation – that is, budget, restaurant classification, average clientele, revenue expectations, cellar conditions and so on.

As for convincing patrons of the 'value' in these wines, it shouldn't be too fast, especially with lists like those on Wine-Searcher at your disposal. In other words, the accolades accrued by wines from this region over the past four decades speak for themselves.

Next, even though it may be a tad wallet-emptying on your part, you have to start tasting these wines for yourself. They're damn good after all. Try to distinguish which varietals mesh best with your taste buds and how Californian wines differ from those made in, say, Italy or France. Then, through rigorous 'trial and error', find a few wineries that you would deem as 'easy drinkers' – those that aren't too pricey and can work for a variety of occasions. It's going to be rough, but I believe in you!

Remember, the ultimate goal of building your wine list and cellar is profitability. Your wine pricing should reflect and be proportionate to your entrée selling prices. True, one or two 'badge' bottles might seem exciting, but remember that there are carrying costs on those inventory items that rarely turn, if at all.

In Vino Veritas: A New Zealand Nosh

Viticulture in this small, remote, agrarian nation was less so a matter of naturally suitable terroir and more so happenstance. When the Brits ended their exclusive trade agreements for New Zealand meat and dairy products in 1973, it left quite a few Kiwis scrambling for creative ways to stay solvent.

If there's a will, there's a way...especially when alcohol is involved. In under a decade, clever farmers had successfully adapted sauvignon blanc to select, rain-shadowed pockets on both the North and South Islands. Sandwiched by the Coral Sea and the Pacific Ocean, New Zealand still has a maritime climate, imbuing its grapes with different flavors. Specifically, the persistent wetness and cool summer nights result in less sugar concentration and lower acidity.

Within 50 years, New Zealand has emerged to rival many other producing nations, both in quantity and quality. While the country is still experimenting and diversifying the varietals it grows, when it comes to presenting the average customer with a Kiwi Vino-USP, we are essentially talking about sauvignon blanc and pinot noir from the Marlborough region near the northern tip of the South Island, which accounts for over three-quarters of the country's production.

What I've found is that these two varietals along with the third most common, chardonnay, are all consistently delicious and reasonably priced. I've long been a fan of New Zealand wines, but it wasn't until last spring when I had the opportunity to sample them in full during my first sojourn to Auckland.

As a long-time-drinker-first-time-caller to the island nation, my suggestion for you as a budding oenophile is to taste-test Kiwi pinot noirs and sauvignon blancs against their counterparts from other premier appellations. Match a New Zealand pinot against ones from NorCal and Burgundy and you'll find that the lower acidity is immediately palatable, with the Kiwi bottles further distinguished by their earthy, savory and full-bodied notes.

For the whites, many already consider New Zealand sauvignon blanc to be the best in the world of this varietal, but it is nevertheless worthwhile to compare a drop or two with those produced in the Loire Valley, or, if you are in the mood, Chile, South Australia, the Western Cape and Ontario (Canadian patriotism in full effect). Quintessential sauvignon blanc, most Kiwi labels are light on the tongue with clean notes of tropical fruit and melon – ideal for salads, white fish or wine neophytes. They also tend to be steel cask aged, adding to their feathery taste.

While the island nation undoubtedly has a lot more to offer than this one growing region and two varietals, the purpose of these articles is to help you enhance wine sales and meal satisfaction. For that, it's best to present customers with only a few, well-distinguished options. To this end, supplementing your list with a New Zealand pinot noir is a great alternative to the French or Californian equivalents, while a Kiwi sauvignon blanc is always a versatile addition.

In Vino Veritas: Piedmont Power

For those of you who haven't visited Italy yet, fake an injury and hop on the next flight out. Well, maybe don't go that far, but, as an Italophile, I maintain that the country should be on your bucket list. The beauty of Italy lies in its vast depth of history and culture as well as the exceptional qualities of its individual regions – remember that Italy as a modern, unified nation has only existed for just over 150 years.

One of these regions is the Piedmont in the northwest, centered on the city of Turin with the main appellations in Montferrat around the cities of Asti and Alessandria. For a very long time, it was a part of the Duchy of Savoy, meaning that it still has many cultural links to France. As far as winemaking goes, I wrote a previous article on Tuscany – which is often first to mind as the main producer of Chianti and other Sangiovese delights – but the Piedmont is more than its equal with barolos, barbarescos, dolcettos and many other excellent varietals made here.

To understand the Piedmont is to first know that the region has some of the best geography for viticulture. Its flat grasslands and rolling hills are ringed by the Alps in the north and west, and the Ligurian range in the south separates it from the Genovese coast. All told, these mountains effectively trap the summer heat with sunny, humid days easily passing 40 Celsius – conditions that also happen to be perfect for concentrating sugars and flavor in thick-skinned grapes.

What's important to keep in mind with these particular varietals is that the wines take a long time to mature and the taste shows substantial changes year-over-year. The cream of the crop (in my opinion), a decent Barolo, with its hearty, tar-filled drop, can take a decade to reach the semblance of maturity and is best paired with meats and other heavy cream-laden dishes. The Dolcetto exudes a tangy, fruity red flavor, perfect for *pomodoro* pizzas, light pastas, spicy foods or strong parmesan-esque cheeses. Hungry yet?

The Piedmont has many other excellent bottles worth a taste or a purchase. Many of the reds are based on the nebbiolo (which translates as 'little fog'), barbera and the moscato bianco which is the basis for the sweet champagne usurper moscato d'asti.

I could go on and on about the wonders of Piedmont wine, but the only way to get to know this region is to experience it yourself, ideally by traveling there or, as a runner up, visiting your local liquor store and sampling a few bottles. Instead, I'd like to devote the rest of this article to tabling a bigger idea than just a preview of one wine region.

Like many other countries with a strong viticultural heritage, Italy also has many proud culinary traditions, with each region contributing their own delicacies and unique dishes to the overall picture. As a resident of North America, Italian cuisine is more often than not lumped into the broad, countrywide categories of antipasti, salads, pizza, pasta, mains and dolce. Not that this is boring per se, but this arrangement doesn't excite the eyes, chiefly because every other bistro, pizzeria or trattoria is doing the same thing.

Instead, how about arranging the menu items according to their respective region of origin? Then, of course, wine, as a fantastic complement to any such dinner, would also be matched accordingly. So, you could have barolos and moscatos paired on the page with Piedmont specialties like *bagna cauda* or, as a dessert, some *gianduja* chocolate. Or how about a Ligurian white matched some of Genoa's other homegrown creations like focaccia, or pesto and *salsa di noci* (walnut sauce) lathered over pizza or pasta? Similarly, Milanese cuisine is renowned for its risottos and *ossobuco*.

To this day, it still sits with me the way the menu was organized at the Meritage Restaurant in the Boston Harbor Hotel, where foods were grouped with the types of reds and whites that are best matched. Why can't you do the same, say, with the French café on your lobby floor? In this case, you might bifurcate the menu into Provencal and Lyonnais haute cuisine, and Northern French, Breton and Normand dishes. Yes, there is the possibility of confusion, but the greater idea here is to be different and therein create an impression.

In Vino Veritas: Beautiful Bordeaux

I'm surprised that I haven't included Bordeaux in this series before, but it seems only fair that we discuss wines from perhaps the most prestigious growing region in the world – just don't make that claim to anyone from Burgundy, Italy or NorCal.

Bordeaux wines range in price from ten dollars for table drinkers to tens of thousands of dollars for a well-aged first growth vintage. Even though these esteemed premier cru bottles are mind-blowing in flavor and complexity, Bordeaux has over 7,000 recognized chateaux, and there are many gems at the mid to low tier. With huge production spread across 60 appellations, it takes a sommelier course to learn all the intricacies of Bordeaux wines. But for the average drinker, most of that doesn't mean anything.

Occupying the southwestern portion of France, Bordeaux is renowned for having the 'perfect' climate for wine – not scorching hot during the summers and just the right amount of cool Atlantic breeze. Geographically, what's important to know is that the vineyards are clustered around the banks of two tidal rivers stemming from the Gironde estuary – the Dordogne to the north and the Garonne to the south. Estates north and east of the Dordogne on the 'Right Bank' tend to produce different varietals and blended wines than those on the 'Left Bank' to the south and west of the Garonne, and centered around the actual city of Bordeaux.

Knowing the specific location of the appellation – Left Bank, Right Bank, Between Two Seas or Tides – determines the dominant grape in the blend and will thus play a role in what wine you recommend to a guest. All Bordeaux wines, oaked or not, are a mix of Merlot and cabernet sauvignon, with nominal percentages of cabernet franc, malbec and petit verdot thrown in for balance and a certain je ne sais quoi. Right Bank wines err towards Merlot dominance, making them softer, fruitier and easier to drink at a younger age. Left Bank bottles are primarily cabernet sauvignon, meaning that they are darker and heavier with sharper tannins and are better suited for aging.

Bordeaux also produces white varietals, the most notable result being Sauternes dessert wine. Most of these sweet delights are comprised principally of sémillon with sauvignon blanc as a minor constituent and the rare addition of muscadelle. Outside of Sauternes, when the average person thinks of Bordeaux, his or her first thought is of excellent tasting reds, so that is where you should focus your attention.

Beyond directing customers to a cabernet sauvignon or merlot dominant bottle, there are five chateaux to commit to heart – those being the First Growth Bordeaux wines of Haut-Brion, Lafite Rothschild, Latour, Margaux and Mouton-Rothschild. While these may be the most famous, there have been many revisions of the region's classifications to highlight other world-class estates. As such, you might also want to augment your Bordeaux lexicon by knowing a few of the more prominent appellations and communes like Barsac, Graves, Margaux (both a chateau and a growing commune), Médoc, Pauillac, Pomerol, Saint-Émilion and Sauternes (dual naming for the type of wine as well as the commune).

Once you've gotten used to some of the terminology, you next have to ask yourself what it means to have such prestigious wines on your menu. It's unlikely that anyone will ever order a *premier cru* with a price tag of several thousand dollars, but stocking them does come with a certain badge of honor. When guests peruse the wine list and see a first growth at the top of the page, they will think, "Jeez, if this restaurant can shell out for world-class vintages like these then the food must be top notch as well!" It's a form of vicarious status, in other words.

That, and the wines taste incredible – if they didn't, they wouldn't be worth what they are today. So, while you're pondering whether your restaurant needs a boost of Bordeaux's 'prestige by proxy', try a bottle yourself – if only to test the purple waters, so to speak. And as a resolution, be sure to educate your servers on the region's wine story because if they can get patrons excited about Bordeaux, then it'll translate to a healthy flow of beverage revenues.

In Vino Veritas: Eastern European Wines

When we picture vineyards in our minds, our first thoughts are probably going to be along the lines of bucolic, sunbaked hills and a lush Mediterranean climate. Even though it was in these lands where today's most popular grape varietals were first developed and where most of the world's produce still originates, let's not discount the ingenuity occurring in small pockets across the globe that is allowing for some rather tasty bottles to emerge.

While some people may consider Austria and Greece as a part of Eastern Europe, I've already covered those two nations in previous articles. This entry concerns Hungry, Romania, Bulgaria and, to a certain extent, the Balkans, all with quintessentially continental climates. That's quite a bit of territory to cover, but as far as your guests are concerned, you only need a cursory knowledge of the region, largely because many of the names are unusual and thus intimidating to the average Western consumer.

Up until a few years ago, if you were to ask me about wines from this region, I'd be drawing a big white blank. But where there's lack of knowledge, there's also the opportunity for learning, especially given the fact that Eastern European wines are in vogue right now. And so I educated myself, which meant lots of drinking.

Full confession: I was highly skeptical when I first heard about this latest trend. I reasoned that the impetus for all this hubbub was the pursuit of cheap liquor that doesn't immediately reek of skunk vinegar and taste even worse. What convinced me, though, was a sturdy reminder that the entirety of this region below the Danube was once Roman land and the imperialists were quick to import their viticultural traditions. Romanian is, after all, a Romance language with many of its words derived from Latin.

Not only do Eastern European wines still boast many of the same growing practices and vine lineages as their ancient Greek and Italian trading partners, but, ever since the collapse of the Soviet bloc, capitalistic enterprises have also flourished, resulting in vastly increased production and better tasting products overall.

So, let's brush over a few highlights from the region so that you in turn can better sell these exotic and relatively inexpensive bottles.

Starting with the 13th largest producing country, Romania, its three main wine regions are Murfatlar, adjacent to the Black Sea, and Dealu Mare and Tarnave on the southern slopes of the Carpathian Mountains, all of which have widespread penetration of the international grapes. Because of this, you might consider stocking a familiar varietal from a strange land to ease guests into the purchase. But higher quality indigenous varietals like Feteasca Neagra, Feteasca Alba, Negru de Dragasani and Tamaioasa Romaneasca are emerging as niche exports – easy names to remember as neagra and alba denote black and white respectively while the third is the country's namesake.

The best way to sell Romanian wine is to appeal to a patron's sense of heritage; they have been perfecting their craft for thousands of years. The region has now almost fully recovered the cultivation hiccup that was the latter half of the 20th century, but the prices have yet to keep pace relative to quality. This vending notion also extends to the wines of most other European Eastern nations like Moldova, Georgia, Armenia and even Russia where jug wine producers are slowly upgrading their practices for a better tiered selection.

Next on the highlight reel is Hungary, and for all intents and purposes this means whites, sparkling wines and dessert wines from the renowned Tokaj region, which is a volcanic-soiled plateau in the northeast with a well-shielded microclimate resulting from its location within the concavity of the crescent-shaped Carpathian Mountains. The only other prestigious contributor worth mentioning briefly is the Bull's Blood of Eger – Egri Bikavér in the local tongue – a bold red blend of Germanic and French varietals.

Although dry Tokaji are beginning to make an impression in the marketplace, when these Hungarian wines are mentioned it is assumed that the discussion will pertain to the nectar-sweet bottles made from Furmint, Muscat and Harslevelu grapes, often harvested around November and nobly rotted for enhanced sugar concentration. In addition to their popular namesake, many Tokaji have a topaz or stark amber coloration which can be used as an additional selling point as it offers a visual demarcation from other whites, and thus the heightened perception of a differentiated drinking experience.

Tokaj wines' stellar reputation isn't built on mere hype; they taste fantastic! Of all the nomenclature thrown around in this article, if you had to choose just one cellar addition, you would most likely opt for a Tokaji. They're consistent and they have the most recognizable name. A caveat before you stock up: these wines are incredibly sweet. In fact, much like French champagnes, they are graded on a sweetness scale. Be sure to test out your comfort zone – as well as that of your guests – on this scale before purchasing en masse.

Moving deeper the Balkan Peninsula, we arrive at Bulgaria. Even though their reputation as a producer has slid in the past few decades, let's not forget that their winemaking traditions were incubated by Greek colonists many centuries before the Romans arrived. Much like the Carpathians, the Balkan Mountain Range, which horizontally bifurcates the nation, acts as a barrier from the cold continental winds sweeping off the Russian steppe. Aside from a heavy penetration of international varietals, the heroes worth stocking are wines made with Mavrud grapes. Originating from the Greek word for black – in fact there's an outstanding Greek wine with a similar name called Xinomavro – Mavrud bottles are both highly tannic and quite spicy.

Without overstaying my welcome, I hope this is enough to entice you to consider perusing Eastern European wines for your guests when your cellar starts running low. There are quite a few hidden gems for bargain prices, and the quality will only continue to improve as modern practices take root.

Larry Mogelonsky

In Vino Veritas: Champagne

Once you pop, the fun don't stop! In most bars and restaurants, when it comes to the bubbly, champagne represents the status quo for taste and class. I see no reason why your servers shouldn't be able to easily help patrons at your hotel restaurant with their sparkling wine selections and convince them of this elixir's worth.

For most, champagne is an expensive and sugary treat, served in fancy tall, thin glasses otherwise known as flutes. The backstory is, of course, far from boring.

First off, you and your team should know how sparkling wines are produced. This is done by bottling regular wine made from grapes lightly pressed so that – for 'white' sparkling wines at least – the skins don't become a factor and bestow their colors on the end result. Then, a little bit of extra yeast and rock sugar are added so that a secondary fermentation process occurs as the fungus feasts on the simple carbohydrates, thus creating alcohol and carbon dioxide gas.

Centered on the Marne River around the towns of Reims and Epernay roughly two-hours' drive east of Paris, the Champagne growing region traditionally uses the pinot noir, pinot meunier and chardonnay grapes in the production of its bubbly varietals. As one of the most northern appellations, this means finicky summer conditions and an early harvest. And for the record, only sparkling wines made in this area can technically be called champagne, even though many use the two terms interchangeably.

The reason why the Champagne region became famous for its sparkling wines is due to a longstanding rivalry with Burgundy, whereby winemaking houses in the former decided to bow out from the race and differentiate their viticultural enterprises by focusing on bubbly concoctions. Many of the table names we use today stem from this divestiture: Veuve Clicquot, Moët & Chandon, Pommery, Dom Pérignon, Laurent-Perrier and Tattinger, among others. As is customary for all major growing regions, there's a controlling body to ensure adherence to quality production standards and to grade the final vintages in accordance with the classic French system of Grand Cru, Premier Cru and Deuxième Cru.

Aside from any classifications or a customer's previous knowledge of one branded house or another, what's most important with champagne is to meet one's desire for a dry or a sweet bottle, which is determined by the amount of sugar added prior to the secondary fermentation and the residual amount after this process has finished. You and your team should learn by heart the following:

- *Extra brut* – very crude
- *Brut* – crude
- *Extra Sec* – very dry
- *Sec* – dry
- *Demi-sec* – semi-sweet
- *Doux* – very sweet

One aspect of this system that still baffles me is that the *sec* grades – originating from the Latin for 'dry' – aren't at the bottom of the dryness scale, but are instead midway through after the *brut* label, which comes from the French for 'crude'. This might cause some bewilderment, so be ready to alleviate any customer confusion; I try to remember that 'dry' is smoother than 'crude'.

There's a lot more going on that factors into the taste of sparkling wines. Aside from anything terroir-related, the finest champagnes have specific vintage years, but many do not because they are blends. The rule of thumb is that these wines drink best ten years after the year on the label. Moreover, some believe that champagne fermented in magnums – a larger offering between two to three times the size of a regular bottle – taste better because of reduced surface area. All these factoids should serve as good fodder for an upsell.

As a final image, imagine yourself witnessing the time-honored champagne tradition of *sabrage*. The adjacent table orders an expensive bottle of sparkling wine and, instead of simply popping the top, in one fluid stroke the server slashes the head of the bottle with the blunt end of a saber (or other readily available large knife). Talk about a quick visual surprise to add to the overall experience; it might even be enough to push you over the edge and compel you to order your own bottle!

251

In Vino Veritas: German Giants

For those of you who can't take the time off work to travel to Munich for Octoberfest, there's a lot you can do to bring the spectacle home for your guests to enjoy, both for the duration of this quintessential German celebration and for the rest of the year.

The title of this blog series denotes wine, but our first thoughts about Germany and Oktoberfest lean more towards beer. After all, the nation does have a proud and deep-rooted heritage of brewing, so you won't be buying bland beer by stocking one or more golden lagers from the big six sponsor breweries: Augustiner-Bräu, Hacker-Pschorr, Hofbräu, Löwenbräu, Paulaner and Spaten.

Outside of Bavaria you'll find a plethora of delicious beers of all varieties ranging from white (*weiss*) or wheat (*weizen*) to pilsners, lagers or dark lagers (*schwarzbier*). These are perfect for any themed Oktoberfest party you might plan for your restaurant or as a regular addition to the menu. Keep in mind that many 'old world' beer makers don't add preservatives or other artificial ingredients and as such their serviceable delivery range is quite limited, but this detriment comes with the lofty benefit of enhanced flavor.

German wines shouldn't be sidelined either. Many of their varietals and vineyards rival those of the more preeminent wine-producing European nations of France or Italy, even though the volume isn't quite there. The fact remains that, like countries of the Mediterranean, Germany has been making wine since Roman times, and in the modern era they've been especially proactive in bringing their quality up to match that of the leading winemakers.

Most German wines are produced along the Rhine and its tributaries in the western states of the country. Regions including Mosel, Nahe, Main and Neckar have breathtaking landscapes of vineyards on steep 45 to 70 degree verdant hills rising up from the broad waterways. If you ever have the opportunity, take a cruise along the Middle Rhine starting near Koblenz, where vineyards and lush forests mix with preserved medieval towns, cathedrals and hilltop castles.

To keep things simple, the dominant grapes to remember are riesling, pinot gris (locally known as Grauburgunder), Silvaner and Müller-Thurgau for the whites, and pinot noir (called Spätburgunder) and Dornfelder for the reds.

As both pinots are more appropriately discussed in relation to French and Burgundian wines, the centerpiece of any German selection should be a riesling. The second most-produced white, Müller-Thurgau, is based off the riesling and shares many of its properties. Typically sweet, dry, acerbic and with a pungent dose of citrus fruits, these wines pair best with seafood, pork, cream-based sauces or spicy dishes. A tad more unusual, Silvaner can be compared to the main Austrian varietal Grüner Veltliner with a milder, floral taste great for chicken, fowl or desserts.

And when it comes to Oktoberfest and delivering a genuine German experience, you might also want to consider throwing in a few local dishes as accompaniments. Think *sauerkraut* (fermented cabbage) and *bratwurst* (grilled sausages), but also *knödel* (potato dumplings), *sauerbraten* (pot roast), *rotkohl* (braised red cabbage) or pretzels with horseradish mustard as a snack. German cuisine is very filling and when paired with a hearty lager or glass of wine, you can't go wrong.

Larry Mogelonsky

In Vino Veritas: I Heard It Through the Greece Vine

If a nation happens to have an ancient god of wine, then you know that grapes are indeed important to the culture. Such is the case with Greece, one of the oldest wine producing regions in the world and home to our dearest, drunkest Dionysus. In fact, it was in Mycenae – Greece before it was called even that – where our modern breed of grape vine was developed and perfected for growth in the dry summers, ample sunlight and mild winters of the Mediterranean.

While the country pales in comparison to the big three in Europe (Italy, France and Spain) in terms of total output, that hardly precludes it from offering many eloquent drops. Greece currently boasts more than 300 varietals from 28 appellations, all with quite uncommon names. This means that whatever your choice of acquisition from this land, the label is destined to be a niche product and a head-scratcher for almost all patrons who come across it on a wine list.

Some will be more adventurous and seek out esoteric bottles from smaller countries like Greece while others will be outright intimidated and stick to the more internationally renowned grapes. As our focus in this series is not only on education but also, and more importantly, increasing the purchase of wine in your hotel restaurants, let's narrow our focus on a few key selling points and the four top varietals for you to consider.

First, Greek wines make a good case for appealing to people's sense of heritage. After all, who wouldn't want to share a bottle from a region with over 6,000 years of winemaking traditions? Next is terroir; many Greek wines are cultivated on islands laden with volcanic ash-rich soil, imparting a distinctive earthy flavor and mineral structure. Lastly, many of these same islands were unperturbed by the phylloxera blight of the latter half of the 19th century, meaning that several of the nation's varietals in use today are truly original in terms of delivering a quintessentially firm and acidic 'old world' taste.

As for the four grapes to remember, these are Assyrtiko, Moschofilero, Agiorgitiko and Xinomavro, two whites and two reds respectively. Originally from the former volcano that is now the island Santorini, Assyrtiko is a steely, aromatic (and phylloxera-resistant) white with dry, citrus-blossom characteristics like Riesling. Second comes Moschofilero, which is lighter and quite floral relative to Assyrtiko, making it a better match for desserts or sugar-dominant snacking foods.

On the darker side, Agiorgitiko is the most popular export, with a transparent ruby body and composite flavor profile akin to Pinot Noir. Xinomavro, the other red, is bolder with its opaque violet color and generous burst of sour fruit and tannins in the same vein as many reds from Piedmont. It also ages quite well if you're looking to sit on some cases for a few years.

I could go into more detail here, but this is the cursory level of knowledge your servers should be able to quickly pass on to guests. Anything information beyond this can be quite intimidating and should be left for the aficionados and sommeliers amongst us. Any way you put it, though, there's lots to discover in this ancient land, so do Dionysus proud and pour yourself a glass!

Larry Mogelonsky

In Vino Veritas: Chocolate and Wine Pairings

Let's explore one more elegant way to satisfy your guests for Valentine's, or any other getaway weekend. We all know that chocolate is a highly romantic food (it's an aphrodisiac after all) and, of course, wine goes with just about any meal, so why not bring the two together?

While you might not have as many options as, say, with a wine and cheese tasting, pairing chocolate with these grape-based liquors may be just the ticket to winning the hearts and minds of incoming guests. You can apply this concept as a small-plate amuse bouche, an appetizer, a dessert or as part of the main if a key ingredient is some iteration of the cocoa bean.

Furthermore, much like any other edible staple with a bourgeois cachet, chocolate is also in the midst of an artisanal revolution. There's now a plethora of high percentage dark, organic and single-origin providers, with culinary specialists all over the world concocting playful and delicious blends of quality chocolate and some very esoteric enhancements.

As such, not only can you offer a range of chocolates organized by purity (90% or 65%) or country of origin (Cameroon versus Ivory Coast), but also some outright wild horizontal tastings from the same chocolatier. As a start, include common additives like caramel, nougat, ganache, mint, cinnamon, nuts (beware of allergies!), berries, peanut butter or liqueur. Then, look beyond to real standout ingredients like tropical fruit, ginger, maple syrup, bacon, wasabi, popcorn, pretzel bits, tea leaves and flower petals. With all these options, you may only need to consider a chocolate-only tasting and leave the digestif to the guest's discretion.

In contrast with the perfunctory cheese pairings, you must take note that chocolate has a strong, sweet and bitter taste with none of the creamy or stinky notes that dairy provides. As such, there's far less latitude when it comes to wine accompaniments. You need a pungent drop to make a copacetic match. Even though I live by the motto that any wine is better than no wine, I still wouldn't recommend pinot noir, sauvignon blanc any other soft, dry varietal for this job.

To give you an example of how this might work, look to Lindt's Paintings with Excellence in collaboration with the popular Californian winemaker J. Lohr. While softer bottles like pinot noir and merlot are still on the menu, they are appropriately countered with tangy confectionaries while their fruitier chocolate products are paired off with fragrant, sugary white wines (chardonnay and riesling).

And then things get complicated when you consider white chocolates, milk chocolates and desserts lacking any cocoa ingredients, but that should nevertheless be included in any move for a wine-themed upsell – think crème brûlée, panna cotta or cheesecake. As such, my final piece of advice is this: You can't go wrong with good chocolate! Creating interesting and diverse pairings, and your guests will be more than happy to go along for the ride.

Larry Mogelonsky

In Vino Veritas: Apéritif or Digestif

My typical day at the office: two to three hundred emails (including spam that somehow the filters can't handle), back-to-back meetings, and a constant barrage of phone calls to interrupt all down time. By the time I scrape myself off the office floor around 6pm, I'm loopy, hungry and in need of a stiff drink. Sound familiar?

While some call this 'mandatory pre-dinner throat and brain lubricant', the French were kind enough to bestow on us a more elegant term: the aperitif. And for symmetry's sake, they also gave us a word for its after-dinner counterpart: the digestif. As beverage sales have tremendous markups and represent a fundamental part of any restaurant revenue stream, understanding these two terms and how to leverage them may be just the ticket.

Let's start with some simple questions. How many of your guests know what these two words mean, and how many of those can differentiate between them? How you do, as a restaurant, visually demarcate the two, for instance, with separate aperitif and dessert menus? And lastly, how are you encouraging patrons to buy drinks specifically for before or after the meal?

To answer these three questions and to connect them with our two French terms, what we are talking about are nudges – those inconspicuous and seemingly innocuous suggestions that have a remarkable influence on our behavior.

Quick: Don't think of pink polar bears. You've probably heard this one before as it's such a great example. By simply planting the idea of an oddly colored ursine, you are much more likely to dwell on it for a moment or to picture one in your head.

So, what nudges can we give our restaurant-faring clientele so they imbibe at a greater frequency beyond what's ordered for during the meal? Many of the basic tactics are already perfunctory in our industry – separate drink menus left out on the table during the meal and regular server prompts are two that come to mind. Both are proven effective and I would never recommend you abandon either without due consideration.

Understand that nudges are almost a form of subterfuge that can help us augment these two tactics, however, and offer a few extensions. For instance, the art is in how the server prompts your patron about their hopefully forthcoming libations. Instead of asking a consumer, "Have you decided on drinks?" lead with something softer like, "Have you had a chance to look at the drink menu?"

The first question requires a monetary decision to be made; the customer should read through his or her drink options and make an actual choice. And we all know that the harder the decision, the more likely the outcome is to be rejection. The second question only stipulates that said patron browse through the drink list...how hard is that? But, by reading and touching the menu, it's recruiting the brain and subconsciously committing it more clearly to the possibility of a purchase.

Sly but effective. Obviously, there are those consumers who already have their alcohol agenda preformed before being seated, but for those who are on the fence about ordering an aperitif or any meal accompaniment, subtle shifts like this may be all that's needed.

Another tactic has to do with timing. People come to restaurants because they are hungry! This means that from the moment they sit down, getting food is more likely to be of a higher priority than getting drinks. Hence, you have to start them off on the right foot before they jam their heads into the food portion of the menu. Ask guests right as they are being seated if you can start them off with a 'quick' drink (yes, the adjective is important here). Moreover, drink menus should be readily available on the table, and in fact more readily available than the food menus, lest they succumb to the will of their stomachs.

Alas, the French have come to the rescue yet again. Aperitif is used mostly to describe beverages, but it also can refer to little morsels of food to begin the digestive process. If this morsel is complimentary, then it would be called an amuse bouche. So, if most people when entering a restaurant first and foremost strive to satiate their hunger, then would an amuse bouche work reasonably as a nudge to induce more beverage sales? Pondering along these lines, how would your beverage sales be affected if you were to seat diners and immediately put a basket of fresh bread and a drink list, but no food menus, in front of them?

All this, though, is shunning the after-meal libations, the digestifs. The primary trick here is to ask and you shall – sometimes – receive. If your servers make similarly clever inquiries about drinks at this juncture as they would when first seating their customers, the results will be markedly improved. Another good nudge is to plant the seed of a digestif before the meal or before clearing the plates, either by asking outright or by leaving dessert menus on the table. This works because by the time the mains have been consumed, your patrons have already started to think about heading home; you have to prompt them to think differently before this sets in.

There's much more we can discuss on the matter, but I'll leave it to you to figure out how to get people to incorporate aperitif and digestif into their vocabularies. Lastly, while this article is all about cajoling more liquor sales to boost the overall health of your business, you should nevertheless encourage your guests to drink responsibly, and this notion must be a part of any training protocol.

In Vino Veritas: Small Batch Liquors

Alcoholic beverages are far more than a vehicle for inebriation. They are a pillar of the dining experience. While wine and beer are the two most common meal accompaniments in this category, there's something interesting happening in the world of spirits and other distilled elixirs. Much like microbreweries and limited-barrel wines, small batch distilleries are making a resurgence, and it's an opportunity you should seize.

Why? Simple: product differentiation.

Your restaurant or bar may be differentiated from your competitors by its décor, its view, its ambiance, its food menu, its cocktails, its executive chef, its live music, its onsite events or a host of other features, but this is one emerging area where you can now make an impact. All of the previously mentioned aspects held constant, what will distinguish your bar selection when you all stock the same standard liquors – for example, Johnny Walker, Jim Beam, Bacardi, Jose Cuervo or Smirnoff?

I'm not slighting these brands – they wouldn't be household names if they weren't high quality – but rather, because they are so prevalent around the world, they aren't doing you any favors insofar as providing your guests an exceptional dining experience. It's easier to confuse two nearby pubs with the same drink slate than mistake one offering standards with one which exclusively serves liquors from small batch distilleries. These spirits may not be available at the neighborhood liquor store and they may require some craft in sourcing.

In a lot of cases, the rarer the better, although too rare may make it near impossible to continually stock. This trend has caught on, with many of the more prestigious small batch distilleries already selling out their whole supply to purveyors both domestic and across the pond.

In this sense, these liquors further your restaurant's or bar's reputation amongst its competitive set. Many of these boutique liquors may have imperceptible taste differences when compared to the household brands, but true aficionados will be able to tell.

In fact, many consumers actively seek out local or unique spirits and their resultant cocktails – give them a reason to choose your establishment over all others.

And yes, you read correctly. The locavore trend isn't only for foods; it extends to your beverages as well. The microbrew renaissance over the past decade is case in point of this. Be sure to let your patrons know on the menu where all your drinks are sourced.

In Vino Veritas: Are You a Cider Provider?

Yes, this series is supposed to be about wine. But ever since humankind discovered that the sugars in ANY fruit juice can be fermented to generate enough alcohol to kill off bacteria like the ones that cause dysentery – common in drinking water when there's no sewage system keeping it clean – we've been tinkering and experimenting to conjure up ever tastier beverages. Wine from grapes is the most popular, but we also have such delightful libations as blueberry wine, raspberry ice wine, gin from juniper berries, schnapps, brandy, sherry, perry from pears and a whole rainbow of liqueurs. Thirsty yet?

Then there's cider, made from apples and especially popular in the United Kingdom, other Commonwealth nations, Germany, where it is called Apfelwein, Ireland and the United States. It's this last territory which fascinates me the most, as the US has a total population greater than all the others combined and its cider sales are currently on a sharp uptick. And you might as well ride this newfound popularity all the way to the piggybank.

Interestingly, cider used to be the bee's knees in America, with annual production and consumption easily dwarfing that of beer. But then they passed the idiotic Volstead Act in 1920 and thousands of acres of apple orchards were burned to the ground to snuff out the 'demonic spread of rampant alcoholism'. Those apple growers who were left were convinced purely by economic forces to switch to other crops to put food on the table. The result was that by the time prohibition was lifted in 1933, most of the bitterer cultivars best suited for cider production were lost. Beer quickly filled the resurgent demand for mildly intoxicating brews because wheat and barley take far less time to reach maturity than apple trees.

It is only now that producers in the United States are rediscovering the bitter varietals that lubricated the nation's throats from the colonial era right through to the Roaring Twenties. While many current estimates put cider at around 1% of the liquor market in the United States, with this comeback, you must ask what will happen when it reaches 2%, 3%, 5% or even 10%. While the last percentage is unlikely any time soon, a 1-2% increase in market share on this scale nonetheless represents millions of additional pints consumed, and perhaps a few savvy capitalists eager to invest in orchards or craft cider mills.

On the hotel level, this industry ramp up may present a lucrative opportunity to differentiate your beverage services from the competition. While other bars and restaurants strive to meet the modern oenophilic and cerevisaphilic demands with fancy Wine Emotion installations and expansive craft beer lists, there's an opening for you to become a veritable 'cider center' and deliver the best in breed to this niche market. At the very least, consider testing the alcoholic waters this summer by offering some specially imported craft or local ciders during happy hour so that customers know you are a leader in this regard.

On a side note, while the range in cider taste profiles may be less diverse than beer or wine for the time being, apples are nonetheless used throughout the culinary world, which could make for a fun theme by which to organize such a promotion. With cider as the centerpiece, you might accent it with apple butter, apple marinades, apple cider vinegar marinated meats, apple-bourbon barbecue sauces or apple ice wine for dessert. And did I mention that apples are high in healthy pectins and vitamin C while cider was used as a traditional remedy for colds?

In Vino Veritas: Visit Eataly

During a recent four-hour stopover in Chicago, I had time to do two things: have lunch with my sister who was also traveling for work and visit the titular Italo-foodie Mecca that is Eataly. I've been to Chicago and New York City dozens of times before, and the store locations in both cities have been on my list since their respective openings.

Founded by the Italian entrepreneur, Oscar Farinetti, in 2007, Eataly takes a Williams Sonoma approach to grocery shopping whereby high-end products and fancy, spacious displays trump the need to pack every available shelf. They serve food as well; the two-story space I toured had a Lavazza café, *gelateria* and a Nutella waffle kiosk on the main floor with formal seating areas and bars – yes, they have a liquor license – mixed in between the grocery aisle on the mezzanine.

For those who haven't graced the halls of an Eataly franchise, make plans for a lengthy sojourn when you are next in Chicago or New York. You can easily spend half a day there bouncing between the wine section, the hundreds of cheeses and all the compiled cookbooks. Although Eataly has 16 locations in Italy proper, 11 in Japan and a few others sprinkled across the globe, there are unfortunately only two in North America at the present. More are in the planning stages.

What fascinated me most about Eataly, and the reason for why I've devoted a whole article to it, is that the store takes an educational approach to grocery shopping, thereby adding a new dimension and depth to the consumer experience. In store, there are maps – one for truffle picking by season, the other for grape varietals by growing region. What is apparent from these maps is how they both serve to visually convey the great geographic diversity of Italian produce.

How many of you know the difference between white and black truffles, and the best time of year to visit certain provinces of Italy to partake in the annual traditional of truffle picking? I didn't, but after perusing the maps adorned throughout the store, I have a better sense of what the answer is. Moreover, it got me curious; I wanted to learn more. It's these little 'did you knows' that stimulate patrons' minds in a different way than the sights, sounds, smells and tastes of a fine dining establishment.

Nowadays, there is a demand for F&B awareness and education beyond simply serving a fascinating meal with equally excellent service. People want to know where ingredients are coming from, what their health benefits are and how cuisine is prepared. It's this same principle that helps explain the rising popularity of restaurants with kitchens that are open to their diners; customers can see every part of the cooking process. Further, look at market-style food shopping. It's not just a matter of pulling stuff off the shelves, but of being able to converse with the vendor in order to guide your end purchase.

So, how can we apply this 'Eatalian' learning to your restaurant and your wine list? Simple: they're also about paying the knowledge forward. Educate your servers about the food and wine that are offered so they can pass along a few morsels of information to the consumer. Additionally, you can infuse your written menu with little factoids about ingredient sourcing and preparation.

The second big lesson to take away pertains to regional specificity. If you can't be locally authentic – a buzzy hospitality term these days – then this is the next best thing. For example, how can an Italian restaurant in, say, Seattle be locally authentic to its namesake? Instead of this outlet flying the broad banner of just Italian food, why don't the operator and chef plan a menu solely around Trentino cuisine – Alpine fare from the north of the country?

As I learned from my trip to Eataly, a Sicilian marinara can have vastly different ingredients than tomato sauces from other regions. Some recipes even call for the inclusion of almond paste! The same goes for cheeses, wines, meats and literally everything else that you'd want to put in your mouth. Nor is this a phenomenon exclusive to the diverse regions of Italy. For example, Provençal and Savoyard cuisines are as disparate as apples and oranges – well, more like oranges and grapefruits – even though the two regions are adjacent to each other.

As a hotelier, this sense of wonder and curiosity can be applied to nearly every other aspect of your operations, so maybe a trip to the nearest Eataly is the inspiration you need to put things in motion. Or, if you have the money, do yourself one better and get on a plane to Rome!

TECHNOLOGY

The Mandarin Oriental Barcelona has defined itself in the local market as a food-inspired destination with multiple, Michelin-starred outlets.

Photos copyright of the hotel and cannot be reproduced without its permission.

Larry Mogelonsky

The Technology Has Caught Up with the Ideation

Great hotel managers not only work incredibly hard to lead their teams and propel their respective properties to new levels of success, but they must also keep a pulse on where the industry is headed, especially regarding technology.

This 'tech' word can be broad, though, with so many new devices and software options becoming available each quarter to help managers increase guest service delivery and make better business decisions. It can be hard to narrow your field of vision and focus on any one aspect of emergent technology. However, where I've spent the bulk of my career – and where it is imperative for all managers to have at least a basic understanding – is understanding the evolving electronic tools that get guests to stay at your property. Because if you can't get consumers onsite, then no other technological upgrade matters.

To this end, I was fortunate enough to land an interview with John Hach, Senior Industry Analyst at TravelClick, a company that needs no introduction. Ebullient and razor-sharp, John outlined what he's observed about the hospitality world based upon the priority information afforded to a person in his position. Overall, he proudly declared that when it comes to hotel websites, booking engines and all other digital processes, the technology has caught up with the ideation.

This means that if you can think of something you want your web presence to capture or express, there is a technology that can now fulfill that need. It's indeed a very good time for hoteliers to reinvest in their electronic channels, but it also means that traveler expectations are likewise escalating. Hoteliers should act prudently to move in the same slipstream as their consumers, particularly regarding mobile and responsive design, in order to keep direct reservations.

As a booking engine pundit, John explained that the industry has almost entirely moved to digital, both in terms of how customers are first introduced to hotel brands as well as the overall usage of e-commerce channels. Moreover, we are currently witnessing a split in user behavior whereby those people seeking a quick trip of less than a week prefer a more transactional 'one screen, one click' booking process. He's observed that an additional click during the sales funnel can cost up to 50% of customers. On the other end of the spectrum, longer stays demand the creation of an experience and a 'sense of discovery' during the booking process.

While a website should load quickly, there is a steadily increasing demand for video content – a trend that John has been privy to observe following TravelClick's acquisition of hotel video solution provider TVtrip. These video enhancements are becoming excellent tools for differentiating room types and for boosting upgrade sales and ancillary revenue streams like amenities and F&B.

As additional areas of differentiation, John touched on two lucrative opportunities. The first was the need for personalization of the travel experience via mobile app CRM software. And next was the near-future milestone of extreme localization. That is, with every building now mapped on cloud-based GPS mobile apps, properties can enhance their competitive advantages on a microscopic level. For example, if you are located directly across the street from a convention center when your closest competitor is over one block away, reorienting your web appearance and SEO to clearly express this minor proximity advantage will allow you to moderately heighten your ADR. Other top localized differentiators include museums, retail destinations, beaches, top-rated restaurants on Yelp or TripAdvisor, airports, train stations and business hubs.

To reiterate, if you can think of a physical property advantage or have an idea to make your onsite product more unique, there is a technology that can reflect this and effectively tell this aspect of your story to consumers.

Addressing my current two favorite industry culprits – Airbnb and the OTAs – John remained optimistic yet cautious. From his analysis, there appears to be enough business to accommodate alternative providers such as Airbnb without rampant erosion, except for compressions such as massive citywide events where there is a statistically substantial impact. We hoteliers must remain vigilant, however, as this erosion may drastically increase once the OTAs unveil their own alternate lodging booking engines.

And speaking of the OTAs, whereas I'm a believer in driving direct web sales by any means necessary – that is, converting business from third-party sites – it may be better to reach a symbiotic co-dependency with these companies, as their marketing efforts can be a powerful force for hotels. Moreover, as John remarked, many customers will always opt for the convenience of a one-stop shop that also includes airfare and car rentals. These travelers are likely to never convert to booking direct or to becoming loyal to a specific brand. It would be better to focus your efforts on optimizing your property's display within the OTA system to best attract consumers with this behavior.

To finish off, John shared with me some statistics from early 2016 that give a better picture of how the hospitality world performed in 2015 and what market segments will present growth opportunities in the future:

- Committed occupancy for the full year was up 3.1% compared to the previous year
- New commitments added over the last month (pace) were up 5.3%
- Nineteen of the top 25 (76%) of North American markets showed committed occupancy increases compared to the previous month
- The group segment was up 3.5% in committed room nights over the same time the previous year
- New group business added over the last month (pace) was up 11.1% over the comparable period the previous year
- Transient room nights booked were up 2.0% over the same time the previous year
- Business demand, which includes weekday transient negotiated and transient retail segments, was down-3.6%
- Leisure demand, which includes transient discount, transient qualified segments and transient wholesale, was up 6.1%
- Average Daily Rate (ADR) was up 4.0% based on reservations on the books

What a Mature Tablet World Means for You

Today, tablets are a mature technology product. What this means is that there are many competing devices in various sizes available for purchase – even those besides the industry leading iPad – and that many consumers have already or plan to make such an acquisition. Moreover, true mobile and smartphones already fulfill many of the tasks that the larger tablets are best suited for.

Tablets aren't as light as mobile devices, making them a tad more cumbersome for transport, and on the other end, they aren't as adept at handling typing, multi-tab browsing or a host of other functions as the full-fledged computer. So, as the middle child between desktops or laptops and smartphones, where does that leave tablets? Now that the novelty has worn off, what uses do tablets have in the hotel space?

In a broad sense, you should look for uses that take advantage of the tablet's portable nature as well as its large screen size – a size that makes the screen sharable amongst two or three viewers as opposed to the cell phone screens which are smaller and designed for only one pair of eyeballs. Along these lines, here are some ideas for you to consider:

1. **Mobile check-in.** This one is obvious, and for good reason. Consumers are increasingly looking to bypass the front desk altogether by checking in via their smartphones. As well, new technologies are emerging which allow guests to safely use their smartphones as their room keys. If these options aren't possible for you now, consider the tablet compromise. Desks can be impediments to developing rapport, so why not have front desk clerks roaming the check-in area with tablets, ready to assist arriving guests? In this capacity, such clerks might double as bellboys, signing guests in while simultaneously hauling their bags. Alternatively, how about just setting up tablet kiosks for check-in, no staff members required?

2. **The everywhere concierge.** Building on the last idea of how tablets can allow for role overlap, you might also consider other such mergers, like having your valet or doormen act as pseudo-concierge staff. I'm not suggesting that you abolish the concierge position altogether, just that, when armed with tablets, the ability for such team members to assist and further satisfy visitors greatly increases.

Here's a situation for you to think about in this regard. It's a heavy downpour and the doorman stands at the ready under the main entrance carport. A couple blunders outside; the husband quickly looses an expletive, having not realized that it's raining. They turn to the doorman, inquiring about the fastest walking route to their prearranged destination. Sure, the staff member could point them on their way with clear verbal directions, but as many of us are visual learners, it would be more effective if the doorman called up a map on his or her tablet for guidance.

Dedicated concierge staffers can also benefit from using a tablet instead of a desktop or laptop. For one, there's the sharable factor – two people, guest and staff, side by side looking up a request versus those same two conversing over the unintentional barrier of a desk. Because of this, your concierge team won't need to be chained to a station or area but can respond to guests by meeting them wherever they happen to be. Moreover, accessories like attachable keyboards – think of the Microsoft Surface – might help your team members use tablets while also having a bit more of the functionality provided by a computer.

3. **In the restaurant.** There are a few possibilities here. First, servers could use them to record diners' food and drink selections, although many always-on-the-move staffers might find such devices to be a tad clunky and burdensome when compared to the basic notepad and pen. Similarly, they might be used on the back-end to relay orders through various parts of the kitchen or for inventory management.

Lastly, they could be used as menus via dedicated preloaded apps.

Yes, patrons can view the menu on their own smartphones from your website, but this just doesn't have the same pizzazz as having all your dining options neatly lined up in a slideshow or turn-book-style app alongside some beautiful high-resolution photography of the food. There's plenty of rigidity to this idea due to startup costs and the potential for theft, but because very few are currently executing this concept, imagine the impression you would make on diners by being the early adopter.

4. **In guest rooms.** You might find this surprising, but this is one area of the hotel experience where I wouldn't recommend tablets. Many properties have already completed such installations and are using their devices as universal in-room remotes, able to control the HVAC, lighting, phone, television and room services calls, in addition to other now obligatory functions like access to web browsers or gaming. However, the clear majority of guests are not only more comfortable using their own devices in the private space, but they also aren't keen on learning a new operating system during their downtime. My solution here, when considering tablets, is to provide lots of easy access recharge stations as well as complimentary WiFi.

5. **Travel research.** To finish off, it's important that you think about how consumers are utilizing their tablets at home. While many statistics point to a slim majority of online bookings still coming from the computer, the smartphone is on the cusp of being the leader in this area, and tablets are increasingly being used for preliminary travel research. Hence, any brand.com revisions you do must take this platform into account. Are you simply porting over the existing website? Or have you incorporated responsive design elements so that your brand.com is optimized for this class of devices?

Larry Mogelonsky

Weird Wellness Coming to a Hotel Near You

The 20th century was filled with prominent science fiction writers constantly throwing wild and prophetic ideas out to the world. The 21st century is where some of those ideas become reality.

We've already seen the rise of smart phones, smart watches and tablets – all predicted in some way or shape long before their mass market acceptance – and many more useful devices will reach consumers in due time. Now it is time for hotels and smart hoteliers to be the true benefactors and incubators for all these emergent technologies. Those that survive and thrive tend to be those that enrich our livelihoods in one way or another, whether it's through enhanced communication, entertainment value or increased productivity.

One area where we are just beginning to make a dent with all our fancy new electronics is in personal health care. Yes, we already have powerful MRI machines at the hospital, while our handheld devices have pedometers and calorie counters. But hospitality properties are rapidly discovering an underserved niche in wellness that aims to not only enlighten guests with better bodily self-awareness, exercise routines and dietary regimens, but also to enrich one's health based upon one's own DNA.

I remember several years ago when I signed up to 23andMe.com and had my DNA sequenced. Expecting only a rudimentary analysis, the results shocked me. They not only identified numerous and specific diseases which I was genetically predisposed to acquire in my geriatric years, but they also pinpointed where in the world my ancestors were from for each of my four grandparents.

Now that the concept of DNA sequencing is relatively accepted – that is, it's not breaking news – hotels are ideally placed to build upon this recognition by guiding and coaching guests on ways to maximize their genetic potential. It's like taking the spa to the nth level, with treatments, procedures and after work all personalized to your exact conditions.

Incremental Upgrades

Before we dive into this Gattaca-esque development, it's important to highlight some of the other advancements hotels are making on the wellness front, especially regarding guestroom design. I address these because, as incredible as onsite DNA sequencing and counseling may be, it's just not feasible for most hotels. For the average hotelier, smaller, incremental upgrades must suffice.

A much-vaunted recent guinea pig has been the Stay Well rooms at the MGM Grand Hotel & Casino in Las Vegas. And there's no better place to test out sleep-enhancing features than a 24-hour gambling hall where weekend-long benders and erratic slumber cycles are the norm. The rooms start by reducing potential irritants via the use of hypoallergenic cleaning products and air purification systems. Next, blackout shades and special lighting systems have been installed to better imitate natural sleep conditions so that guests can maintain some semblance of a proper circadian rhythm amidst all the craziness of The Strip. Last, but not least, there are the highly publicized vitamin C showers which ostensibly act to neutralize chlorine for softer skin and hair.

Taken individually, each of these features isn't anything to write home about, but as a package they represent an excellent USP for the property and a model to emulate for hotels wishing to build their 'Wellness Guestroom' programs. Most upgrades along these lines seem to involve some form of sensory modification:

- Lighting that stabilizes daily melatonin cycles by not interfering with this hormone while it's peaking during sleep via warmer, natural hue projection or fancy LED nightlights
- Aromatherapy via massive air purifiers or the subtle release of mood-altering scents
- Healthy mini-bar options and nutritional F&B menus that are not only enjoyable for the taste buds but also beneficial for the waistline and energy levels
- Hygienic or organic materials in furnishings that not only reduce skin irritation but are also more pleasant to touch

- Water filtration systems for smoother skin or cleaner drinking water
- Sound dampening materials or noise reduction via smart room and furniture layout
- Using magnets, negative ions, photo-catalytic patinas or other electromagnetic manipulations for a variety of functions (although based on my past experience as an engineer, this to me is verging on pseudoscience)

In-Room Fitness

One of IHG's latest unveilings, EVEN Hotels, takes in-room wellness upgrades a step further. Aiming for 'repose-conscious spaces' in their guestroom configurations means the use of natural materials and mood-enhancing colors – think 50 shades of green. This Zen approach extends to the lobby, lounges and gym facilities, with indoor plants and plenty of sunlight on top of the previously mentioned improvements.

The visual 'meat' of this concept, however, comes via the chain's dedication to in-room exercise through multipurpose accessories such as a coat rack that's also a chin-up bar and a luggage bench (an overlooked guestroom feature in its own right!) that can be converted into a workout bench. These two examples are at the upper end of costs for potential fitness upgrades, but there are easier routes for the average hotelier to excel in this area. For instance, how hard is it to stock yoga mats, foam rollers, medicine balls or resistance bands in each closet, or attach a TRX Suspension Trainer to the back of a sturdy door?

In-room fitness is more than just exercise, though. It's more holistic. Another compelling feature of the wellness rooms at EVEN Hotels is the pebble walk path on each balcony for reflexology – that is, the purported calming effects generated by stimulating certain nerve endings on the hands and feet. Although the science behind reflexology is still questionable, there's no denying that such a pebble walk makes for a striking first impression upon arrival. Yes, water and air purifiers are fantastic upgrades, but they are invisible; they aren't exciting from a visual standpoint, and this is a major issue when considering upgrades along these lines. If guests can't see or feel the presence of such improvements, how they are supposed to develop a positive emotional connection to the room and to the hotel?

Building on the ideas of holistic fitness and visually palpable upgrades, any accessory that augments sleep and alertness can also be lumped in this category. Proper sleep is, after all, paramount for weight loss, muscle growth and hormonal balance. The Stay Well rooms have subtle red lights so that guests can navigate to the washroom without having to turn on any bright, melatonin-disruptive lamps. EVEN Hotels have specially shaped posturepedic beds. Then there are dawn-simulating alarm clocks, vibrating sleep trackers and a host of other 'smart' devices soon to be revealed.

The Pinnacle of Personalization

With this survey of incremental upgrades out of the way, let's refocus on those pieces of code in every cell of your body: your DNA. Imagine for a moment that you have in your wallet or purse a credit card or thumb drive that provides quick access to your entire genome. Bring it to any doctor, dietitian or physiotherapist and they can give you recommendations specific to your unique DNA, making for more effective results from their treatments or prescriptions. Looking at where we've come in the past two decades in terms of technological advancements and social interconnectivity via the internet, it isn't farfetched to say that these sorts of DNA dealings may soon be commonplace.

I was first put on to this topic when I learned about TheBodyHoliday at LeSport, St. Lucia. Not only is the Caribbean location hard to beat, but through their BodyScience program, guests are subjected to DNA sequencing followed by a battery of tests and regimes to de-stress, detoxify, bolster digestion, optimize exercises, promote weight loss and reverse aging, all individualized to each consumer's genes. Plus, there's far more perceived value than what's provided by a one-off wellness retreat. Yes, guests at The BodyHoliday are pampered to the nines, but because of this highly personalized approach, guests come away learning valuable insights about their own bodies, thus making the experience near impossible to forget.

Although this may appear to be a novelty, as personal genomic mapping becomes more socially acceptable and less expensive, I wouldn't be surprised to see more resorts adopt similar wellness programs, followed soon after by abridged versions at urban and business hotels. What's most important to remember from all this is that these futuristic and esoteric wellness programs are emerging to meet a demand that's already there.

As we delve deeper in the 21ˢᵗ century, this consumer desire for more health-conscious hotels will only increase. Espousing wellness will require experimentation – some features will heighten guest satisfaction while others won't have any effect – but it is a worthy direction to nevertheless consider for your property. Incorporating DNA-centric amenities may represent the pinnacle of this trend, but my hope for you from reading this article is that you are aware of the multitude of other options also available in the wellness camp.

When Time is Money, Drop the Restaurant WiFi

This may seem counterintuitive, as offering WiFi to hotel guests for free is a great way to increase guest satisfaction. However, this is a specific instance where promoting complimentary wireless internet access may not be the prudent method of garnering consumer advocacy.

Unlike hotels, where the primary components amounting to profitability are ADR and occupancy, many eateries live and die on the number of turns per day. And what we are seeing now is that, due to the prevalence of smartphones, ready access to the internet is slowing down how quickly a server can deliver meals and turn tables over for the next group of patrons. Even minor, incremental distractions add up to an insurmountable sum of lost time, including:

- Diner is seated and immediately checks, say, a social network instead of looking at the menu and deciding upon his or her order;
- Diner asks about free WiFi access and spends time trying to log in instead of looking at menu and ordering;
- Diner has trouble connecting to the WiFi service, thereby arresting the ordering process and taking up server's time as both attempt to solve the problem;
- Diner is so engrossed by a smartphone that he or she makes a mistake or is unclear in communicating the order, and then sends the food back when it arrives;
- Diner stops to take mediocre pictures of his or her food instead of diving right in;
- Diner takes longer to eat because he or she is responding to email or bombarded by text messages that 'absolutely must' be answered at that instant;
- Diner finishes food and, instead of signaling server for the bill, goes right back on his or her phone and ignoring the world;
- Diner pays for meal but then lingers a few minutes to check a social network once again, thus preventing the server from swooping in to clean the table and get it ready for next group.

All these actions may only be one or two minutes in length, but together they can effectively chop the total number of turns at a restaurant during breakfast or lunch hour in half. And that's a lot of money! Of course, one may counter argue that diners will want to use their smartphones to talk about your restaurant in social media, TripAdvisor or Yelp. A valid point, but in my experience, rarely is this done at the dining table.

Mitigating this modern problem is difficult as you can't stop people from going on their phones, especially the tech-addicted millennials. Or can you?

As a start, dropping the restaurant WiFi is entirely in your control. That way, when a patron does inquire about it, your server can reply with a definitive "No." followed by, "Are you ready to order?" This alone will help move the sales process along, as many with limited data plans will be discouraged from going through their cellular network when WiFi isn't available. And to speed this up even further, signage stating "Sorry, No WiFi Available at This Time" may also do the trick. It may sound draconian, but you might want to give it a try.

While banning certain guests for excessive time wasting is an extreme measure, I have seen several restaurants institute a no cell phone policy. Right now, this appears to be an action relegated to the lofty Michelin or other haute cuisine establishments where exorbitant prices also connote a higher degree of dining etiquette. But as operators wake up to how much smartphone usage is adversely affecting turns, such a policy may become more widespread, and thus more readily accepted by the masses.

Note that you can purchase WiFi, 3G and 4G blocking technology, so that even if your patrons want to go on their phones, your restaurant will be a dead zone. But this is not recommended, and it may put you in legal jeopardy. You should consult your attorney if you plan to take this route, as a blocker is indiscriminant and will probably affect your neighbors as well. Or, you could place your restaurant in a subbasement bunker underneath a couple hundred tons of concrete and rebar. While these last two ideas are almost entirely impractical, cutting out the complimentary WiFi is not.

Using Uber to Understand the Airbnb Challenge

In 2016, the Ontario provincial taxi cab and limousine drivers filed a class-action lawsuit against Uber seeking over $400 million in compensatory and punitive damages. This marks just one instance in a long series of opposing activities against this game-changing and rapidly growing company. Putting aside personal judgments on this case or any preceding one, there are many parallels to Airbnb and its disruptive impact on the hospitality industry.

Even though they exist in mutually exclusive spaces, a snapshot comparison between the two organizations yields uncanny similarities. Both founded around 2008-2009, they now operate on a global scale with valuations in the tens of billions of dollars and strong growth fueled by mounting consumer acceptance and new product offerings. Uber is an usurper to traditional car services, while Airbnb challenges traditional accommodations, and yet they are both largely mobile and urban-centric with flawless apps and two-way user review accountability checks.

With so much in common, would it be reasonable to also say that Airbnb's legal foibles might follow a similar path to Uber's? More importantly, what can we, as hoteliers, learn about how traditional car services have fought back against and adapted, or not, to this ferocious new entrant? Can hotel properties coexist with this highly unregulated, free market enterprise, or are we on the path of extinction?

Sharing Economy or Taking Economy?

The phrase 'sharing economy' is what's used to describe this new market shift away from traditional forms of service and transaction. In order words, the old rules are out the window, the playing field has been leveled and practically anyone can 'share' their goods – cars, apartments, parking spaces and so on – for a profit, all through a simple, user friendly website and with minimal barriers to entry.

These sharing economy systems, Airbnb and Uber included, let buyers and sellers meet on the open market, where decisions can be made on the fly and without serious penalties. To me, this sounds more like the 'Taking Economy' as it encourages consumers to say to themselves, "Hey, I've got a smartphone and I want everything without lifting a finger, damn the consequences."

Airbnb and other companies with this non-traditional modus operandi now pose perhaps the single greatest threat to the hospitality industry. From quaint beginnings as a website mainly for coach-surfers and backpackers, the company has emerged in the past few years to offer accommodations that rival every hotel in the world. They still have plenty of products targeting the low end, but they also have ultra-luxury houses and condominium units available for booking, as well as an impressive corporate travel program.

Think of what you go through to set up and sustain your commercial enterprise: occupancy permits, employee background checks, health inspections, fire alarm testing and so on. Airbnb has almost none of that, serving to disrupt an established system that not only protects the consumer from harm but also employs a lot of people across multiple fields in the process.

Next, consider what your city is losing in destination tax levies as well as state and property taxes. Think about how all that money cycles back through the local economy in the form of infrastructural upgrades, urban renewal, capital for new attractions and support for tourism bureaus. In the short run, endorsing Airbnb may translate into heightened travel to a region due to increased room supply, but thinking long-term, years or decades from now, without large-scale periodic upgrades shepherded forward by governmental institutions, a municipality's incoming traveler numbers may go into decline.

Yes, left unchecked, we are all expecting significant erosion to the traditional accommodations market as a result of these sharing economy outfits – the model is too enticing not to draw away members of our target consumer set. But there are other, more selfless reasons beyond the four walls of your property for you to join the fight. Neighborhoods need constant repairs, and without proper taxation to underwrite this upkeep, a 'tragedy of the commons' situation is likely to ensue. A good first step is to recruit your CVB or local hotel association to see what can be done as a collective on behalf of the district.

Rise to the Challenge

While these above paragraphs may appear to be wildly anti-Airbnb, it is better to give this the glass-half-full perspective. No matter what courtroom rulings or injunctions occur within the next decade, Airbnb is here to stay – it's too entrenched and its gig-based exchange structure is too perfectly aligned with our capitalistic systems for it to dissolve.

Moreover, have you tried Airbnb? It's impressive! The website and app work flawlessly, and they have some truly remarkable rooms available. There's a reason why it's hit a multi-billion-dollar valuation mark just beyond the first decade of its existence; it gives customers what they want. Try it for yourself to see. And rather than wait for external actions to correct the issue, you best treat this company as a legitimate, bona fide competitor to your business.

Bringing it back to the current state for taxis versus Uber, you could make the argument that these cab services have 'done it to themselves'. Uber beat them to the punch in terms of developing a fluid mobile app that allowed for wallet-less transactions, GPS location tracking, better accountability via a driver-rider rating system and oftentimes cleaner interior vehicle cabins. What have taxi companies done to augment their product offerings since the arrival of Uber? What would compel, for example, a millennial with the Uber app on his or her smartphone to go back to the old ways of calling a cab?

Instead of complaining about Airbnb, this is your opportunity to rise to the challenge. Make your property the best it can possibly be and wholeheartedly authentic to your territory so that there is no question in the consumer's mind as to who provides the best choice of accommodations. Just as third-party review sites have shone a spotlight on all operational deficiencies, so too is Airbnb forcing us to improve our products. There's only one solution to this sharing economy problem, and that is to be better hoteliers.

Is It Too Late to Fight Back Against Airbnb?

Despite what many have dismissed as a mere blip on the radar, Airbnb is a force to be reckoned with, and we have yet to see just how widely it will impact our livelihoods. But before we discuss this disruptive company and its effects on the hospitality industry, let's look to Uber. The vehicle for hire industry underestimated Uber by not adapting to the new paradigm of internet and mobile-based transactions, and my fear is that we are making the same mistake with Airbnb.

It is not only a hotel service for backpackers or those looking for esoteric accommodation experiences. Not anymore at least. As new listings come online, the doors are opening for more and more key population groups to find something they want on its website, even in areas previously deemed 'off limits' like traveling for business or the ultra-luxury market.

Airbnb is now a household name, but it is only just starting to supplant its 'millennials only' image. Along with the bargain hotel prices provided by the OTAs, this online service has increased the worldwide demand for travel by making it more accessible. Soon, though, it will target all the same consumer types that we depend on to stay in business. And it may already be too late to stop it!

Airbnb's Website Beats Any Hotel

You love your website, and you've spent tens of thousands of dollars on it. But, frankly, it pales in comparison to Airbnb's web venture. Not only does it have a booking engine that shows you all upfront costs, but it also fluidly integrates comments from its own user data. The commentary and description of the rooms being sold reads like a storybook written by people who truly care. They are not selling; they are trying to make your travel more interesting. Moreover, the presentation is seamless on mobile, tablet or a laptop computer.

Social media was meant for Airbnb, or is it the other way around? When you are contemplating booking a room, you don't research your options through some third-party gateway such as TripAdvisor, but directly with members of the Airbnb community – both the users and the purveyors of the product. This provides a level of confidence in the buying decision that is very difficult to match. The site even reports on how long it took for the buyer to post the rating. Confidence is assured.

Ever visit a city for the first time? Not sure of where you are staying relative to where you want to visit? Airbnb integrates a map function directly into every search. You can see all participating properties and instantly select based on availability and location. This makes Airbnb both intuitive and logical. You end up searching the full range of accommodations just for the fun of it, especially when you browse in the $1,000+ range.

Lastly, Airbnb reveals the complete rate breakdown: room, cleaning fee and commission. We all like to feel we are getting a bargain, and with Airbnb you see the net price along with all add-ons. Imagine if your hotel site showed the net rate, then the housekeeping fee and the third-party commission.

Dispelling the Myth

Worrisome for the luxury market is Airbnb's wide range of product offerings. Yes, you can still find some low-end rooms to book. In fact, the low to middle ranges – the supposed 'bottom feeder' customers – comprise most of what's available. But Airbnb's accommodations stretch up to multi-bedroom homes and into some of the world's most exclusive locations. Heck, you can even book luxury treehouses on the site!

It is this premium segment that will eventually make significant inroads into the luxury hotel market. If a cardinal rule of the upper echelon of travel involves the creation of vibrant and exceptional experiences for guests, then Airbnb has it in spades, especially once it fully rolls out its aptly named Experiences program, which connects travelers with local guides and activity operators once they've booked their accommodations. Each selection is 'unique' as it isn't a part of a branded hotel but contains the personal styling of the individual landowner or renter.

Along these lines, consider the baby boomer market. Airbnb might be a table name for them, but it still holds the perception as a forum for the afore mentioned bottom feeders. As this demographic looks for more profound experiential vacations to satiate the ample free time made possible by retirement, Airbnb offers 'badge-generating' alternatives to hotels. Why stay where everyone else stayed? Airbnb not only provides a truly unique travel experience, but also bragging rights to boot.

What Can Hoteliers Do?

First and foremost, study Airbnb's website and business model. Learn all you can about it in a general sense and, more specifically, the properties that are being offered in your vicinity. Understand the price points that you are competing against and see where you stand. You don't want to necessarily change your pricing structure or your amenity packaging. Rather, try to understand this new competitor and treat it with the same respect and acknowledgement as other properties in your comp set.

Second, take a good, hard look at your own website. Look at how it 'talks' to your audience and the convenience factor. See how friendly it is to use and navigate as well as how many clicks it takes from arrival to confirmation of booking. Torture test it on a mobile device. Additionally, ask the same from your web agency. Encourage them to learn from Airbnb and make recommendations as to how you can enhance your site's profile and sociability. Then run, don't walk, to properly fund the necessary work to make your site more user friendly. This may not be a quick fix, but it is worth it.

Next, get involved with your local hotel association and make sure all the other hotels in your constituency are participating as well. The issues pertaining to Airbnb are very political, meaning that tax dollars are at stake. Hoteliers want a fair share: Why do individuals checking into your property pay local and state taxes, yet those checking in with Airbnb do not? What about local tourism levies, health, insurance, fire and safety code issues? And does the Airbnb location being offered violate any municipal codes? Meet with your local representatives. Calculate, then identify the losses in tax revenues – ditto job losses. You're not arguing for some sort of tax reduction or special favor, only an equal treatment for everyone in the accommodations sector.

Airbnb Is Going To Improve

It is not going away, so deal with it! They already have some outstanding rooms available and will increasingly become an important factor in all segments. The push for the premier end of the market is compounded by the launch of the Airbnb's quarterly magazine, *Pineapple*, which released its first issue in November 2014. Printed with barely any distracting advertisements and showcasing only a few prime cities to focus its awareness profile, this new venture will soon be a strong adjunctive to the company's luxury-seeking strategy.

With all this, it's nearly impossible not to view Airbnb as a somnolent hospitality giant about to scarf down its first coffee of the day. Sure, it's not for everyone. While you may be appalled by the concept of buying your hotel room in this fashion, millions are finding it increasingly acceptable. And these are the people who will not only encourage others to give it a try – they will also make it part of a habit-forming behavior.

Larry Mogelonsky

HITEC: Why You Must Go

Full disclosure: I love tradeshows. The exhibitors bring the excitement while the throngs of attendees build the energy to a fever pitch. I marvel at the glossy displays and all the fascinating new products ready for sampling.

Yet, despite encouragement from me – the-ultimate fan-of-tradeshows fan – I was saddened that very few of my colleagues – general managers, asset managers, owners, sales and marketing directors and so on – attended the most recent HITEC. Your responsibility as a hotelier does not stop at your lobby door.

In the days of yore, the big tradeshow for the hotel industry was the International Hotel Motel and Restaurant Show (IHMRS), now called The Hotel Experience (HX), perennially staged at New York City's Javits Center. That's still a great opportunity to look for hard and soft goods, kitchen equipment, amenities and pretty much everything you need to fill and run your property. If you're shopping, remodeling or considering the same, this show is for you.

HITEC is different. While there is some overlap with other trade shows, this is the one event that makes you truly think. While IHMRS focuses on the present, HITEC has its eye on the future. The fun part of your job is not only plotting the next six months to a year, but gazing through your crystal ball to think of what the hospitality world will look like in a decade's time.

There is no other place on earth where you can see, touch and hear ideas and products in their infancy or those just on to market. As you move across the exhibition floor from booth to booth, you will find yourself talking not only with intelligent vice presidents, but also passionate engineers and product designers who have a clear vision for how they hope to change the way we do business with our guests.

But it's even better than that. Spend some time with your suppliers and learn about what your systems can do for you. You will quickly realize that you've barely tapped the capabilities of your PMS. It will only take one 20-minute conversation to open your eyes to all the intricate new features that go into the latest versions of these software suites. Next, visit some of the smaller booths and see burgeoning ideas that may or may not bloom in scale as their products take hold. Third, attend some seminars to gain some added insight and to discuss the current technology issues facing hospitality. And last, look at the age of the participants – were we as enthusiastic at that age, and how do we reinvigorate our hotels with that same energy?

All told, you'll return to your property brimming with ideas and likely execute one that pays out for the entire journey. Importantly, show some proactive leadership – your team will respond in kind! At the very least, plan to send a knowledgeable 'scout' in case you cannot personally attend.

We're fortunate that our industry has HITEC, a one-stop shop for all our technology needs and desires. As Winston Churchill said, "A pessimist sees the difficulty in every opportunity; an optimist sees the opportunity in every difficulty."

HITEC: Lessons for Your Outbound E-Marketing Efforts

Attending HITEC as a member of the press, I was bombarded with e-blasts and emails from vendor representatives vying to have me drop by their booths or set up a meeting. I received close to a hundred emails in the month leading up to and during the week that was the tradeshow. That's a lot to read – too much in fact for someone who also has a full-time job outside of his hospitality writing. As such, most of these emails received only a cursory glance and were summarily dispatched via the DELETE button.

But herein lies a very powerful lesson. When someone is harried, stressed and managing multiple projects at once (as I'm sure you all are if you are doing your jobs rights!), you just don't have time for much else. So, how do you get a stranger's attention in an email, even if the call to action is something as minute and innocuous as 'Visit our booth!'?

Before I answer this question, let's start with what not to do. Understand that these are my own personal preferences and should not be considered gospel.

- **Walls of text.** Looking at a computer screen for work all day is tiring enough on the eyes; the last thing I want to do is struggle through an eight-line paragraph explaining what your product is. It's downright intimidating. Keep it short – two to three lines, max.
- **Saying you're 'the best'.** At least a quarter of the introductory emails I received purported their company to be 'the best', 'leading', 'preferred', 'foremost' or another similar expression. Guess what? If everyone says they're the best, then no one is, and your use of such verbiage rubs off as deceptive – not a good way to start a business relationship.
- **Unsolicited attachments.** If I'm struggling to read a wall of text within the email, do you think I have time for an unprompted PDF? Be they press releases – and yes, this is

coming from a media person – branded white papers or other supplemental materials, while I'd like to read them, I just don't have the time, and your lack of empathy for my situation is bothersome.

- **Excessive graphics.** Seeing lots of shiny logos or embedded images is an immediate turnoff as it indicates a lack of personalization. Such graphics cue me to think of the email as a catch-all e-blast with no regard to my personal state of affairs. Again, if I'm hard-pressed to keep pace with the business correspondence addressed to me personally, how do you think I'll have time for the impersonal emails?

- **Excessive bold, italics, underlining or text coloration.** These font stylizations are the spice, not the main ingredient. When used too much, it all blurs together and makes the email appear highly impersonal and ignorable. The most appropriate uses I saw were to highlight the booth number or the most pertinent details about the product on display.

- **Using a 'bolt on' personalization.** The body of the e-blast starts with a personalized salutation then goes directly into the text of a dense and complex press release which has nothing to do with me. This isn't personalization, this is spam in content's clothing, and I'm too busy to read a series of eight line paragraphs. Trash basket!

- **Too many three letter acronyms.** I am a professional engineer and a bit of a tech geek. But many of the releases were so complex that even I couldn't follow them. Get another set of eyeballs on any outbound e-marketing campaigns to ensure that the ideas are succinct as well as comprehensible to the layperson.

That said, you know what gets my email mojo going? A straightforward, three paragraph letter with each paragraph comprised of only one sentence. The first sentence must indicate that you know something about me so it won't be immediately interpreted as a 'bolt on'. In the next line, spell out the logline of your product – that is, tell me what you do in as few words as possible, leaving out the ineffective bells and whistles. Last is your call to action, inquiring about a time to visit your booth, arrange for an offsite meeting or establish whatever objective intended by the letter.

I took several dozen meetings while at HITEC and each started with a simple email in this format. I wasn't picky about who I met with – I wanted as broad a perspective as possible. But when there are thousands of people vying for your attention, you have to set certain criteria, and mine was a legible, personalized email. In this age of digital marketing, consumers are bombarded by e-blasts on a regular basis and many people have become numb to this channel. Use these inscribed lessons to help guide your future efforts.

HITEC: A New Hope

With another *Star Wars* movie opening every year from now until who knows when, it seems only fitting that we borrow the original 1977 film's subtitle to describe HITEC.

The weather outside was sweltering; the mood inside the convention center had never been brighter. Exhibitors were optimistic and enthusiastic while the throngs of attendees were eager to learn about how the new products only display would not only increase a property's bottom line but also improve the overall travel experience for guests.

Yes, competition is fierce in the technology sector, but the general undertone on the tradeshow floor was collegial, collaborative and eternally hopeful. We all know that there are many external forces working to seismically shift how accommodations are purchased by consumers. And not all influencers are good news for hotels – the two most discussed were the exorbitant commissions of the OTAs and the rapid expansion of Airbnb.

The exhibitors acknowledge these issues and are here to help hoteliers with some highly innovative solutions. I suppose the real question now is: Can hoteliers help themselves?

After all, I would consider everyone I met and saw at HITEC to be one of the 'smartest guys in the hotel room'. That is, these are the people who are not resisting the revolutionary changes soon to come to our industry. They move with the flow, recognizing that the only constant is change itself and that technological upgrades are the only way to stay apace with ever-shifting consumer behaviors.

I could drone on and on about the new capabilities of predictive algorithms to enhance just-in-time marketing, advanced Big Data modeling or frictionless capture, but my chief takeaway from a week's time in Austin is that there is no magic bullet for the hospitality industry. You need a cluster of solutions, and it's not one size fits all. Each individual property requires a detailed analysis of the going trends and the unique strengths, weaknesses and opportunities to determine which technologies are worth investment and implementation.

For me, HITEC is always a revelation. There is and will always be hope for hotels in our modern, tech-savvy world. If you did not attend the tradeshow, I suggest you seek out those vendors present to see what solutions they might offer and make plans to travel to next year's conference.

INTERNET MARKETING

The COMO Metropolitan, a remodeling of the Traymore Hotel, perfectly melds the art deco qualities of Miami's South Beach with a modern ultra-luxury sensibility.

Larry Mogelonsky

An Obituary for Search Engine Optimization

In its heyday, search engine optimization (SEO) meant that the entire left-hand side of the viewer's screen was devoted to these free listings. But this may soon no longer be the case. These 'organic' listings are derived from the websites themselves, rather than paid search – also known as Google Adwords for the masses who utilize this search engine juggernaut – which are currently relegated to the right-hand side of the screen as well as the top and the bottom of each page.

With SEO being the buzzy acronym that it is, everyone is still determined to have their site found 'on the first page' for any important search term or browsed keyword. A whole cottage industry has also emerged to service this desire. Fueled by the recognition of the importance of being discovered on the internet, countless organizations and purported gurus have developed their own techniques in a mad dash to reach for the top of each listing.

Google has, however, responded with a series of rules for the search game, each aptly named for a different member of the animal kingdom: Penguin, Panda, Hummingbird and so on. These Google bulletins give hints as to what Google is prepared to release on 'how' or 'what' is important in their ever-evolving and secretive search algorithm. But at the same time as the marketing world is scrambling to find ways to get their sites picked first, Google is busy selling the prime 'organic' space to the highest bidder. First, ad space (sponsored links) increasingly dominate the top of the left – the supposedly free – column on the page. Then, as the right-hand column has been replaced with Google Local (another profitable product), paid ad space continues to expand through the left-hand column.

In the pecking order for hotels, the big omnibus sites – Expedia, TripAdvisor and other OTAs – are primed to take up these dominant ad spaces simply because they have the budgets for exceedingly high bids. The result is that the front page of any search result is pretty much closed off for any individual property hoping for a free search-engine-optimized listing.

Ever wonder how Google's share price moved from $54 to more than $700 within a decade? They did not reach that number by giving away free space on their search engine, but rather by selling these much-vaunted positions to the highest bidder. And the best way to sell us more Google Adwords is to limit, reduce, eliminate and literally kill the free (organic) search space allocation on the eternally critical front page.

Many of you still encourage your web marketing teams to seek a first page ranking on Google through a comprehensive SEO program. While a full court press may indeed deliver a first page ranking for some search terms, is it worth the effort nowadays? How much extra time is your marketing team spending trying to reach for this Holy Grail instead of pursuing other fruitful goals?

Moreover, as a senior manager, should you encourage your team to improve your website's viewer experience and make the site better not just in Google's eyes but in the mind of the guest? Or perhaps you might undertake a bold, new social media campaign and spend your scant advertising dollars through those channels? Regardless of the strategy, you can all but guarantee that, in the next few years, Google's gradual conquest of the organic search results section of the first page of a query will force us to seek new means of reaching consumers, and anyone who relies solely on this cost-heavy system will be left behind.

Larry Mogelonsky

Broad Strategies to Persuade OTA Customers to Book Direct

Do online travel agencies (OTAs) have you frustrated? They certainly do me. On the surface is their commission rate, which can squeeze a property's margins and force unsavory cuts to service levels. But there's a bigger factor lurking in our midst, and it all comes down to branding. The OTAs' marketing machine is huge, larger than any single hotel or chain entity can commit to. They advertise across all major communication mediums while we struggle to balance one or two, swaying consumers one by one until we reach a tipping point.

For those unfamiliar with the term, a 'tipping point' is defined as a threshold in a continuum where habits or events can no longer be restored to their original position. The concept of the tipping point has been well documented recently in the press with respect to climate change and global warming. When applied to the accommodation distribution network, has the hotel industry's adoption of the OTAs reached a tipping point from which there is no return?

The topic is a constant source of discussion when I meet with owners, general managers, marketers and revenue managers. Apart from those properties in the five-diamond range that do not wholeheartedly engage this channel, there seems to be unanimous frustration expressed on many levels, primarily concerning the OTAs' commission structure, followed quickly by the lack of brand or product differentiation on their search result pages.

But no one who engages this distribution method seems able to reduce their dependence on the steady stream of generated revenue. The OTAs work hard to deliver an efficient product delivery system, reinforce their branding with high levels of effective advertising and create their own packaging, promotion and loyalty programs. No wonder hoteliers are frustrated; they're practically helpless in putting into action a viable solution. Thankfully, there is a three-step system that may be the answer you need to eliminate any agency aggravation.

Step One: Understand Your Real Revenue

The first aspect to address pertains to revenue implications. The old model of ADR and RevPAR needs to be replaced with Net-ADR and Net-RevPAR – numbers which reflect the deduction of distribution costs from all revenue sources. In other words, using net calculations instead of gross will level the playing field.

With this approach, the property moves distribution costs out of sales and marketing, or wherever else they are hiding on your statement, and onto the top line. This lets you examine every external cost impacting ADR – definitely the OTAs, but also GDS charges, traditional travel agent commissions, third-party group commissions and even, albeit nominal, booking engine costs from reservations made on your brand.com.

Years ago, this might have been difficult to do, as accounting systems were less sophisticated. But with today's ability to look at every kernel of data, I suspect that your controller or CFO will relish the opportunity of surgically cutting into the cost accounting, especially if it means ultimately uncovers ways of improving the bottom line.

Once the data is revealed, you can work to evaluate the relative advantages and disadvantages of each channel as they correspond with each property's individual situation. Through a meaningful understanding of the relative return of each channel and the allocation of resources needed to influence consumers, this becomes the first step to shift business into those channels you find most profitable.

Step Two: Reduce Decision Fatigue Through Clear and Concise Branding

Hoteliers are frustrated, but consumers are as well! More to the point, they are confused over each brand and sub-brand's unique selling proposition. Few brands stand apart, which makes the research harder and the final purchase decision exhausting. A travel experience should be anything but frustrating – especially given that navigating airports and flying in general are both nightmares – and alleviating this anxiety begins well before arriving at a chosen property.

By streamlining selections per the primary purchase driver – price – all on one search results page, the OTAs make travel research simple. To understand the psychological mechanism at play here, you should familiarize yourself with the term 'decision fatigue'. Neurologists have found that decision making is the most energetically taxing job on the brain. Yes, lifting weights may drain your muscles and temporarily lower oxygen levels, but decisions use up far more sugar neuron for neuron.

To understand this concept, think first about a grocery store and that rack of sugary snacks immediately adjacent to the cash register. If you go shopping with a list, the decision work has mostly been completed prior to entry. But without a list, you leave what ends up in your cart to memory work and on-the-spot decisions. It's tougher to do, so much so that by the time the latter customer is ready to checkout, his or her brain sugar levels have been depleted to the point where they are subconsciously compelled to buy a little boost right as they exit.

Give a person a choice of two options – do I follow the list for this item or do I improvise? – and the decision is easy. Give a person 25 options and it's a headache. In this sense, the OTAs are the rack of chocolate bars abutting the cash register, aggregating the hotel purchase choices in such a way as to minimize the additive anxiety of deciding amongst the many competing properties at a single location.

The solution here is to simplify your brand so that its unique traits can be more readily understood by potential guests. In this age of lightning fast communications, you have a maximum of one concise sentence to express the crux of your brand to consumers. Sharpening your brand to this point may just be the single most important task you do.

There's a systemic problem in the hospitality industry these days whereby instead of focusing on only those characteristics that define a property or brand, companies are taking the shotgun approach – blasting consumers with long lists of features and hotel sub-brands with too much overlap. Quick: what are the nine main brands under the Starwood banner and what makes each exceptional? As a hotelier, if you can't answer these sorts of brand questions off the top of your head then how can you expect a layman to do the same? In short, they won't even try; they'll go to the OTAs which do all the mental processing for them.

While reducing the number of brands may be quite difficult, clarifying the unique differentiators of each is not, or at least it shouldn't be. Simplify the brand message you communicate to the public and make the purchase that much easier. Have one concept and stick to it. That way, consumers can book directly with you instead of through an OTA because they won't have to worry about all things related to the subconscious onset of decision fatigue.

Step Three: Give Consumers a Reason to Book Direct

The first step was all about discovery. The second step was all about clarification. Now it's time to put it all into action – via tactical and logistical issues – which, like most things, is easier said than done. Chief among this, we need to explore some of the ways you can encourage guests to book directly through your brand.com or central reservation system.

But first, let me debunk a statement that I've heard countless times: "I will give my guests such a fantastic experience that next time they will certainly book with me directly." Although we'd all like this to be true, the modern traveler doesn't exactly think this way. Vacationers are bold, traveling to different cities and countries instead of constantly repeating the same excursions over and over. For business and leisure alike, delivering that 'wow moment' necessary to drive repeat visits is becoming even more difficult and requiring escalating costs.

Remember, your contract with the OTAs requires you to maintain price parity through all channels, presenting you with a somewhat paradoxical situation. Your mission is to convert OTA customers to your own, but rendering this transfer can be a rather costly affair, especially considering the transient, globetrotting behavior of today's travelers.

But don't give up; there are several approaches you can consider to sway OTA consumers to the more profitable, direct booking channels. As the lowest common denominator, a key objective should be awareness, so that guests can pass the word along to other potential customers about the substantial benefits of direct bookings. Here are some ideas to consider:

1. **Join our loyalty program and earn rewards.** Remind guests of the advantages of your chain's reward program and identify the explicit advantages of these loyalty systems. For independent hotels, loyalty programs such as Stash Rewards and Voila can fill in this gap quite well. Of course, if a guest books through an OTA, he or she does not earn loyalty points, but they don't know this. It's your imperative to educate them. For instance, instead of sending a perfunctory customer survey email upon checkout, send a letter that informs them in simple language about how booking direct will benefit them. Train your front desk clerks on how best to approach this topic with guests upon check-in, and leave some informative pamphlets lying around or the occasional infographic flashed across a lobby flatscreen.

2. **Lever internet access.** Free WiFi is now unquestionably a top issue for business and leisure travelers. Many loyalty programs already offer complimentary internet access as one of the main features of membership. If your property already has free WiFi, then maybe it's time to change your product mix to make it free only for those who are your direct customers and not those who are OTA customers. Alternately, segment your WiFi with basic (that is, slower) delivery as free for everyone and premium (that is, faster) internet access free only for your direct channel customers or loyalty cardholders.

3. **Free breakfast.** Provide free continental breakfast to those who book with you direct. This can be in the form of a coupon or voucher given to your guests upon arrival,

and it can even be expressed to these consumers in a congratulatory manner to heighten excitement. The vouchers should be dated and personalized to the guest or room number. Why stop at breakfast? As many operators already provide complimentary breakfast, you might consider differentiating your property by offering lunch or afternoon teatime vouchers. Additionally, it is important to subtly tell those customers who go through the OTAs that this benefit has been foregone, and then communicate how they can get this by booking direct on their next visit.

4. **Mobile check-in.** Advances in technology include the ability for guests to check-in through their mobile phones, thereby avoiding any lineups at the front desk. To utilize this technology, a hotel needs to know a lot about the guest, typically through information garnered from a loyalty program database. Clearly, OTA customers have no such relationship and would not be eligible for this advance. Yet another advantage to relay via your front desk clerks to OTA customers who've just finished waiting in a lineup.

5. **All other amenities.** All other features or amenities should be up for grabs as potential perks to offer direct customers at the expense of OTA guests. Think spa treatments, gym access, lobby bar cocktails, telephone, long distance, room service vouchers, gift shop vouchers, free newspapers delivered to the guestroom each morning, complimentary dry-cleaning, shuttle services, facility fees and so on. The cardinal rule is that you must communicate with each benefit that they are receiving the bonus because they booked direct and not through a third party. That way, they know the effect (extra service or benefit) in addition to the cause (booking direct).

6. **Offer monetary incentives.** A promotion code is all it takes. Creating a financial inducement is a surefire way to encourage a repeat purchase. But these packaging actions must be performed adroitly. Too much and you run the risk of creating a new class of consumers addicted to your

promotional packages, refusing to book at the regular rate and holding out for the next price slash. On the other hand, your hopefully sporadic promotions must be enticing enough to elicit more than just a shoulder shrug from browsing consumers. Finding this balance requires tact to keep your margins and avoid breach of rate parity contracts.

To state the hard truth, any plan to encourage booking direct will not be perfect. Remember that many guests will never end up being repeat customers as they may not visit your location ever again. But if enough hotels are creating a buzz about booking direct, the traveling public will soon get the picture and hopefully a collective light bulb will go on, shifting booking habits before we pass said tipping point.

For one last word, many so-called 'experts' think that SEO is the solution. In other words, enhance the visibility of your website on Google searches so that consumers looking for a destination can easily find you and, once they come to your site, become so enamored with your offerings that they will be compelled to book direct. While having a great website is a vital part of the marketing mix, an OTA customer will typically view your property on his or her preferred OTA's results page. And if they indeed go directly to your website, it will often not be to book, but rather to get a look at your rooms and other amenities.

Remember, we're trying to change an ingrained behavior and it will take a lot more than some nifty SEO magic to overcome these obstacles. Old habits die hard after all, and so I wish you the best of luck in your direct booking conversion strategies. Be patient. Start with this three-step plan, and then utilize one or more of the six broad tactics listed above.

The Hunt for Book Now

Every marketing manager you employ will tell you a version of the same story: Your website needs to have a 'Booking Bar' prominently stapled onto the home page and every page thereafter – big, flashy and impossible to ignore.

The central concept is that your site visitors will be compelled to immediately interact with the banner to see what spaces are available, compare guestrooms and even select value-added options to enhance their stays. Another assumption is that site visitors are just too naïve or blind to click a smaller button that says 'Reservations' and that revenues will be lost as a result.

This mandatory element, espoused by most of the leading hospitality web design agencies, may in fact be a big mistake. My belief is that this is one of the key reasons why hotel property websites are losing ground to the OTAs and Airbnb. Before you call me a heretic and bombard my email with contrarian opinions, hear me out.

In *Homo sapiens'* primeval days, we were all hunters and gatherers. Survival was far from guaranteed. It was hard work to bring home even a morsel of food for the family. Men would go out on two-to-three day hunts at a time, starving themselves throughout, while the women would forage the lands of undomesticated (that is, low yielding), and often poisonous, 'edible' plants. Any anthropologist will contend that this brutal cycle persisted for over four million years, from the dawn of *Australopithecus* right up to the start of the agricultural revolution roughly ten thousand years ago. For an erudite and thorough read on the matter, I recommend, amongst many others, Jared Diamond's Pulitzer Prize winner, *Guns, Germs and Steel*.

While humanity has only had a consistent supply of food for a few millennia, evolution acts on a much slower timetable, and our primitive hunter instincts persist to this day. Ingrained in our DNA is a foundation of working hard to get results, achieving satisfaction through said work and being suspicious of things that come 'too easily'.

And this animal instinct hides in plain sight in our modern society; some of us go 'bargain hunting' at malls for the best deals while others peruse vintage stores for that perfect find. Indeed, there is a stronger sense of emotional satisfaction when you search through all the available options – whether it's clothing, cars, restaurant reservations or hotel rooms – and select what you deem ideal to your situation only after prudent deliberation.

So, why are we as hoteliers depriving our guests of the ability to hunt by making it too easy to buy? Selecting a guestroom is very different from standing in the cafeteria line and choosing between browned beef and soylent green – it's a highly emotional purchase. And the more emotional input you have, the greater the need for 'the hunt' and any consequent satisfaction. In the process of simplifying this decision-making pathway, we are mitigating our probability of success, both in terms of bookings and guest satisfaction.

For contrast, I would encourage you to visit the fantastic site created by Airbnb. Here it's 'game on' from the minute you start your search. You begin with a broad location and then slowly chisel away and refine your options in what is often referred to a 'sense of discovery'. Not only do you have to search through a wide range of different facilities and qualifications – styles, location and price points – but once you select a potential accommodation, you also must peruse the reviews and owner comments.

All this to ensure that what you buy fits just right. In other words, reaching that final purchase requires a lot of relatively hard work for what's supposed to be a leisure activity, and as such it makes the journey even more rewarding.

With this, we conclude with two self-evident questions stemming from the anthropological argument above. How is your website expressing this sense of discovery? And how are you making consumers 'hunt' for your guestroom purchases?

Converting OTA Customers

If you've been following my writing over the years, you're aware that I'm not a fan of the OTAs. They are strong marketers, and exceptionally run. In a way, I'm awed by their clout. But, nothing personal, I see their business model as contrary to many hospitality organization's long-term goals. Three key arguments I've inculcated are margin erosion, commoditization and brand dilution. To tie them all up in a neat bow: the design of an OTA website subliminally conditions a user to search for the cheapest room available and not to take into consideration the unique qualities of each hotel brand.

Although the OTAs extol the fact that they are taking on a big chunk of the marketing burden on behalf of hotels, this does not negate the often-gigantic commissions they command, nor does it remedy the psychological effects of becoming accustomed to using one website for all hotel queries instead of visiting branded pages. After a while, hotel customers who utilize the OTAs for research and bookings become the OTAs' customers, not yours.

Spouting hellfire and brimstone like this, however, is not productive. The OTAs are here to stay, so we need learn to work with them. Now that rate parity laws are beginning to show their cracks, and indeed repeals are well underway in some EU countries, it seems like the perfect time to lay down a few of the OTA strategies that I've led discussions about in the past.

1. **Conversion through education.** A fair share of OTA customers simply don't know the advantages of booking direct. The re-education process begins online from the moment you identify an OTA customer that has made a reservation. If you can send them promotional emails prior to check-in, try and find out a bit more about what they are looking for in a hotel – that is, get data on them – and explicitly state the advantages of booking direct next time, such as loyalty points and complimentary upgrades. Once they are onsite, your staff should be specially trained to prompt this topic through conversation and try to get these

customers to sign up for the newsletter. And importantly, make sure your front desk team captures their email data.

2. **Reputation management.** Part of my stink against the OTAs has to do with how the websites display properties. When each hotel is shown in roughly the same page layout with the same colors and fonts, there is very little to visually distinguish one from the other. To mitigate this, ensure that you own your pages and that you keep the property descriptions crisp and brief while uploading the best possible photography. While layout uniformity is an issue, one clear advantage of the OTAs, and of other third-party travel websites, meta-search or social networks, is their review systems. Respond to every criticism in a timely, professional manner and act on the issues addressed – other users will judge you on how you react.

3. **Get around rate parity.** Even though this may not be an issue in five years' time, it is right now for most of us, so we may as well deal with it – at least until it's time to renegotiate these contracts. If you can't compete with the OTAs on price, then offer your guests clear incentives for booking direct. At the most basic level, these perks can include access to fast or premium-tiered WiFi, F&B vouchers, complimentary bar beverages, or free amenity trials.

4. **Disruptive technology.** While I'm not going to mention any specific names, rest assured the OTA dilemma is not something privy only to managers within the hotel ranks. There are quite a few companies working to solve our problems for us, whether it's through image-rich, pay-for-performance apps or advanced algorithms that target the right consumers and personalize each marketing message for maximum conversion. Read the trades, attend trade shows and always be on the lookout for 'the next big thing'.

5. **A great guest experience.** The OTA websites are designed to favor location, price and date searches over specific properties. However, once a guest is onsite, you work hard to impress them and demonstrate why your hotel

is unique so that they will indeed remember you for a return trip, and be likely to book direct for this revisit, and spread your name through online praise and word of mouth. If you have friendly staff with impeccable service delivery and you wholly fulfill the modern demand for a local, authentic experience, then I see no reason why more and more customers won't go to you direct.

Always keep in mind that when OTA customers enter your property, they are your guests, but they aren't your customers, and they don't know that they are not your customers!

Larry Mogelonsky

Speed is King with Mobile Websites

When it comes to a website's mobile presentation, slow and steady does not win the race. You want your web pages to load as fast as possible with a fluid, oft-simple navigational flow that lets viewers easily bounce around to find exactly what they want. It's a different behavior than someone surfing the web via a desktop or laptop. Some of the reasons for this may be obvious while others may not.

It's a given that we all despise the lag while our smart devices' browsers fill our screens. An extension of this is cognitive drift – the point at which we've waited so long we just don't care anymore. We move on to another site, which, in dire situations, might be an OTA or a direct competitor. While statistics vary by device, demographic and one's state of mind at the time, a rule-of-thumb average for cognitive drift on mobile platforms is four seconds. Anything longer than that and you'll risk consumers migrating away from your website out of frustration or not returning for subsequent visits.

Given that consumers nowadays are increasingly using smartphones and tablets for more and more of their daily web-related tasks, designing a comfortable user experience on these platforms must be a top priority. Add to this the fact that website loading is delayed on mobile devices relative to desktops or laptops because of reduced processing speeds, memory capacities and 3G, 4G or LTE setbacks. Not only is cognitive drift a problem, but any sluggishness in this regard decreases consumer confidence in your product; they'll uphold another web address as their reputable source.

As a start, have you ever looked at your website from a guest's perspective? Obviously, this point-of-view exercise is something you embark upon right from the start. Furthermore, have you tried your site out on various mobile platforms? Given that the screen sizes are different, consumers' purposes are likewise different from platform to platform. As it concerns travel, smaller devices are often used for quick information access whereas larger screens are for exploratory research. And if prospective guests cannot utilize your brand.com's mobile presentation to speedily find what they need, then they will look elsewhere while you will lose the chance to subtly build relationships and give said guests the opportunity to discover other pages.

Solutions Abound

While it's great to know the magnitude of this issue, what's better is to have a few solutions at the ready. While this could easily digress into a conversation about behind-the-scenes programming tactics such as consolidating a page's cascading style sheets (CSS), eliminating unused code or utilizing image sprites, let's steer clear of the outright tech talk and focus on what managers can do.

It's crucial, though, that you understand why some websites lag, which should give you a few ideas to remedy the problem. Primary culprits to clog up a browser include large image files or robust plug-in attachments. For these two, reducing the image dimensions to thumbnails and installing smaller, singular-purpose plug-ins might do the trick. Consider dedicated pages or pop-up scripts for hi-res photographs or embedded videos so they don't automatically load on the more trafficked areas. The problem might not even have anything to do with the end user's internet connection; your host servers may be the offender, in which case an upgrade to one with a stellar query speed is in order.

Oftentimes, however, it's not the downloading of information that causes the congestion but the number of HTTP requests your website requires. To explain this in layman terms, when a user types in a URL, the website does not stream in a single chunk. Rather, it is divided into separate resource files, each of which entails a connection that's opened between the viewer's browser and the host server. Forming these individual connections frequently takes longer than downloading the files; hence, reducing HTTP requests is the way to go.

There are many ways to execute solutions along these lines, and after analyzing your website's code, any good developer will be able to offer a variety of opinions (and costs). One other option that my agency has had experience with has been building a compression engine in the CMS.

Think of Flow

The previous section mostly addressed solutions that pertain to speed, but another approach is to tackle the problem through flow. That is, you must be able to track the breadcrumbs by which consumers are moving through your various pages and see if you can reduce the number of clicks needed to access any given information. It goes without saying that a website's design must be intuitive, but often what's intuitive for a mobile user differs from a desktop user. Furthermore, what's intuitive for a manager or a developer is not for the consumer.

This recalls what should now be considered the age-old argument of responsive mobile website versus dedicated mobile app. The latter runs much faster because of its smooth, streamlined design and content preloaded onto a device. Obviously, the chief drawback is its price tag, both in initial launch and in upkeep. While responsive web design (RWD) will ensure that a site is properly framed on all devices, it doesn't necessarily diminish the size of the content or the number of HTTP requests needed for a page to fully render.

The hybrid solution between the two is to build a separate mobile website, one that's still not an app because it functions within the browser. Because of this, the new site could be made lean and aligned to the most common queries of smartphone or tablet users instead of those from desktop visitors. While you're at it, tweak the site map to simplify the layout and flow. The key question: Is this page necessary for the mobile-framed site? If not, you can still keep the page, but don't code it for smaller devices. Let it retain the clunky desktop formatting and link to it via a gateway script that informs users that they are leaving the mobile site.

For this reinterpretation, a good exercise is to assemble the site map as a large, printed flowchart, and then look for incongruities or branches that can be amalgamated. Web analytics are also a great tool to help you discover where your mobile consumers are browsing and what sections they are ignoring entirely. Again, cost becomes an issue, as this requires more programming hours than a basic RWD port.

314

Further Options

You might also consider contingencies for slow visitor internet connections. That is, if your server detects bandwidth problems on the client side, a page can be scaled down with less content loaded so that speed isn't compromised. Discuss this with a developer as it may not be possible for certain advanced functionalities or it might be out of scope for your web budget.

Another potential solution comes by analyzing your website from a search engine's perspective. While this is an important task regardless of mobile discussions, you must understand that many people nowadays will seek to access a desired page under your brand.com's umbrella directly from a search engine rather than enter via a landing page and click through to arrive at that same domain. Having accurate and up-to-date SEO will help make individual pages readily accessible from a search engine to better satisfy this behavior pattern.

My final suggestion is that you learn from the best. That is, look to the most palpable winners in the mobile space and pay attention to how they lay out their pages. Beyond scrutinizing your immediate competition and the major chains, I'd cite Amazon.com and the OTAs as good starting points for analysis. Yes, the OTAs have marvelous websites and apps for mobile platforms, and this can help explain why so many customers decide to book through them! As for yourself: What can you glean from their designs? And more importantly, what can you apply to your own mobile website?

Happy Black Friday!

American Thanksgiving and the Friday after – the now notorious Black Friday – come but once a year, a day of midnight rushes to the mall and wading through the hordes of shoppers for those mega-deals. When it comes to Black Friday, it's all hands-on deck, with developers testing the website to make sure there are no hiccups while the marketing and senior management wait for the final tallies on revenues.

Arranging for a fruitful Black Friday takes lots of hard work and a minimum of a month's prep time. If you're hoping to scrounge together a last minute ad hoc promotion, take a deep breath and save that gusto for next year. Moreover, the postmortem on individual consumer spending habits is equally as important as the gross figures. Who is visiting your website? Where is the traffic coming from? Who is buying? Why is this group of people buying instead of other groups? What other pages are visitors clicking to on your website? What are people saying on social media? Have you asked them what they think?

If you've missed out this time around or if you aren't meeting your Black Friday revenue target, rest assured that there are more upcoming sales opportunities before the ball drops on December 31st. It's best to think of Black Friday as a consumption primer. It's the first signpost to indicate to shoppers that it's time to spend on gifts and treats in the lead up to Christmas. You can differentiate yourself by offering another sales period outside of the traditional Black Friday to Cyber Monday promotion window.

With consumers already 'primed', a standalone promotion for one or two weekends following Thanksgiving may present a good option to drum up more sales. Keep in mind that more important than the timing is the promotion design; if it doesn't entice then it won't work today, next week, next month or next year. Put your heads together and build a package that offers something different and you'll be bound to generate interest.

Living in the Review Age

Corporate transparency, social responsibility and responding to customer reviews in real-time are but three examples of 21st century business practices that have transitioned from value-add to consumer expectation in under a decade. It's this third instance that concerns us today as we descend into a literal 'Review Age' where everything under the sun can be given an online user evaluation. Moreover, when it comes to hospitality, guests will also pass judgment on you, as a hotel operator, for how well you curate your property's online criticisms.

Respond too slowly to reviewers who cite operational problems and it makes you look like you aren't allocating the proper amount of resources to electronic monitoring or, worse, that you don't care about guests' needs. Don't thank past guests for their positive support and it may earn you contempt. Respond emotionally to a negative critique and it draws suspicion as to how you would act if this grievance were brought up in person. Don't respond at all and, well...

The bottom line is that hoteliers are expected to rigorously monitor all digital review channels and chatter – be it through social media, OTA websites or the juggernaut that is TripAdvisor – and manage the written responses as well as any onsite follow-up activities. Living in the Review Age means that your online persona casts a strong reflection on how you operate in the flesh. For example, a well-curated TripAdvisor page with effusive gratitude and assurances to mitigate cited grievances will inform future guests that this property cares.

It's a reflection of your guest services and your brand. And this process is largely star-rating-agnostic, too. Responding properly to boost consumer appeal is an action that can be carried out by economy roadside inns, ultra-luxury resorts and all in-between.

Alas, this is treading on common ground. The importance of third-party monitoring and management has been written to death in industry publications. But there are new evolutions in this Review Age that have yet to be given the spotlight.

Namely, prospective travelers are wise to the ways of internet trolls – those who let their emotions get the best of them and unfairly ridicule a property or those who purposefully seek remuneration by way of an exaggerated condemnation. Yes, consumers will still judge you on your response – primarily by rewarding you for remaining non-defensive, consummately attentive and not stooping to their level. But with consumers now readily able to sniff out trolls, they are much more likely to disregard such an angry person's criticisms as partially or wholly fabricated.

In other words, we are headed for a two-way rating system. Your property gets judged, but the users themselves are also tacitly assessed on such things as grammar, tone, length and how constructive their reviews are. Taxi-usurper Uber is paving the way with a mobile platform that lets its drivers rate their passengers. Imagine if the OTAs had a similar system whereby a property could append a guest's bill after his or her stay based upon the linkage between credit card information and said guest's profile on the OTA's database. Hoteliers could then jot down whether this guest was, say, overly demanding, a constant complainer, excessively messy or prone to towel theft. Other hotels could then decide whether having a guest with 'baggage' is worth accepting in the first place.

Such a two-way system is tricky to implement and not without a heavy dose of controversy, but if Uber can do it, then undoubtedly Expedia or Priceline – as billion-dollar corporations with the prerequisite technology already largely in place – can undertake such a monstrous coding project. Major chains might install similar platforms, using them to see if certain individuals are worth signing on to their loyalty programs or granting a room key.

It all gets a little 'actuarial' when you think about how a person's online reviews and commentary can be compiled and extrapolated to give hoteliers a cost-benefit analysis report on every prospective guest. This isn't science fiction either; there are companies with proprietary big data algorithms that benchmark individuals' social media usage to effectively determine whether they are suitable for promotional targeting.

After all, why even waste your time on those customers who are predisposed to causing trouble? Given the influence that such websites like TripAdvisor have on the travel research phase, it is worth two nights of room revenue for a potentially scathing online critique in return? If you are a believer in the 80/20 rule, where 80% of your problems come from 20% of your customers, then identifying and sidelining trolls and interlopers may reduce your revenues but save you tons more in the process.

While we've endured through the lightly regulated 'Wild West' years of third-party review sites, guest-hotel equality is on the way. Living in the Review Age means that everyone is accountable for what they write online. My one piece of advice: always be kind and always be helpful. Or, in other words, be genuine hoteliers and everything will be fine.

Larry Mogelonsky

Musings on Amateur Reviews

Life used to be simple and somewhat orderly. Hotels were classified as one through five stars or diamonds by reputable agencies such as AAA or Mobil/Forbes. Classification was based upon a very specific set of criteria for both service and physical operations. Annual inspections were exciting times on property with staff anxiously awaiting any changes in classification, for better or for worse.

No one believes that inspections only take place once or twice per year. Every guest that crosses your transom is an inspector, fully capable of providing an instantaneous blow-by-blow of their stay. Furthermore, these ratings often include personal or emotional bias, something that would never be included by a professional evaluator. I have read many of these often slapdash or maligned reviews, and perhaps you have your own war stories in this regard.

Take, for example, a one-time billing incident, leading to an assignment of a three-star rating, even though the guest admitted it was a terrific stay. But one issue – one not even highly or marginally repeatable – nevertheless lowered the overall score significantly. Or another example, where the hotel rating is substantially downgraded by the restaurant's shortcomings, even though the F&B outlet is a completely independent, standalone entity. And even if the restaurant's ownership was the same, what does this have to do with the physical accommodation's efficacy?

Many of us tend to look at the average score or ranking. Take wine: the higher the score, generally the better the product. We know how highly Wine Spectator's ratings (out of 100) are prized by wine producers. A wine that delivers a score close to 100 (perfect) is voraciously sought after. Hoteliers are looking for this perfect score too. I have been in planning meetings where managers quote their TripAdvisor rating as if they were quoting Robert Parker of 'The Wine Advocate' fame.

Like wine, most hotel ratings are simple to understand, with a maximum score of five stars. The challenge is that all hotels and resorts are lumped together in the same database, just like wine.

320

So, it is quite possible to have a Holiday Inn Express ranked in direct comparison to a Four Seasons Hotel within the same city. Even without passing judgment on either brand, any hotelier knows that the guest experiences at these two properties will not be the same. Yet, it is possible to have the two rated very similarly, or the HIE rated, numerically, even higher. Why? One easy explanation: The Four Seasons' guests have much higher expectations than those frequenting the HIE, and they will punish the luxury hotelier for any perceived impropriety.

To understand why ratings are deceiving, consider two hotels: Property A and Property B, respectively 4.2 stars and 3.8 stars on an online review site. Say you're traveling to a city where you have zero experience. Now, for a moment, pretend you are not a hotelier, and you have very limited knowledge of hotel brands – say they were all in a foreign language.

Based on the two ratings above, would you choose Property A or Property B? Without knowing the details, I believe we all would gravitate towards the higher-rated property. That's common sense. Next, add the possibility that Property A is lower priced than Property B, and you might think that you have uncovered a bargain. Remember, you know nothing about either property other than what you see on the review site.

Now try again: Property A is a limited service hotel whereas Property B is full-service luxury. Same ratings, but now you have a little bit more information. So, which one would you choose? Are you still prepared to go with the higher rated property, even while recognizing that it offers considerably fewer services? How about if I told you that there was no statistical difference between a 4.2 and 3.8 star-rated hotel. Would this change your mind?

The bottom line is this: these are amateur ratings, not done by professional reviewers. Your standards for a 5-star may be different than mine. They are not perfect, and can be misleading to the viewer, so worry less about your actual number and more about what the individual rater says in the description. It's the qualitative that counts millions over the quantitative.

Think about the motivation for amateur review writing. Some are written by review hounds who delight in helping others with a seemingly objective review. But many arise due to emotional extremes – someone who is immensely distraught or someone who is overwhelmingly enamored, both instances where the guest is borderline obligated to write about the hotel. Knowing the motivation – that they write uncompensated and on their own free time – tells you that what they write about will almost certainly be what's top of mind from their stay.

Emotional reviews might not be objective, but they will shine a light on any issues that are especially bothersome to guests. In other words, if a visitor takes the time to draft a review online, then what they comment on should be considered imperative to improving your hotel. Thinking qualitatively – and, of course, look for commonalities in the reviews – and you will undoubtedly boost your overall rating and increase bookings.

The Future of Facebook

Over a decade old, Facebook is a mature product. No longer the rebellious upstart of 2004 promising to change the way we connect, it's now the status quo. For better or for worse, it has done its job in this regard. With over a billion users, Facebook's monthly growth rate is now close to flat. We all know about social media, understand its potential for reaching consumers and most of us have registered on one network or another.

As a part of this status quo, it's vital that you think about how the network's maturation affects consumer perceptions and interactions. In line with this, many of us may feel obliged to maintain an account on one of the more popular social media like Facebook because of how entrenched said networks have become within groups of friends. My question to you: How does something that's viewed as 'compulsory' change how we interact with it? Moreover, how are branded pages perceived on established, supposedly 'uncool' networks versus on newer networks with a lot more buzz? These are just a couple questions that every savvy marketer has considered.

Just as Facebook overcame the astounding growing pains of accruing, managing and bringing value to hundreds of millions of active users, now it faces the additional obstacle of continually placating stockholders with steady returns. The challenge is in balancing the wants of these two groups. Even as the site continues to deploy new features to heighten the user experience, much of what we have seen in recent years indicates that the shareholders are winning as Facebook increasingly becomes an advertising-fueled and acquisition-hungry corporation – recent examples include Instagram and WhatsApp – hamstrung by a need to buoy its own stock price.

Yes, Facebook has changed, and the way consumers use it has as well. The social network is far from dying – as many have purported – but it is certainly evolving into a beast with a wholly different source of sustenance and primary user behaviors. This transition can be a headache for hoteliers attempting to understand where their social media resources would best be allocated and how to best entice fans into spreading the good word. Here are five top-of-mind issues for you to consider as Facebook moves into its second decade of existence.

1. **Uncool doesn't mean obsolete.** True, the teenagers have migrated to Snapchat and Instagram, but everyone keeps and periodically checks their Facebook accounts. The latter is too multifaceted and rooted in today's culture to ignore. Tagging, newsfeeds, comments, pages, events, private messages, groups, places – there are always updates worth a user's eyeballs, and this relevancy cuts through a wide swath of demographics beyond the tail end of the millennials. While a person's login frequency may be higher for the dedicated picture and video social media, eventually he or she comes back to the mothership that connects all other networks, and at present this happens to be Facebook.

2. **Geolocation supreme.** Many of the latest feature rollouts on Facebook have been designed to engage smartphone users based on their current locations. This includes 'Nearby', which suggests proximal locations relevant to a person's interests, as well as 'Local Awareness Ads', which is an elegant form of advertisement geo-targeting. As these features become more prevalent – and indeed as overall smartphone utilization increases – the prudent hotels will be the ones that are both connected to their neighborhoods – via features like inbound links, cross-promotions and local events – and have promotions that are specific to and convenient for passersby. There are many options here beyond selling rooms – restaurants, bars and spas are a good start.

3. **Analytics.** Posts, likes, check-ins, shares, searches – they accumulate over time and contribute to something far bigger. As the record keeper of the ceaseless online interactions on its network, Facebook is primed to leverage its big data archives to glean some fascinating observations about its subscribers, its businesses and overall consumer behavior.

Hotels will be a key benefactor of these refined advanced analytics features as they will allow us to more efficiently connect with the right types of customers, those already eager to learn about hotel brands.

4. **Personalized recommendations.** White noise to one consumer is gold to another – it's all in the eye of the beholder. Building on the last two points, part of the vision for Facebook is to deliver more value for its users by increasing the precision and ranking of its interest-based, location-based, and retargeting search and suggestion services. This will also become a prominent factor in the network's advertising functionality as such tools like Boost Post and Promoted Posts come to increasingly hinge on previously endorsed content. While these audience customization and algorithmic changes may seem to favor users in terms of not bombarding them with white noise, they will also help hotels avoid consumers who aren't already receptive to a business's posts and promotions.

5. **Social media is earned media.** In the advertising game, you pay for people's eyes and ears, albeit temporarily, with the hope of generating excitement for your product or, at the very least, a base level of awareness so consumers will investigate further. Even though Facebook has pay-for features that companies can use to garner more attention for their posts, engagement is less a direct result of money down and more correlated to the quality of content generated. In other words, converting users to fans and fans to customers requires trust – something you earn, not buy. This will become progressively more important as the amount of daily content increases, all of it vying for the spotlight and creating an abyss of digital white noise in the process. The foremost tactic in developing this relationship is to consistently deliver valuable content for the end user. And social media advertisements are not exempt from this trend; they'll need to be highly creative and well-targeted to thrive.

Larry Mogelonsky

Photobomb Marketing

For those living under a rock, a photobomb is when photograph is ruined by someone unexpectedly appearing in the background, distracting from what was originally intended for the image's framing. Typically, photobombs occur in crowded areas frequented by oblivious or harried passersby, or when interlopers commonly spoil pictures as a practical joke. Definitions aside, photobombs seem like something for drunken college students. What do they have to do with hotels?

Photobomb marketing is a very niche tactic housed under the greater banner of experiential marketing, and it harks back to the relationship between the onsite experience and social media usage. The primary goal of this enterprise is to generate positive electronic word of mouth (word of mouse) to obtain strong third-party approval for your hotel with heightened brand awareness and new customers as outcomes.

With smartphones inseparable from their users nowadays, it's easy to presume that while guests are at your hotel, the odd pose and camera flash is bound to occur, with a summary posting to Facebook, Instagram, Snapchat or any other preferred digital avenue. This is a form of people 'experiencing' your hotel after all.

However, unless a user specifically earmarks your property via a caption or hashtag, it may a tad hard for outsiders to identify where your guests were when they were having all this fun. Your mission, should you choose to accept it, is to ensure that these candid shots are taken in such a way so that the photos are irrefutably set at your hotel and not any other.

A casual browser on social media should scroll through a friend's most recent pictures and, boom, immediately know that they were staying at your abode. While photobomb marketing may appear to be exclusive to leisure travelers, don't dismiss business guests so quickly; people snap pics wherever they go, especially when there is something worth photographing. Five key tactics come to mind to accomplish this.

1. **Background logos.** Getting your hotel's logo in the background is almost the same as laminating an image with a watermark. You want to strategically place your logo at certain key points around the property where photos are already a common occurrence. That way, when pics are snapped in the future, your logo subtly appears in the background. This can be tacky when done to the extreme, so proceed gingerly. As well, ask yourself whether your logo is picture-worthy. That is, is it elegantly simple so that it photographs well, even when off center and taken through a granular smartphone camera?

2. **Objects of curiosity.** People want images of themselves as well as any objects that they feel are worth remembering. Think moving pieces of art, sculptures or even decoratively presented food – physical things that guests will want to capture. Once you've identified these, subtly (or not so subtly) put your logo nearby so that the property in question is apparent. For art, put your logo on the adjacent description label. And for food, while printing your logo on plates and glassware is a tad expensive at this point, another option is to present it in edible form; that way, your logo becomes the actual object of curiosity. Not that it isn't already, but food photography will become more prevalent once cinemagraphs catch on.

3. **Sense of place.** More like surroundings of curiosity, a striking sense of place awes a guest and all but demands that they capture the moment in a still image: beautiful floor arrangements by the front desk; opulent chandeliers illuminating a grand ballroom with stone columns and wall frescos; fountains and an air of tranquility as you walk towards the elevator bank. These are the settings that inspire; these are the settings worth photographing. While a million-dollar makeover is probably out of the question, a smaller budget just means you have to get more creative with your solution.

4. **Environment.** Looping back to what was discussed with background logos, think hard about where on your property guests are most likely to take photographs. What are their motivations for engaging these places over others? Are there any creative ways that you can insert your logo into the background? Off the top of my head, could you mold your image into the scenery via a sculpture or artistic landscaping? Or, perhaps you could prompt guests to include a hashtag with some well-placed signage.

5. **Promotions.** Running a photo-sharing promotion can be a great way to generate a social following in a fun and interactive way. For these sorts of contests, you must give people adequate incentive; a prize that people actually want is a basic requirement, while you must also focus on conveying your property's unique experience and telling a story through photography in order to deliver 'moving' images. A quick Google search will yield dozens of examples of this working on both a large-scale, chain-wide, as well as a single, independent property level.

The Future of Social Media is Advertising

Whoever said that advertising is dead is either horribly misinformed or merely drumming up controversy as part of a self-promotions agenda. This section is a rebuttal for all those naysayers and managers who are slashing their advertising budgets in favor of newer and supposedly cheaper methods of building their businesses. The fact is that advertising is thriving – and will continue to thrive – through online platforms, social media included. Yes, traditional mediums have slid from the limelight, but digital channels are more than ready to pick up the slack.

Once we have long passed the initial fervor surrounding these new digital channels, we will come to see that social media is simply another form of 'media', and paid advertising is but one tactic for using said media alongside public relations and customer relationship management.

The adjective 'paid' in that last sentence is an important modifier because the conversational nature of these peer-regulated websites essentially transforms all forms of communication into advertising. Paid advertising – what we now define as traditional insofar as it involves contractual agreements with money changing hands in exchange for services rendered – is what's directly quantifiable and active in the pursuit of consumer awareness, while all other actions are forms of passive marketing.

In the future, all online activities undertaken by a brand will function as advertising, whether direct, passive or somewhere in between.

Now that these social networks have expanded their reach to global and billion-user proportions, we need to take a big collective step back and look at how we interpret our usage of these digital channels. At the present, it's fashionable to classify or pigeonhole channels by specific purposes; for instance, defining one social platform as a relationship management channel or another as a personalized sales channel. Instead, it is wiser to deem all social media and electronic areas of consumer interaction as capable of handling a spectrum of distinct objectives.

The future of social media is not one of segregation of goals and objectives by individual platform, but rather a holistic integration of all networks where, as we are progressively realizing, content will be king. The back-end programming for blogs and social networks will soon be completely seamless so that posting on one platform automatically forwards and adroitly adapts content to fit all channels. Gone will be the days of social media experts and gurus; all that will matter is what value you give back to your fans and how you sway potential consumers through focused advertising.

Explanations Through Examples

Some examples will help illustrate what is meant by this paradigm shift. And there's no better place to start than with Facebook.

Many hoteliers mistake this platform as a one-to-many sales channel, against the advice of social marketers who advocate that it is a relationship management tool. They're both right and they're both wrong. Facebook can serve as a one-to-many broadcast system if your objective is to rapidly increase the base level of brand awareness. But it can also serve as a means of passive marketing and a concierge adjunctive by having specialized staff members regularly post content and respond to fans.

In this sense, posting content gives continual value to those who have already liked your property, thereby sustaining healthy relationships with fans, reinforcing your brand's benefits and increasing your depth of sale. On top of any ancillary SEO gains, this tactic also serves as a marketing tool for those who are in the midst of online travel research and want to check for any recent happenings or upcoming events – all part of the modern-day vetting process. An active social network with the right type of content demonstrates to consumers that your property is all it's cracked up to be; that there's congruency between the onsite experience, the impression your website makes and the promises conveyed in your advertisements. Hence, a prompt and courteous reply to an online fan's comment is more than just a reply; it's advertising for all to see that indicates that you are a diligent and attentive brand.

While Facebook is the most versatile and multi-functional of all social media, it's best to look at some of the more singular-purpose websites to flesh out this explanation. Namely, let's look at YouTube, Vine, Instagram, Insta-video and Snapchat.

Using the former as an example, the content intended for a paid advertising campaign on YouTube should have a completely different tone and appearance than videos destined as supplemental information. Promotional content needs a strong hook and must tell an emotional story that speaks in terms of emotional benefits and not necessarily features. The expectation is quality video production with seamless graphics and a clearly structured narrative. This is in sharp contrast to any videos produced to 'give the lay of the land', which are often recorded by a camcorder or a smartphone in one uncut chunk. These should be candid, matter-of-fact and largely untouched by the editing bay, diving into the desired information without any fluff and held together by the sparkling personality of a hotel spokesperson.

One medium, two completely different approaches. And yet both are ultimately designed to 'advertise' your brand. The first is active – either by reminding viewers of a brand's positive attributes or through a specific and immediate incentive – while the second's promotional value is indirect, giving value to current or future guests without a direct sales line or call to action.

Online travel agencies and review websites are not exempt from this 'omnipresent advertising' model either. With internet travel research as popular as ever, all hoteliers worth their weight know that positive user endorsements on these sites are a significant factor driving the final purchase. While these reviews are excellent resources to help a property affirm its exceptional qualities and refine its service shortcomings, they can also be thought of as a form of passive marketing. Every time a manager replies to a user's critique, it demonstrates to all other future readers of the page that the hotel cares about this user's opinions.

The key here is to be polite and helpful – two characteristics that a guest would expect from staff when speaking face to face. In fact, how a hotel approaches and curates its presence on the OTAs is indicative of how it should handle social media in general. Timely, gracious responses to user inquiries – including their comments on your posts, tweets or pictures – reflect how you'll interact with visitors once onsite.

Fundamentally, your online behavior is a permeable advertisement for what a guest should expect when he or she arrives. In fact, every interaction you have with consumers in the online realm should be thought of as part of the sales process. My suggestion to you: Set the tone for an excellent experience by having a great online presence.

Advertising Will Always Be Vital

In this digital age, social media and advertising are two sides of the same coin. The problem with narrowing your gaze to only a social media strategy is that it becomes much harder to breach new social circles.

You need advertising to get your foot in the door and generate that initial excitement for your brand. Yes, social media is integral for managing relationships with your customers as well as for healthy SEO. And I am certainly not recommending you abandon these channels; far from it, as these days you need social media to build fans up to the point where they are ready to pounce on your latest promotion or to book a return visit.

However, your reach on social media can only go so far and most of the time – that is, for everything that doesn't 'go viral' – it organically spreads at a snail's pace. This happens for several reasons. First is white noise; there is such a multitude of data flowing through a social network at any given time that a single update stands a reasonable chance of being lost in cyberspace. Many networks now offer a method to counter this issue – by having you pay! In this sense, social media again resembles two-way advertising channels in that you broadcast to many consumers outside of your immediate social circle and then allow your fans to speak directly with you.

The second pertains to one's emotional proximity and shared history with his or her online connections. Suppose a fan interacts with a picture your hotel posted online, thus allowing all of that fan's friends to likewise see his or her activity. This fan may have hundreds or thousands of personal connections through this social site, but most of those users aren't primed to listen to what brands this fan finds appealing. Yes, we will listen to what brands our immediate family members and close friends endorse, but not the college dorm friend who we haven't spoken to in earnest for years, the estranged cousin who lives on another continent or the acquaintance you met at a party without any follow-up communications to progress the relationship. Just as not all of your friends have the same importance in your life, the same goes for the digital world. The activities we see from these pseudo-friends often amount to data points on a list; they barely have any influence on our purchasing behavior.

Advertising in its traditional sense allows you to talk to consumers about your product's features and benefits, but it also allows you to imbue your brand with a strong sense of emotion so that people will at least be 'emotionally aware' of your raison d'être. Whereas the impact of social endorsements is dependent on how close two people are, traditional advertising is relationship agnostic – it relays the same emotionally charged message to everyone. Whether they are receptive to it or not is entirely their choice, not yours.

Conclusion

In the old days, whenever a client would scrutinize me over the efficacy of a particular ad campaign, it would serve me well to sometimes counter with the question: How do you quantity a billboard? If this vector doesn't work, then why are there are so many of them and why do firms pay exorbitant fees to display their products on them? It can't all be accounted for by company ego.

Nowadays, we must think about this question in terms of how we quantity the real impact our online social presences are having with consumers. But if you fundamentally change your point of view to think of all social interactions as advertising for your hotel, then it will make you more effective at both aspects. You won't be burdened by a need to inculcate your fans with a direct sales message and you'll understand the significance of building quality relationships.

Advertising and social media should be equal parts in any comprehensive marketing strategy plan. The best way to think about it is in terms of experiences – online and offsite, or promotional and tactile respectively. As we become accustomed to social media pervading every part of our daily operations, it will soon be time to lose the 'social' adjective and instead bring these channels into the more comprehensive 'media' fold where advertising is once again a lucrative tactic.

Experiential Marketing for Hotels

The world of hotel marketing is changing. Internet sites, OTAs, social media and other new channels hold the limelight, while print advertising, radio, rack brochures and other 20th century staples fall out of practices. In these ever-evolving times, however, it would be folly to abandon the old ways entirely.

Instead, an integrated approach works best via a circular strategy called 'experiential marketing' that is comprised of three broad components. Like a virtuous circle or a golden triangle, each equal part feeds back into and reinvigorates the other two. To understand and apply the principles of experiential marketing, you must grasp how each component acts on its own.

1. Onsite / On-Property Excellence
2. Relationship Management
3. Advertising and Public Relations

Onsite / On-Property Excellence

While the latter two require some elaboration, the first item on this list should not. We are hoteliers, and our ability to drum up future business is only as good as the products we offer. Package or glitz up your hotel in whichever way you like; if you aren't offering a hospitality experience that surpasses the competition on more than just price discounts, then you will forever be fighting an uphill battle because of how much harder it is to gain new consumers as opposed to retaining existing ones.

So, what makes for a great hospitality experience? While I'm sure you all could write a 300-page manifesto to answer this question, let's boil it down to a few key points. At its most fundamental level, you must deliver a good night's sleep for each guest – clean, quiet rooms and helpful staff are a good start. Looking slightly beyond that, expectations pertaining to other operations like enjoyable amenities and quality restaurants must also be met.

But this is just the foundation. It's not going to win you any awards. What defines excellence is what you do to go above

335

and beyond, from the property-wide scale to the littlest gestures of kindness and appreciation. These are the 'X factors' or 'wow moments' that consistently stir up happy emotions and irreversibly lodge themselves in consumers' minds.

They can be anything from an immaculate lobby with striking furnishings, frescos or statues to establish a strong sense of place right down to the personalized handwritten note a manager leaves in the room prior to a guest's arrival. It might involve a complete makeover of your premier restaurant's dinner menu, or it could be the addition of a colorful local ingredient or some culinary artistry to the dishes which makes patrons double-take before diving in with their utensils. Think vegetable and herb gardens in the eyeline of passersby. Think effervescent staff with sharp, distinctive uniforms.

True hospitality isn't about meeting guest expectations; it's about exceeding so that you make an impact on consumers. And at the core of experiential marketing is just that – the experience. If you can't conjure something that consumers would suggest to their friends and relatives, let alone inspire them to come back for a repeat visit, then nothing else matters. Keep your house in order by constantly asking yourself the question: am I exceeding what guests expect of my hotel?

Relationship Management

Guests need to be wooed, both to be satisfied by their onsite experience and, ultimately, to become pundits on your behalf. Building and managing relationships between customers and staff members represents the primary force for these two broader goals. You can have lavish décor and enough amenities to make any hotelier drool, but if these efforts aren't supported by an attentive and motivated team, then it's all for naught. Unlike many other products, emotional and lasting connections to hotels are formed through personal bonds, not just on features and amenities alone.

To put it another way, you need personnel excellence, not just material excellence. This relationship management occurs onsite and online, and it should not be confused with the human aspects which contribute towards a great guest experience. Rather, relationship management comes down to how you value each guest as an individual, whether that involves remembering and anticipating specific requests or exuding that same friendly, helpful personality on your social network pages as you would in-person.

The purpose of this second component is to facilitate the conversion of consumers into fans and fans into pundits who are willing and able to market your property on their own volition. After all, there's no better way of convincing new customers to vote with their wallets than through the face-to-face advice of a close friend or relative. In this age of constant media bombardment and audiences who are ever better at ignoring or seeing past impersonal brand endorsements, the oldest system of recommendation — word of mouth and by extension its internet cousin, word of mouse — reigns supreme once more.

To accomplish this — that is, to discover and build an organic and fervent fan base — you must deliver guest satisfaction. This we already know. Next comes two actionable follow-ups once you've discovered these new pundits lying in wait.

First, kindly ask them to spread the good word on your behalf. Ask and you shall receive is what the good book says, no? Permission cannot be granted if you don't request it.

Train your staff and social media team to think of scripts along the lines of, "We're so glad you feel that way about hotel! It would really mean the world if you would tell your friends and family about your experience with us." Try to instill the belief that they can genuinely help your brand through their actions. I would advise against advocacy incentives in most cases; you want to earn pundits who like you for the experience you provide, not those who are only galvanized by remunerations.

Second, you must give your fans a soapbox to broadcast their support. Social media should immediately come to mind here. Whether it's retweeting on Twitter, facilitating more activity on your Facebook fan page or writing warm replies to good reviews on TripAdvisor, your fans must know that their efforts are appreciated. Make your website the hub for this activity by putting up testimonials in addition to all the proper social media icons for easy access. Again, there's nothing wrong with asking your fans for a little help.

Advertising and Public Relations

Many would argue that traditional advertising is dead. As an advertiser and marketing consultant, my opinion here is biased, but I must absolutely disagree with this statement, and I lump public relations into this decision because it is a form of broadcast targeting many people at once.

The proponents of this advertising RIP speculation often cite the rapid diversification of channel offerings as well as the rampant success of viral marketing, to name two factors. To the latter, I say that this is the exception not the rule. And to the former, this segmentation simply means that you must hone your tactics and distribution to highly specified demographics and psychographics. We are moving towards a world of endless niches, not one of several catch-all buckets.

To understand why advertising is still essential to any business growth plan, you must look to the tribal nature of human beings. Yes, you may have over a thousand connections on Facebook or LinkedIn, but how many of those are actual friends who you could call this instant and request a favor requiring serious effort? In actuality, we still more or less abide by the nomadic way of life where you can only really know and influence less than 50 people. And this is a conservative overestimate; many would argue for the 'power of seven', whereby we can only truly remember intimate details and care for up to seven people.

Even if you dominate your comp set at converting consumers into fans, eventually these relationship management efforts will run out of steam in isolation. There's a ceiling to how many friends and relatives one fan will influence without monetary incentive, that is, without the impetus to step outside his or her immediate tribe. You need advertising to breach new social circles, ones with little to no Venn diagram overlap with other social circles for which you already have pundits in place.

Advertising is the 'foot in the door' for new social circles. But looking behind this adage will give you a better sense of comprehending why such marketing tactics must be perpetual endeavors. Afterwards, you still need to be seated on the living room sofa and give your sales spiel before the customer makes his or her purchasing decision. Whatever traditional advertising channel you have been using as your 'foot in the door' vehicle, you will nevertheless require another dose as your 'hand on the doorframe' counterpart. In this sense, you can't expect a one-off effort to get you anywhere; advertising requires repetition alongside a commendable social media campaign.

Even though it's still indispensable, this does not mean that advertising shouldn't be adapted to the times. Outside of any social media integration, what we are seeing now is a move towards more interactive, less intrusive forms of marketing. These can range from something as simple as clear calls to action in all your one-to-many channel pursuits, to smartly programmed gamification platforms on your brand.com, loyalty program website or custom mobile application (oh yeah, mobile is the future, in case you hadn't already noticed). The key here is to look for ways to seamlessly incorporate advertising into the user's content stream so that it builds on the overall consumer experience.

Putting It All Together

In a nutshell, experiential marketing is the process of using consistent and creative advertising to spur new customers to stay at your hotel, and then, once on property, overwhelm them with how good your product is to the point where they feel compelled to tell their friends and families about their outstanding experience.

One vertex on the triangle feeds into the others, from advertising and PR to onsite excellence, and then to relationship management or the triggering of fans to share your product details. This is not only a linear path, however, as your successes in the latter two will make others more receptive to your advertising campaigns as well as heighten their willingness to reveal constructive criticism so that you can improve at all accounts.

What's critical here is that you cannot think of any component of experiential marketing – or your whole operations for that matter – as isolated events. Every part aids the others and therefore they must all be considered as a part of the bigger picture, which is to drive revenues and occupancy through your own endeavors as well as through those of your fans.

EXAMPLES OF EXCELLENCE

One of Canada's iconic landmarks, Fairmont Le Château Frontenac recently underwent a complete revitalization of its public spaces that fully integrates a historic archaeological dig site.

Photos copyright of the hotel and cannot be reproduced without its permission.

Examples of Excellence Section Introduction

As a hotelier, it would serve you well to be ever-vigilant when you travel, as you never know what you might learn. Every hotel and resort you visit, whether for business or leisure, represents a full team of professionals who have worked tirelessly to make their particular operation function at its best.

I have been blessed in that my career has afforded me the chance to stay at some truly unique properties around the world in addition to some of the most expensive and some of the most inaccessible. Overall, I can say without any doubt that there are lessons to be had from each new property that is visited. It is only a matter of whether you are receptive to them and of how you might adapt these teachings to your own hotel.

This section is devoted firstly to the most exceptional properties that I have frequented, with many of these helpful examples coming in the form of interviews. More importantly, though, this section is dedicated to the intricacies that make each one so exceptional and the takeaway lessons for you to not only apply to your current property but to keep throughout your hotelier career.

A Tale of Three Italies

A recent trip to Italy for a speaking engagement afforded me the opportunity to stay several nights at three different properties in three different cities – and in a way, three different eras! While creating a travelogue for other hoteliers might be of some interest, the learning and applicability to hoteliers around the world is the focus here.

After landing in Bologna, the Grand Hotel Rimini on the Adriatic Coast literally transported me back to *La Dolce Vita*, as this property was a perennial hang out for Federico Fellini, the director of this classic 1960 Italian film. The property décor, with a few modern technical touches added in, looks unchanged from the 1950s. It's a bit of a shock to someone used to the vanilla, made-in-China-décor of today's typical North American resort or any newly constructed chain address.

Everything about the property of 108 rooms says grandeur in its size and personality. Of course, we're dealing with a property that is over a hundred years old, so one expects the over-the-top approach of the decadent imperial era: 14' ceilings in guestrooms, 15' wide corridors, a lobby large enough for an Italian opera, and lavish patios and gardens.

Yet, despite the aging of the physical product, the most important guestroom requirement was nevertheless to deliver a good night's rest. In this respect, the hotel delivered: mattresses were new, sheets of exceptional quality, pillows soft and all amid pure silence.

Even with this impressive hard and soft goods display, however, the lasting impression was staffing excellence. In the face of limited speaking abilities in the native tongue, the team worked hard to respond to our needs without any sense of delay or miscommunication.

As an example, my wife and I arrived on property at an awkward time – an hour before the restaurant opened for dinner, which was 8pm as is common for Mediterranean cultures. Sidling up at the bar, we told the waitress we just wanted some food. Without looking at the menu, she immediately transformed a bar

343

table into a dining facility, with a fresh tablecloth, linen napkins, a floral display, bread basket, cutlery and china. Next, she poured us glasses of Prosecco while presenting the full dinner menu. How can you resist this level of unanticipated service?

Next was the Relais Villa Armena, a Small Luxury Hotels of the World establishment, located in Buonconvento, Tuscany. What a contrast! Everything at Villa Armena was like living in a jewel box, especially given that there were only ten guestrooms. While the Grand Hotel Rimini was quintessentially Old World, Villa Armena was classically modern, a total rebuild of a farmhouse completed only a few years ago.

Interestingly, this was a wholly family affair: design, construction and management all under the same roof. The feeling here is one of intimacy and a close relationship between the guest and owner. I was impressed with the approach insofar as it showcased understanding guests' needs and a palpable gusto for the art of hospitality.

For an example, while we were in Tuscany and undoubtedly expecting a wide selection of great local wines, Villa Armena went one step further, offering wines off the list based upon a personal consultation. Then the next day, without asking, wines were served that extended the previous day's knowledge and experience. To my surprise, the bottle labels were removed, pressed and given to me at checkout as a memento.

All of this was expertly and personally handled by the patron, the *mama* of the general manager, as she managed the entirety of the F&B experience. The family aspect coupled with professionalism was endearing and gave a genuine authenticity to the hotel experience. Moreover, having this proximity to the ownership made me feel as though my stay with them was of the utmost importance.

Last came the Park Hotel Villa Grazioli, another Small Luxury Hotel property, located in Frascati, a Roman suburb, which is more museum than hotel. Built in 1580 as a cardinal's residence, the property embraces its culture and history in every aspect. The principal rooms – 62 in total: 20 in the villa, 42 in adjoining buildings – are large and laden in elaborate Renaissance-themed frescos, bringing a quaint sense of place to the experience.

In common with the other two properties is the overriding concept of service excellence. The staff members were just finishing the cleanup of a full-house wedding when we arrived, and yet they were gracious, giving us a full tour of the facilities, even as the moderately inebriated celebration stragglers were leaving. This included a brief tour of the common rooms and an explanation for why the site was chosen by the original architects – a completely unobstructed and breathtaking view of St. Peter's Cathedral some eight miles away.

Food and beverage, again, was superb (when isn't it in Italy?). Despite this ancient setting, though, the menu presentation was unorthodox, served on glass plates and as exceptional as anything in a chic modern restaurant. For instance, the lemon gelato with vodka dessert was served in a champagne flute with the consistency of a milkshake, made only as ordered from egg whites, fresh lemons and, of course, ample quantities of Absolut.

To conclude, no matter the size, no matter the geographic location and no matter the property's age, service is always the critical determining factor in a guest's evaluation. After all, you remember people over objects ten times out of ten. Additionally, you cannot separate food and beverage from the hotel experience. This is especially important when traveling in a foreign country where it's a tad intimidating to venture beyond the hotel grounds for a nosh when all the roads are labyrinthine and the signage is in another language.

Larry Mogelonsky

Emotional Luxury at Raffles Le Royal Monceau, Paris

When a hotelier thinks of Paris, they naturally make references to the ostensible palace properties around l'Avenue des Champs-Élysées: Le Bristol, Four Seasons George V, the Ritz, Hôtel de Crillon, the Peninsula, Shangri-La and Raffles Le Royal Monceau. So, it was not too much hardship when I had the pleasure of meeting the last hotel's General Manager, Serge Ethuin, to learn more about this property, what makes it distinctive and to see what lessons we as 'mere mortal hoteliers' could take away from one of these citadels of European service culture. Mr. Ethuin is relatively new to the property, having come from the Cavalieri Waldorf Astoria in Rome, and is looking forward to the challenge of 'palace-management.'

But first, a little bit about the property: 149 room and suites, two restaurants, bar, private 99-seat movie cinema, art gallery, a spa with the largest indoor hotel pool in the city, cigar and smoking lounges, bespoke stores (one for fashion, the other for sundries and books), and spacious meeting areas. Art everywhere, by the way.

Reopened just a few years ago after an exhaustive renovation under the direction of designer Philippe Starck, Le Royal Monceau was literally reinvented in homage to the creative arts. Starck, known for his playful adaptations of form and color, has created a delightful masterpiece of contrasting ideas. Some examples: carpets that are slightly off kilter, desks that seem to be astray, paintings that are resting on the floor rather than hung, unique wall coverings, custom railings, a guitar and objets d'art. One must embrace it – this is not a hotel for tradition.

This property takes some getting used to. I feel as if I am in sensory overload.

Indeed, there is a lot here – a feast for your eyes, not something that you see every day. And that is the point. Our current – it changes on a regular basis – lobby floral display is not traditional, but rather an installation art piece of paper flowers. But look carefully, and you will see that the flowers are made from the maps that are used in our guestrooms. Or, the oversize Annie Leibowitz photo book in the lobby, designed to demonstrate the power of portraiture. In fact, everything has a place, and one element plays into the other. Together, we hope not only to make a lasting impression on our guests, but also to stimulate a deeper creative sense. We call this emotional luxury.

Does this creativity override service or get in the way of a service culture?

Not at all! We use our space as a creative base, but are dead serious about the delivery of outstanding service. Creativity is not a substitute for exemplary delivery, not just of the hotel basics, but going beyond. For instance, when a guest is departing and asks for a wakeup call, we not only make that call at precisely that time, but call back again ten minutes later to make sure they have not fallen back asleep (it has happened). Then five minutes after that call, we follow up with fresh coffee and, optionally, our croissants delivered piping hot to the guestroom.

Speaking of food, you have two, Michelin-starred restaurants here.

Food touches everyone's lives. It is another dimension to demonstrate our emotive creativity. Our restaurants start with Starck's design: playful, lively and feature-rich. The depth of detail is self-evident. This has carried forward into the menu design and the dishes served. And both of our two restaurants operate independently: one classically French, the other uniquely modern-Italian. Experiences in our restaurants respect the senses and contribute to our emotional positioning.

How do you translate this emotional luxury concept to your staff?

Training, learning and more training. Our staff meets and discusses all aspects of the guest experience on a regular basis. We work together to anticipate our guests' needs, researching new arrivals and renewing acquaintances with past guests. Our database provides the foundation of our efforts to make their stay exceed expectations.

Speaking of technology, what steps have you taken to embrace the mobile era?

We have created our own mobile app. Multi-language, the app not only provides the basics, but also serves as the nucleus for the guest's stay in Paris. In keeping with our creative core, users can find all they need to enrich their stay through galleries, museums, theater and performance arts. And, of course, they can also link to all the available attributes our hotel offers.

I read about your Art Concierge. Is this so that I can purchase the art that I see in my guestroom, the dining room or the lobby?

Not exactly. We do not sell works of art that form part of our private collection. Rather, our Art Concierge works with our guests to ensure that their artistic passions are fulfilled through our gallery or through many of the galleries, both public and private, throughout the city. If there is a piece that a guest finds irresistible, we will suggest close alternatives.

What differentiates Le Royal Monceau Raffles from the other Parisian palaces?

Each of the Parisian five-star properties has their own unique approach to luxury. Like any property worthy of that top-echelon recognition, each supports their concept of luxury through delivery of those little things that go beyond the basics, those unique touches that become exclusively theirs. We believe that our creative or emotional heart – and the support of this positioning through cuisine, service and décor – will form a lasting memorable moment for our guests – one that will generate positive opinions amongst their peers and strong repeat visit levels. If you are a five-star hotelier, or for that matter any hotelier, you need to find your own unique way to create an emotional bond with your customers.

The Power of London

When one thinks of The Savoy in London, one recalls high tea, formality and maybe even an episode of Masterpiece Theatre's famous series, *Downton Abbey*. Serving as a bastion of society and refinement for 125 years, The Savoy remains a landmark of British heritage as well as world-class hospitality.

Relying on the prestige of the past isn't the hotel's only card. Far from it; managers are forging the way towards a modern interpretation of classic British service concepts. The Savoy was acquired by Fairmont over five years ago. Closed for more than two years, the property underwent an amazing transformation. While protecting the structure and many of the fixtures, all the workings — heat, air, electrics, plumbing, electronics — were totally replaced.

Presiding over the hotel's team is Managing Director Kiaran MacDonald, coming by way of Fairmont's Waterfront (Vancouver) and Scottsdale properties. Fully steeped in North American luxury, he now holds the reins of one of the properties recognized as a world leader in service. Thus, my meeting with him was to learn more about the influences the 'new world' has had on the 'old' and what he sees as the differences. (Note, since the interview Kieran is now Managing Director at the Fairmont Princess in Bermuda.)

Scottsdale and now London? Wow! Talk about a difference.

There's no question, there is a significant difference in the two climates! But the guest needs and the responsibilities of the hotel in performing the tasks necessary to meet those requirements are very similar. In every hotel, the staff only have a few minutes to interact with the guest. These interactions are golden moments and we need to ensure that we take full advantage and that we do our best to support them. At one time in house, our guest list could include locals who have been coming here for decades, businessmen wanting to take advantage of our location and first time visitors from all over the world — many with families in tow. We also welcome a great deal of high profile guests to The Savoy. For each group of guests, their hotel needs are different. Our colleagues have to be able to understand and adapt to these individual needs. Exceptional service is both about anticipating a guest's needs – when possible we pride ourselves on being able to fulfill requirements before a guest has even made their request – and staying in tune with what the guests of today want while ensuring we can deliver it to the highest standard.

I always thought of The Savoy as formal, unbending to the times and the last bastion of the British Empire.

The Savoy has been part of the fabric of London for 125 years, but whilst we are incredibly proud of our rich history and heritage, we consciously strive to stay relevant and forward thinking. We continue to respect tradition, which can be seen in colleagues' uniforms for example (our team dress a bit more formally than in North American properties), but this sense of tradition shouldn't be mistaken for rigidity. Our team recognizes that many of the old customs only create roadblocks in service delivery and we are also very aware that our typical guest, if there is such a definition, is savvy to the ways of the world, and is probably more comfortable around a smartphone than a dinner plate surrounded by a dozen pieces of flatware.

Give me a demonstration of the new Savoy, and contrast it to the Savoy of old.

Our Kaspar's Seafood Bar and Grill restaurant offers an informal setting, in response to the changing expectations of London diners, yet still retains our traditions of the highest quality ingredients and service. Our monthly dinner dance gives an opportunity to blend old and new. Our American Bar combines modern cocktails with many classics, while the Beaufort Bar, open since our restoration in 2010, offers an entirely new and unique cocktail offering while paying tribute to the Art Deco roots of The Savoy and its past links to theatre and music. Our rooms and suites are totally redone with modern technology, yet many of the decorative touches harken back to our heritage.

Do you see technology as a replacement to service?

To the contrary, technology can aid traditional service. Whereas I do not see an iPad or other tablet device taking the place of our concierge, I do see tablet devices as a means of enhancing our ability to provide guests with information on a faster or more efficient basis. With mobile capabilities, our team can synchronize their efforts and provide a more seamless guest experience. However, under no circumstances will we let technology form a barrier between our staff and our guests.

The irrefutable knowledge base of the Savoy butler: fact or fiction?

We do indeed offer 24-hour butler service for our suites. While our butlers are extremely knowledgeable, exceptionally trained and seasoned in the art, they are not infallible. New skills are added all the time. While they are still adept at finding last minute seats for the latest West End Show or fitting a tuxedo at the last minute, they have added new skills, such as linking a new computer to WiFi. In particular, our butlers are trained in the art of knowing when it is appropriate to extend the services of a more traditional butler versus behaving as more of a personal assistant to our guests.

What can every hotelier learn from The Savoy?

Our team is continuously searching for ways to further enhance the guest experience. To the hotelier, true service means staying just one step ahead of the guest, anticipating their needs and demonstrating how we can be of help. We want their stay, regardless of type – leisure, business, group or social event – to be the best it can be. The Savoy is the destination and the conduit by which great memories have been, are being and will be made. Find your balance. Learn what you can from the old and translate this into a new way of meeting guest needs.

Becoming a Gastronomic Destination

Several years ago, I had the opportunity to stay at the Mandarin Oriental Barcelona (MOB), where I remarked upon their exceptional service culture. Lucky enough to recently find myself in the Spanish metropolis, I returned to MOB where my mission was to assess their new approach to food and beverage.

Having experienced their 36-seat, two-star Michelin restaurant, Moments, during my last visit, I was now ready for the signature 15-course tasting menu. Suitably priced well into the upper atmosphere, I waded through each Catalan-inspired dish with bliss, reverence, satiety and anticipation for what would come next. For those who have not yet had the privilege to consume a two-star Michelin meal, know that each course was magical with an extraordinary confluence of elements and senses.

But does a property need to strive for a two-star Michelin rating for its signature restaurant? Even with the exorbitant prices charged and staffing efficiencies, Moments is probably not a substantial profit silo on its own. What advantages does such a prestigious F&B program bestow upon its parent hotel?

MOB does not stop with their signature restaurant. The main floor restaurant has been transformed into Bistreau by Angel Leon, a gourmet yet slightly casual eatery dedicated to seafood. As well, La Mesa operates three nights a week for a dozen lucky souls ready to embark upon another highly pelagic-focused, 15-course tasting menu.

"Our goal is to create a gastronomic destination," noted Greg Liddell, the property's Managing Director. "By offering three (four in summer) unique, world-class dining experiences, we differentiate ourselves from the other five-star properties that make our city famous."

At the luxury end of the spectrum, guests have, well, luxury standards and expectations. When wealthy travelers become accustomed to shelling out hundreds of dollars for each night's stay, they assume that the guestrooms will be flawless, the lobby awe-inspiring, the fitness center state-of-the-art, the spa sensational and the level of service emotionally uplifting. Luxury by itself does not exclude a hotel from competition.

As Liddell continued, "There is an increased sophistication level for the top tier traveler. No longer is it simply good enough to have a fine dining outlet. For the Mandarin Oriental Barcelona, we set out to challenge ourselves, to take the risks with dishes that have never been offered before."

As I've stressed repeatedly in the past, unique F&B offerings get people talking and can work to heighten overall guest satisfaction. By taking its restaurants many steps further towards creating a 'gastronomic destination', MOB is extending its USP well beyond its core of providing luxury accommodations.

So, how do you distinguish your luxury property from the competition? Setting location aside, you have architecture and décor, brand name and loyalty program. All of these play an important part in creating your positioning.

Broader still, is it possible to create another extraordinary characteristic to define a property, regardless of star rating, without excessive capital expenditure? Just as an army marches on its stomach, in the world of superstar properties, the marquee restaurant (or two) presents a critical differentiator. Exceptional F&B is, however, a goal attainable for any hotel class, and this unto itself should prompt you to reconsider a program if you haven't done so recently.

Food can be the soul of your property if you give it the love it deserves – 'love' as expressed through proper funding, renovations and team empowerment. Kudos go to MOB for realizing this opportunity.

In Search of Hotel Excellence: Four Seasons Hotel, Sydney

Midway through a whirlwind tour of Oceania, I find myself lodged in downtown Sydney, Australia for a couple of nights to visit my wife's family. Forgoing complimentary accommodations with the relatives, I opted for one of the city's hotel marvels, the Four Seasons Hotel, which stands as both a pinnacle of urban luxury and an oddity within the FS brand. At 531 rooms, it far exceeds the usual 175-225 rooms one expects in a Four Seasons.

And yet, the General Manager, Rudolf van Dijk, assured me during our brief morning chat that the property's size has not stopped them from delivering a flawless guest experience. Traveling the world with his family under the Four Seasons banner, Mr. van Dijk is adamant that the key to success at the luxury level always boils down to a team that is motivated, engaged and passionate, regardless of the hotel's size. With that as lead in, I had a few more questions to help hoteliers understand how this property excels.

How important is F&B to the operation of a luxury property?

Our F&B outlets provide another way for guests to enjoy our product and service in-house, so it's essential that we are providing the best possible experience for them – both food and service wise. Pei Modern opened in late 2014, and since then we've had some incredible feedback from our guests who not only enjoy the quality local and seasonal Modern Australian food, but also the intimate space and high level of service. Our bar, Grain, has been performing consistently since it opened in 2012 and has won 'Bar of the Year' two years in a row by Tourism Accommodation Australia. It's popular not only among our hotel guests, but also local Sydneysiders who have embraced it as one of Sydney's small local bars in The Rocks.

And yet FS Sydney has only one restaurant. Do you find this at odds with the traditional luxury hotel, which includes a good and a great (typically special occasion) outlet?

Our location, in the heart of Sydney's historical district of The Rocks, boasts a number of very high quality restaurants right outside our doorstep. Because of our location and our market, I don't believe we need more than one restaurant in the hotel. Our guests also make use of our international room service menu, which is convenient for business travelers.

Do you utilize the OTAs?

We do utilize OTAs and they are an important partner for us in this game. Our strategy has always been to work cooperatively with OTAs as we know a lot of our guests use these sites to book their accommodation. However, we do prefer our guests to book through our website and, to that end, we have made enhancements to our website to make it very easy to book direct. We have also created some special occasion packages that are only bookable through the Four Seasons website and enhance the guest experience through prominent value-adds.

Do you see Airbnb having an impact on the luxury marketplace in Sydney?

I believe Airbnb appeals to a market that is quite different from the market that looks for a hotel stay. Their needs and wants are different. Both Airbnb and hotels have a place in the overall lodging industry.

In Search of Hotel Excellence: The Langham, Auckland

As I sit down for afternoon tea in Palm Court, the lobby lounge at The Langham Auckland, I'm astounded by the immaculate presentation, the flawless service and the attention to detail in every corner at this incredible New Zealand hotel. It's a luxury property that feels quintessentially European and yet is about as far away from the contintent as is possible.

After acquiring the property in 2005, the Langham Hospitality Group spent over $12 million to refurbish the 411-room hotel, in addition to many other subsequent upgrades, and model it after The Langham London with its grand tradition of Victorian elegance and sophistication. Look no further for evidence of this than the exquisite Langham Afternoon Tea at Palm Court or a formal gathering at The Great Room which can seat 900 guests. To help elucidate readers on how this property excels and what differentiates New Zealand hospitality, I met with The Langham Auckland's General Manager, Franz Mascarenhas, who brings more than 30 years of experience working throughout Southeast Asia to the job.

Have you experienced a dramatic shift of inventory sales to the OTAs?

The region has generally seen a large amount of internet-driven business, largely due to the strong brand presence from Wotif. com over the past ten years. This has naturally increased with the emergence and growth from the likes of Booking.com and Expedia in our region at the expense of traditional wholesale models.

While we partner with OTAs to extend our global reach, our direct business has always been strong and is one of our highest yielding channels, which shows that our loyal and valued customers have confidence in the Langham Hospitality Group's Best Rate Guarantee. The company has also recently invested in a group-wide rollout of our new website with great feedback from our customers.

Have third-party review sites made an impact on business practices?

TripAdvisor is a great tool to better understand what the customer is saying about us, and has ensured that hoteliers must continue to evolve to stay at the top of our game. It has allowed us to actively engage with customers, both satisfied and dissatisfied; gives the consumer a global voice and the hotelier the opportunity to listen to our guests' needs and ultimately exceed expectations to deliver a truly luxurious experience. Consumer reviews across other third-party OTAs, while not as strong, are still an important tool for the hotel to understand what our mutual customers are saying.

How do you maintain a high service culture amongst staff in a relatively small market?

Our focus on quality begins with the recruitment process, wherein efforts are made to ensure we are recruiting the right people for the job with commensurate remuneration. New recruits have the benefit of extensive orientation and training programs to equip them to provide our guests with a high level of guest experience. The Langham Group also provides all its hotels with training tools such as comprehensive brand standards, which then ensure a consistency in service levels right across the globe.

What steps do you take to manage costs?

Import duties, for example, are not excessively high and are just absorbed as a cost of business. The largest single cost within our business is labor, especially when we consider The Langham Auckland has the highest staff-to-guest ratio of any large hotel in New Zealand. We believe management of costs, though important, is secondary to our focus on quality, as this ultimately drives our customer satisfaction and consequent profitability.

How have *The Lord of the Rings* and *The Hobbit* trilogies influenced your business?

Although it is difficult to draw specific correlation with the films and our business, it is without doubt that they have provided our country with immense positive publicity, especially in the US. We have seen an upsurge in travel from the US in recent times following the economic downturn of 2008-2009 and have a very positive outlook for our industry in the years ahead.

What are the key differences in hospitality operations between properties in New Zealand and those in larger markets?

New Zealand provides a more relaxed approach to hospitality, with genuine heartfelt service but without the formality you would experience possibly in some European countries. I believe this is a positive differentiating factor for us. Alongside this aspect, hotels such as The Langham Auckland provide guests with a strong value proposition, primarily due to the competitiveness of rates we offer as compared with other major cities. We provide the same brand standards as our sister hotels in large markets, the same quality amenities and the same service standards, but at one-third the rate of, say, London or New York City.

In Search of Hotel Excellence: Crown Towers, Melbourne

During a brisk tour of the Land Down Under, I found myself in Australia's Second City – the begrudging nickname belonging to none other than Melbourne, a metropolis that's in a near perpetual rivalry with Sydney. While conducting travel research for downtown hotels, it's all but impossible to avoid hearing or clicking on one of the many Crown Resorts properties in the greater Melbourne area.

As an entertainment and gaming corporation that is characteristically Australian, it was an easy choice to decide to stay in the heart of the action with a local hospitality provider. That choice was the Crown Towers, a five-star property with over 480 rooms. Needless to say, the experience floored me and left a fantastic first impression of a city that I must now visit again.

As is customary, I sought out the upper echelons of the hotel's management to delve into the secrets of their success. To this end, I sat down with the General Manager, Shaun d'Cruz.

How do you maintain the high level of service quality?

Simple. Setting clear service expectations and standards. We review these standards on a regular basis to ensure all the practical elements of our business are aligned. We conduct regular training for our team, which covers every aspect and ensures we run as a cohesive team. In recognition of our wonderful staff, we have a formal recognition program where we identify and reward those who have excelled in certain areas with awards like Service Leader and People Leader.

How do you keep your staff for such a long time?

We've implemented a range of incentive programs that help to ensure staff members feel appreciated and motivated, including a staff cafeteria with access to nutritious meals, a dedicated onsite staff gym, access to the Crown Social Club and discounted staff parking. All staff members have a review every six months where we identify opportunities for growth depending on their personal goals. We work with each staff member to make the most of their individual abilities and to look closely at succession planning.

We also have strong programs in place for staff development. For example, we have a Leadership Development Program, designed specifically for high potential team members, as well as the Next Generation of Leaders, implemented for supervisors or assistant managers who are keen to set themselves up for a management role. Lastly, we conduct benchmark studies of the hospitality industry to ensure our team members are well remunerated for their contribution.

Do you get a lot of guests who stay at multiple Crown properties?

Yes. We have guests who stay with us here in Melbourne and at our sister hotels at Crown Perth. We have loyalty programs including Signature Club in Melbourne and Crown Club in Perth to reward our regular guests for their patronage. We also have a Milestone Stay Program where guests receive added benefits once they reach a certain numbers of visits.

What advice would you give other hotel operators in terms of how to get such exceptional performance from your team?

Listen to your guests and listen to your team. There is a lot to be gained by encouraging a culture of open communication and constant feedback. Ensure all team members are clear on what the service expectations are to encourage a seamless service. As well, plan to succeed. Ensure goals are set and that all responsible team members are well-versed on what the plan is. Finally, focus on the positives and celebrate success as often as possible.

Housekeeping was flawless in my opinion. What's your secret?

We pride ourselves on being innovative and are constantly looking at new ways to enhance the in-room experience for our guests. We have a robust room audit process and our housekeeping operations manager, rooms division manager and I conduct random, weekly inspections on rooms to ensure the service is consistent. Any areas that require attention are passed on to the team immediately via the supervisory group. Perhaps most important is our quality, year-round training and support programs, designed specifically for our housekeeping staff.

Let's end with F&B. What makes yours great?

Within a complex that has over 20 restaurants, ten bars and multiple nightclubs, flawless cuisine means designing creative menus for each restaurant and delivering superb service throughout via incredible staff. Our motto at Crown is to hire for attitude and train for skill. Each new staff member at Crown takes part in a four-day induction which we believe is critical to our business. It means that right from the very beginning of his or her employment, each staff member has a complete understanding of the operation.

Before we implement new menus into any of our venues, we undertake extensive sales analysis, consider seasonality, seek customer feedback and assess costings. Our finger is always on the pulse of both the local and the international dining scene, ensuring that the cuisine offerings are innovative, diverse and leaders within the market. Staff tastings and presentation sessions are held before new menus are implemented. This process is imperative and ensures that all staff members are completely familiar with the changes and their feedback taken into consideration before we introduce the changes.

Larry Mogelonsky

Using Art as a Point of Differentiation

The luxury customer is a demanding sort. They are well-traveled and have seen a good portion of what the world has to offer in terms of an upscale hotel experience. As such, they have high expectations, and the only way to command their attention is to bring something truly unique to the situation.

Decorating a property with spectacular works of art and becoming a patron of the arts is one viable tactic to this end. Art is visually stimulating and it creates fascinating environments for guests to interact with and remember after they have left, and to talk about later with their friends. When you espouse the arts, you are championing a new point of differentiation to distinguish your property from all others in your comp set.

But where to start? How does a hotel get involved? To help understand some of the nuances of this process, I've recruited the general manager of the Hotel Plaza Athénée in New York City, Anne Juliette Maurice, to lend her wisdom. A boutique property, it is in tune with its neighborhood and has wholly embraced the power of art.

In 2015, the Hotel Plaza Athénée in New York City launched Art in Motion, where select works by Matisse and Picasso, as well as original printer's proofs and signed lithographs of modern artists from the private collection of the Galerie Mourlot, were exhibited in top suites and the lobby. This is but one recent example of the property's intimate relationship with fine art and it is also where we begin...

Why should hotels care about art?

Hotels are part of a vivid urban environment made of offices, homes, parks, stores, galleries and museums. So, hotels should naturally care about art. That is especially true for the Hotel Plaza Athénée, which is located steps away from the Museum Mile on the Upper East Side in Manhattan, which includes the Frick Collection, the Metropolitan Museum and the Guggenheim, along with a range of extraordinary galleries.

Is art only for luxury properties?

Art is for everyone. But for our very specific case, we want to cater to our guests, who arrive with high expectations. When we launched Art in Motion with the Galerie Mourlot, we also wanted to help our top guests by giving them a chance to visit this winter's fabulous Matisse exhibition at MOMA as VIPs.

Art is not only for luxury properties. There are so many different forms of art found throughout the city that can appeal to any individual regardless of their socioeconomic background. The value of art is established through the eyes and its interpretations by the viewer. Our guests are drawn to the more classic art, whereas an economy hotel may be more inclined to focus on local or up-and-coming artists.

What are the best ways for hotels to get involved in the art scene?

We are fortunate that our neighborhood museums attract the most exquisite collections. We are currently partnering with Galerie Mourlot to support and highlight the Matisse exhibit taking place at MOMA. We are exhibiting very rare lithographs by Matisse and other Fauvist painters. This quality of art is expected by our guests and certainly adds to the overall guest experience.

How can hotels develop connections or partnerships with the local art community?

I can only comment on the Hotel Plaza Athénée, and to this end we are working on various partnerships with the MOMA and the Metropolitan Museum of Art to include unique packages and special viewing privileges for our guests. Lastly, we are part of the Madison Avenue BID which provides us with a rare opportunity to liaise directly with local galleries.

What can hotels do to make their art exhibitions or decorations more interactive?

With Art in Motion, we are exhibiting a series of rare lithographs in our suites. On one hand, you have to rent that specific suite to enjoy the art; but you also have an exclusive connection with the art. Only four lithographs are prominently exhibited in the lobby and the Bar Seine – two Picasso and two Matisse – adding a unique quality to the environment for any hotel or bar guest.

What are the best ways for hotels to promote onsite art projects?

The best way is through the guest, mostly via word of mouth, and naturally through marketing and extensive public relations, including past guest communications.

How will the relationship between the hospitality industry and the art world change?

The relationship between hotels and art has dramatically changed over the years. Hotels have focused on integrating art in their architecture, design and décor. So many of the hotels today, regardless of their standing, boast about some sort of art related to their ethos. Hoteliers must remain relevant and ensure they capture the audience relevant to their brand without confusing the guest.

A Single-Minded Focus Delivers Results at the Library Hotel Collection

Let's say hypothetically that you had no legacy commitments to OTAs and other commission-hungry third party relationships. I know this is impossible, but bear with me for a moment. Now, what would you do? If we assume that you would still have guests, how would your service delivery change? What would you do differently if you did not have the pressures of margin-eroding distribution systems?

Chances are that you would put your efforts back into doing what we, as hoteliers, are trained to do: provide true and meaningful guest experiences. Guest service taken to its extreme connotes providing experiences that exceed your customers' expectations. Service of this caliber is generally reserved for exclusive (read, expensive) five-star, five-diamond professionally rated properties, the ones you read about in Travel & Leisure and Condé Nast Traveler, generally inaccessible to the average or even somewhat above average traveler.

Yet, in my travels, I have found a small hotel chain that somehow manages to deliver this seemingly unheard of customer service, and it does so while keeping within the bounds of the upper-middle range of pricing. In doing so, not surprisingly, they are not just loved, but revered by their customers, resulting in TripAdvisor rankings 'well above their pay grade'.

Library Hotel Collection (LHC) operates four properties in Midtown Manhattan. I have now had the privilege of staying at all of them. They are all small, each less than 100 guestrooms. They are not the newest properties, nor do they have the most modern accouterments such as showers separate from tubs, large bathrooms or colossally sized television screens. In fact, looked upon in the absence of their service component, a property inspector might be hard-pressed to bestow a four-star or four-diamond award on these locations.

Yet, there is magic in the air, and before you discuss a multi-million-dollar renovation with your asset managers and owners, a trip to Manhattan might present a bountiful learning opportunity. That's because LHC gets it! They truly understand what today's guests want: to be treated like highly appreciated visitors who have arrived in someone's home and not nickeled and dimed to death. When you check in at a LHC property, your room rate plus tax is the rate you pay. While there are services you can choose to add like dinner, parking or flowers on arrival, guests enjoy a multitude of amenities without adding anything else to the bill.

Their leading concept revolves around what they call the 'club room'. Here, you can indulge in food, snacks, beverages, read the newspaper or magazines, surf the internet, and just relax. Bring a friend? No problem and no additional cost. Want to have a snack in the evening? Why not. Glass of wine? Bottle of water for the trip? But, of course! This is your home away from home, so help yourself. There are no additional charges. Ever. A cash register is not in sight.

So, how do they somehow get this done when no one else seems to get it and when every hotel that I know of is into value-engineering your stay to the point that full-service and limited-service are virtually indistinguishable? In a world of seemingly endless resort fees and surcharges, LHC's approach is truly refreshing.

To help make sense of this dilemma, I spoke to Adele Gutman, LHC's Vice President of Revenue Management and Marketing. Her acumen in this area is both refreshing and eye-opening. "For our New York City properties, we have maintained all of our four properties within the top ten on TripAdvisor for eight years now, but our goal is always to have the top four places. With 450+ Manhattan properties listed, this is a tall order, but we have done it before and the whole team is focused on achieving this again. More than anything else, our stellar reputation is due to our staff members, who are excited to be the object of such enthusiastic appreciation on TripAdvisor. Every positive review motivates the staff to do even more for the next guest."

She continues, "This single-minded goal is communicated to our entire team and becomes the mantra of our organization, with every other metric being secondary. We know that the majority of new guests are generated through TripAdvisor searches. This, plus our past guest referrals, delivers our occupancy goals. And, since all four of our properties receive similar ratings, cross-selling to another location when one of our hotels is full becomes so much easier."

For LHC, the system works, and with new properties outside of Manhattan now under construction, they may be coming to a city near you. Could their approach work for you? I suggest you visit one of their properties and experience their magic for yourself.

Larry Mogelonsky

In Search of Hotel Excellence: COMO Metropolitan Miami

As a hotelier, what does one think of when considering Miami Beach? Perhaps the hustle of the South Beach strip crammed with Art Deco micro-properties. Or, is it the top brass of properties like SLS, ONE, Setai, The W, Ritz Carlton or Fontainebleau?

Leave it up to Singapore-based COMO Hotels & Resorts to take its turn at reinventing the Miami Beach luxury experience with the early 2014 opening of their Metropolitan Hotel. Formerly known as the Traymore, a name that legally remains on rooftop signage and is now the name of the lobby restaurant and bar, the 74-room hotel is the result of a total rebuild that maintains the overall size and configuration of the original.

The scale of the property doesn't overwhelm upon arrival. Only eight stories high with old-world ceiling heights, the Met Miami tucks into a neat space between two modern condominium buildings. Once inside, the jewel box unfolds. As COMO's first hotel in the United States, the best words to describe the sense of place are calm and wellbeing.

The tight-cornered, terrazzo-floored lobby opens into the restaurant-bar and directly to the cabana-pool area. Overlooking the scene is a small, glass-walled general manager's office from the mezzanine area above. Javier Beneyto, a newcomer to COMO, answers the call as the opening GM. While he seems to be everywhere at once, I managed to get a few moments to ask him about the property and his goals for COMO in Miami:

"This is COMO's second property in the Americas, as we have enjoyed good success with Parrot Cay in Turks & Caicos. The addition of a hotel in Miami was a natural, given that this is the transit point for the bulk of guests headed for Parrot Cay. The Met Miami has been designed in the COMO tradition of understated, simple elegance, with our focus on wellness.

This has been carried into many of the elements that we use as differentiators: lemon and ginger scented towels to welcome weary guests upon arrival, our spa-inspired menu items, and our signature COMO Shambala Spa.

COMO is a relatively new name to North America. Yet, surprisingly, we have had a lot of interest right from pre-opening, given the strong brand following amongst Americans looking for a visionary service approach.

We do not advertise, and rely almost exclusively upon past guest referrals. Occupancies have grown steadily as we have moved gradually up to 100% room availability. We are matching rate with our competitive set."

When asked about a success formula for the Met Miami, Javier made it clear: it is all about staff and continuous training. The phrase used on property to describe this philosophy is 'Retour au Source', meaning a back-to-basics approach to hospitality.

Moreover, for many of the team, this is their first job in the industry. They have no pre-conceived notion of service standards. The property creates its own, infusing in these young staffers the importance of meeting and exceeding guests' requirements.

They are constantly reminded that this is all about the little details and executing them to perfection every time. They are invited to share in the COMO philosophy of wellness and are encouraged to participate in the company's long term goals. This is a recurring theme I've witnessed during my years of travel to luxury properties, and the Met Miami is no exception in this regard.

(Since this interview, Javier has moved on to a new COMO property in Thailand.)

Larry Mogelonsky

Weddings Done to Perfection at the Fairmont Grand Del Mar

Weddings are often viewed as an orphan kid of our industry, and special attention to this stream is only given at a narrow set of dedicated properties. Let me remind you, however, that weddings are 'recession proof', whereby every bride wants her day to be as immaculate as possible. But it takes time and commitment to develop a successful weddings program, and to this end there's no better place to look for inspiration then a five-star, five-diamond hotel with a stellar reputation in this arena.

The Fairmont Grand Del Mar is a majestic, sprawling property tucked away in the foothills north of San Diego. When I first visited the resort, I instantly noticed how important weddings were as a major source of revenue. And so I reached out to the Director of Catering and Conference Services, Charles Stuart, to elucidate some key details as to what makes their wedding program special. As always, there's learning for all!

Give us an idea as to the size of your wedding facilities.
All told, we have 25,000 square feet of usable outdoor space and 20,000 square feet of indoor banquet space. The marquis space is our Elizabeth Ballroom, which is 9,700 square feet with 20-foot ceilings and a built-in recessed stage, able to accommodate up to 550 people. Padded, gold-framed air walls can divide this space into three separate ballrooms if needed.

Our Manchester Salon and Terrace has 2,250 indoor and 1,925 outdoor square feet, with 13-foot ceilings and accommodating up to 120 people. Meanwhile, our Capella Room is 3,070 square feet and accommodates up to 160 people with a recessed dais. The unique feature of this space is its dual purpose; it can be used for the reception dinner and dances as well as the inside venue for wedding ceremonies. The décor is that of a traditional chapel with high wood ceilings, inlaid marble walls and floors, stained glass windows and removable ornate wooden pews.

The Llama Is Inn

Our outdoor spaces include the Aria Lawn at 8,160 square feet, which overlooks the golf course and canyon with a unique Mediterranean-themed pavilion. The area is used for the outdoor ceremonies and can double as a space for pre-dinner receptions as well as the dinner venue itself. Next comes our North and South Reflection Lawns and Gazebo which are located around the reflection pool and fountains. These offer another outdoor venue for the smaller ceremonies up to 120 people as well as for pre-dinner receptions.

What's the typical GDM wedding like?

The wedding business accounts for a significant proportion of the local catering business and the weddings range in size from 120 to 550 guests. When quoting an approximate amount, one should budget for between $300 to $375 per person plus service charge and tax. This would cover the food and beverage requirements; décor, entertainment and guest room needs would be in addition to this figure. Great skill is needed in balancing and managing the two families' needs and who is paying for what, along with the bride and groom's plans. Our job is to calm and reassure that everything is under total control and the day is going to be a picture-perfect day.

How many room nights does the average wedding yield?

The number of weddings varies each year based on available space, and whether it is a destination wedding, which, for instance, changes how long people stay. These average between 40 and 45; our peak year was 48. We have seen events where as few as 10% of the guests will stay all the way through to an almost-total buyout of the hotel over the whole weekend when there are multiple events that are planned in association with the wedding, such as rehearsal dinners prior and farewell brunches the following day.

Apart from unique facilities, how else does the GDM uphold its segment leadership?

First is customization. We do not offer all-in packages where a price per person is set and everything is included, as these often limit choice and flexibility. We listen carefully to the bride and groom's dreams balanced with the parents' input, and then offer suggestions with a solid team to ensure flawless service and attention to detail.

Next is the desire to make the bride and groom feel special. We will only host one wedding on any day, even though the facilities could accommodate two or more weddings on the same day. After that is food and beverage quality. As with the resort in general, no frozen products are used, items are made from scratch and ingredients are of the best quality we can find, using organic where possible.

How are weddings integrated into other operations?

As a special surprise for our bride and groom, each receives a personalized Grand Del Mar monogrammed bath robe, beautifully presented in the bridal suite upon return to their room. Special golf days for the groomsmen and special spa days for the bridal party are often arranged. Additionally, themed welcome amenities and gifts have been arranged in the past which tie into the wedding theme and are delivered to each guestroom.

What changes have you experienced in the weddings over the past years?

The booking window has shortened to between six and nine months. Leads are coming in from all types of vendors these days – from photographers, for example, indicating that brides are securing their photographer before other vendors or even the venue. Interestingly, wedding planners are no longer the main source of vendor referrals for weddings.

People are getting away from the old traditions and are customizing their weddings to exactly what they want. With the influx of social media sites such as Pinterest, more brides are becoming their own planners; they have greater access to all the ideas that are trending, and are often looking to incorporate these into their special day. Our specialty is in knowing which concepts will work and which will not when recreating a small snapshot of an idea for a large event.

What other types of events use the wedding facilities?

Our event spaces accommodate all types of events including Bar and Bat Mitzvahs, Quinciñeras, birthdays, anniversary parties, celebration of life events, fundraisers and high profile black tie galas. We customize each event for so many of our clients that it's not so much the type of event but the client's overall needs. For example, we have Bat Mitzvahs that have had as extensive décor as weddings and birthday parties that have outdone black tie galas in both décor and entertainment. In general, though, weddings usually require a lot more setup time than other events due to the extensive amount of décor, floral arrangements and lighting needs.

Why is GDM so popular for celebrity weddings?

The reason is that we are not a wedding factory. It is now common knowledge that LeBron James got married here. He is but one of many celebrities to do this over the years, many of whom are never reported because of how we handle confidentiality for all our guests. Privacy, intimacy and confidentiality are offered in both accommodations as well as the venue itself. The resort is off the beaten track and we can manage who has access to the drive-in. It was quite the accomplishment that it was never released where Mr. James was getting married right up until the party was almost over, much to the frustration of TMZ!

SoCal has quite a few five-star, five-diamond wedding venues. How do you differentiate your product from a marketing standpoint?

Our venue is unique in every sense of the word. Still relatively a new hotel, the old-world design and décor of the property, landscape, and manicured grounds, and the intimate internal ambiance all create a world away from other Californian properties. Many guests liken us to being at a family estate in the Mediterranean; couple this with the unbeatable weather of San Diego and you have a venue like no other.

We focus our efforts on relationship building with other top industry professionals. Much time is spent networking with high-end planners and vendors to build this personalized relationship where understanding and trust is key. In addition to these one-on-ones, we host a memorable FAM trip for these professionals each year where they will be our guests for a couple of days and experience firsthand our level of service and quality of food and beverage. It's fun; it's a blast; we all let our hair down, and they experience what's trendsetting and what sets us apart from the other venues. All this leads to word-of-mouth recommendations from some of the top planners in the country and Europe targeting the marketing at guests who are looking for an exceptional venue with the best service.

Can you convert wedding customers to leisure or other segments?

Yes, we have found that many guests who have stayed with us over a weekend and attended a wedding will return for a special getaway, be it for their own engagement dinner and subsequent wedding or a special occasion such as an anniversary weekend. The brides and grooms tend to be the most frequent returning guests, celebrating their anniversaries each year with a night or weekend stay. Often we will recreate part of their dinner menu or a tier from their original cake for them. One of the main reasons for this is due to the great amenities we offer including golf, spa, tennis, world-class dining and offsite activities. With all these options, we can offer a different celebration for each year and for every visit.

In Search of Hotel Excellence: The Sagamore Resort on Lake George, New York

Recall the movie *Dirty Dancing* starring Jennifer Grey and Patrick Swayze to put you in the mood. Now fast forward 25 years and modernize by adding a lakeside setting with multiple dining and leisure options and you have The Sagamore Resort. And for the record, *Dirty Dancing* was filmed in North Carolina and Virginia.

This 375-room historic property spread out amongst a main building and a series of lodges located on its very own 70-acre island just off Bolton Landing on Lake George, about three hours north from New York City, seems like the idyllic summer getaway. With several pools, a spa, tennis courts and a massive family-oriented recreation center, the resort just may be the perfect destination for a July or August family sojourn.

My two-night stay confirmed this; I haven't seen so many families with kids since my last trip to Disney World in Orlando. Yet, this wasn't a family-only resort – as witnessed by my time in the main restaurant where I could easily point out many couples and even a few business groups taking advantage of the massive 25,000 sq. ft. convention center, all of them dining in noisy harmony.

The property is so large with so many options for guests to congregate that there was something for everyone. The LakeHouse, a lakeside bar, drew the singles and couples, while the poolside seemed to lure families. Another indoor pool attracted the teens like a magnet. And the waterfront held rental boats, jet skis, the Morgan (a large touring boat) and a shallow lakeside swimming area. Even more kids could be found tucked away at the Rec Center, a building housing a myriad of activities for the young folks.

The guestrooms were comfortable and functional but not overly ostentatious. Our room had a great view and was about 375 sq. ft. The bathroom was small and somewhat dated, but not in such a manner as to be considered a major negative. And I could also say that it was spectacularly quiet.

Managing a property of this magnitude requires patience and exceptional teamwork. I sat down with Tom Guay, General Manager, to discuss some of the challenges and processes he undertakes to keep The Sagamore up to its high standard of excellence.

What's the team dynamic like for a summer resort?

Each year, we must reinvent ourselves, as our team rises from about 130 to 630 for the Memorial Day through Labor Day peak season. This means an intensive recruiting effort that starts each November, with our key team leaders visiting hotel schools as far north as Prince Edward Island, Canada and as far west as Niagara. Then, once hired, we have to train them to ensure that they are able to meet our standards. This includes intensive mentoring and shadowing our core team until they quickly 'solo' in their positions.

I've read your TripAdvisor reviews. How do you manage to keep every guest happy?

I wish it was as simple as ensuring that there was a chaise in the sunshine for every guest. And, while this is important (we have over 800 chaise lounges), there is a lot more to it. It starts with an appreciation for the guest and understanding their needs. For example, if you have a family in the dining room, you need to serve quickly. In comparison, a couple dining alone does not want to rush their service. You have to have the necessary experience to anticipate how to manage each type of guest.

Speaking of the dining room, I've rarely seen the combination of families, couples and business groups all cohabitating the same dining space.

It isn't something that is done easily. We do not segregate couples from families. Our experience is that the children seem to rise to the occasion. Somehow, they know to be on their best behavior, and their parents seem to self-regulate their younger family members. Our team members know how to keep things moving and this is something we stress during the training process.

So, how's business?

Over the past five years, we've seen continuous business improvement. Our occupancy levels have been increasing, and this is coincident with higher unit room revenue. While there is always room for improvement, we're convinced that the marketplace approach makes sense.

Larry Mogelonsky

A Personal Autograph at The Algonquin St. Andrews

As a child, I spent many summers in Saint John, New Brunswick. The highlight of my family's 10-week stay was a 90-minute car ride south to St. Andrews by the Sea on the Bay of Fundy, where the grand Algonquin Resort beckoned (no relation to the Algonquin Hotel in New York City). For the 99.99% of readers who have never visited or heard of it, the Algonquin was a Canadian Pacific and then a Fairmont property of historic proportions.

A visit to the resort just after its 100th anniversary in the 1990s was less than inspiring, though. Old and faded, it reminded me of the scenes from *The Grand Budapest Hotel* depicting a luxurious property's fall from grace after years of neglect. While a new, lavish wing was added, the main building was tired at best.

Less than a decade ago, New Castel Hotels & Resorts, based out of Shelton, Connecticut, took on the role of both investor and management firm. With a scheduled opening for Spring 2014, I wanted to be among the first visitors to see for myself whether the 'old lady' would have her renaissance. And indeed she has! The overall curb appeal remains unchanged; the Tudor style and colors are identical. The only noticeable difference on the exterior was the removal of the shuffleboard courts, replacing them with fire pits. No doubt, this is just one minor detail in the strategy of modernization.

Entering the lobby, there is no question that this is a complete renewal. Moncur Design Associates of Toronto has accomplished a visual treat – modern yet still sporting the broad lines and casual feel of a summer ocean side resort. Guestrooms were also treated to a full revitalization. In total, some $30 million was spent to revitalize this 233-room property, which, due to inflation, is many times the cost of the original 1889 construction.

It is not hard to spend money on a renovation. What is more challenging is finding a leader and team who can quickly complete the project and launch into peak season without cutting corners. Getting it right and aligning all staff and operations accordingly is no easy task. Enter Tim Ostrem as General Manager, who has the unique distinction of being the only person I know in hospitality management taller than me! My conversation with Tim focused on the challenges he has faced through this critical launch phase and the first year of operations.

Why a Marriott Autograph?

The Autograph Collection allows us to take the best of the Marriott system, yet maintain our own distinctive branding and identity. You only see the word 'Autograph' on a plaque in the entranceway. This ensures that our guests establish a close relationship with us. At the same time, we enjoy all the benefits of Marriott's reservation system, distribution network and, importantly, their recognition as a group segment leader. They have been a tremendous supporter to us during the opening.

How important is the convention segment to the business mix?

Groups are vital as we plan to be a 12-month resort. The challenge is not to fill the hotel from May through October. Rather, and where groups will be critical, is the period from November through April. This property used to be a seasonal operation, necessitated by the lack of adequate HVAC systems and 100+ year old insulation (or lack thereof for both). We know the challenge that is facing us, and the Marriott support system, as well as intensive sales efforts to local corporate and regional government, will be critical.

This property was closed for well over a year and your team is being built from scratch.

True! The advantage we have is that New Castle has a wide range of properties from which we were able to draw some key team leaders. It is refreshing that the local talent pool is surprisingly strong, yet at the same time our trainers have their hands full. Admittedly, our first few days were a bit dicey, but our initial groups and visitors recognize that we are in startup mode, and the TripAdvisor and direct feedback has been nothing short of exceptional. This is a continual process, and I cannot overstate how important this is given our 'four-star plus' guest requirements.

What advice can you give other developers planning their own launch?

Expect the unexpected. Be prepared for some long nights and keep in physical shape as you might be lifting furniture into guestrooms the day prior to guest arrivals. Inspect things yourself. Be a problem solver rather than a blame pointer. Encourage your team to take action and learn by doing. Oh, yes, keep a change of clothes in the office to greet guests.

What about advice from an ownership-relations perspective?

Keep owners abreast of what is happening so that there are no surprises. Share information with everyone so that there is zero communications breakdown. Never decline offers of support. Keep your REVPAR projections on the light side – that is, don't over commit. Focus on the successes, recognize the challenges and act on the proposed solutions. Remember, a property launch is more about establishing processes than immediate numerical success.

In Search of Hotel Excellence: Halekulani Hotel, Wakiki Beach, Honolulu

A few years ago, I reviewed two resorts – the St. Regis Bal Harbour on the east coast of the United States (Florida), and the Montage Laguna Beach on the west coast (California) – comparing these properties as examples of the finest accommodations that America had to offer. *Mea culpa*. I failed to include Hawaii and Halekulani on Waikiki Beach in Honolulu, which just might surpass both of these continental jewels with its own unique blend of services and amenities unlike anything else found beyond this tropical archipelago.

A property with a rich history, Halekulani has a reputation that has been developed for almost a century. Putting aside impressive historical anecdotes, what's most fascinating is the 'what and how' that this 453-room property delivers to its guests today. Speaking with Ulrich Krauer, the property's GM, who leads a team of 800+, was an eye-opener. Here is what I gleaned over several days in paradise.

What do you think makes Halekulani so special?

It is our focus on longevity. It starts with our owners, and transcends through to our staff and our guests. We have had the same ownership for over 30 years; 30% of our staff has been with us for 20 years or more while one third of that number has been for 30! The same loyalty applies to our guests. It's not uncommon to meet guests that are on their 20th or 30th stay with us, and visitors who stay for months at a time.

Long-term employees and long-term guests: how do you do it?

It's a process, simple but often forgotten. The equation balances how you treat your guests with how you treat your staff. In my mind, there is no difference in the level of understanding, respect and encouragement. We encourage staff to learn the names of the guests and personalize every experience, from enjoying a drink by the pool to a conversation with the concierge and to check-in and check-out – every act of guest interaction provides another opportunity to extend our customer reach. One of the advantages of having an experienced staff is delegation of responsibility. Guest issues – and believe me we have them – can be resolved immediately and pretty much always to the guests' advantage.

Tell me about the property's culture.

Our special-ness (if there is such a word), begins with a culture of service. This culture transcends our staff throughout all levels. It is an understanding of the guest, an anticipation of their needs and a helping approach that is very much Hawaiian in nature. At Halekulani, we embrace this culture, magnify it and focus it on delivering exceptional guest service.

How do you follow social media?

We subscribe to social media and review platforms, and follow reviews for their potential learning. But we do not respond to every social media comment. Why? We know our guests, and our guests interact with us directly. We've been operating this way since well before Facebook and TripAdvisor were in vogue. We really don't need social media to tell us what is going on but definitely use it to continue to enhance the guest experience.

What are your thoughts on traditional versus electronic advertising?

While many luxury properties and even some luxury brands gave up on traditional advertising in favor of allocating most of their resources to electronic advertising – pay-per-click, display ads, SEO, video, and so on – we did not. Why? Because we know that consumers need a continuous reminder of brands and brand values. This comes from all types of mediums, not only digital, but both traditional and digital – mediums that can both communicate our brand message and positioning.

Hoteliers who put all their efforts into Google Adwords, for example, forget to remind their customers of their property's brand values of legacy and tradition, which can't be conveyed from a single line of text soliciting a click through. Are they merely thinking of the short term? Possibly. However, although we need to keep pace with the trends and be technologically savvy, we still need to remain relevant to our customers and each of their different needs.

Food and beverage is often considered the heart and soul of any luxury property. What's Halekulani's point of difference?

Guests have dining options, both on and off property. We hope that they will join us in one of our three restaurants, each targeting different experiences and price points. Our high-end restaurant, La Mer, is the only AAA 5 Diamond and Forbes Five-Star rated restaurant in the state. Open for dinner, this French restaurant is clearly fine dining. Orchids, our mid-tier restaurant, is an exceptional place in its own right, with awards and accolades. And our House Without a Key serves a broader audience in an informal manner with live entertainment. Kitchens are different and menus are unique to each venue, but service is always top of class. The food and presentation is terrific, but service is our differentiator. In all three venues, our hostess takes your information as you enter (most are house guests although anyone can dine here), and from then on all staff addresses each guest by name and takes note of personal preferences.

Hawaii is the gateway to Asia. How does your customer base reflect this?

We have very close ties to the Japanese market, with 40% of our leisure business coming from that country. We cater to this market with appropriately trained staff, many of whom are Japanese speaking. Our menus have Japanese-oriented options. All of our signage and menus are translated, as is our website.

Are you concerned about an aging guest population?

Service and quality truly transcends all ages. While the average age of our guests would probably be approaching 60, we believe quality is ageless. That means everything from food and beverage quality to instantaneous high-speed WiFi with exceptional bandwidth. Our price points are such that we cater to those who appreciate the value of our product proposition, independent of their age.

To finish, care to provide an example of how you differentiate Halekulani?

It is the little things that count. Here are some examples. At turndown, we do not put a chocolate on a pillow or something similar. Instead, we place a small charm (a miniature sandal or a note in a glass bottle, for instance) in a see-through, hand-tied bag. This is accompanied by a short poem on a printed card. And, because our average guest stays four nights, we rotate this turndown item every four days. It's the perfect end to a perfect day.

A Floridian Audit of What Defines Luxury

In the pre-internet-domination days, Forbes star ratings or AAA's diamond ratings provided an immediate litmus test of luxury, with a five star or diamond as an immediate indicator. Regrettably, the sun has set on these traditional bulwarks of quality control. TripAdvisor and other online review agencies have now assumed the mantle of being the traveling public's quality thermometer.

As a hotelier, it may seem counterintuitive that limited-service or economy properties can achieve a prestigious TripAdvisor rating of 4.5+ out of 5. And yet somehow, the public now considers free WiFi and waffles to be more important than evening turndown service or 24/7 concierge availability. The standards for third-party approval are increasingly based upon emotional whims rather than logical systems and checklists.

However much I gripe, the situation is what it is, and instead of fighting the current, we must accept this paradigm shift and adapt accordingly. I recently set out to visit six purported luxury properties throughout Southern Florida. Each of these properties has exceptionally high TripAdvisor scores in addition to four or five-star and diamond ratings.

What was surprising to me was the wide variability in accommodation quality and service offerings. These half dozen properties appeared to be trying to save money, cut corners and scrape by with near-minimum standards. Whether this is a product of decreased overall margins or already knowing what their target demographic of 'luxury customers' wanted and excising everything else in the name of efficiency is still up for grabs.

I did not ask for comp rooms. After all, this was peak season in Florida! Moreover, I wanted an unbiased treatment. My findings are as follows:

1. **A lack of value.** Every room night was over $500. Add to that the compulsory resort fee ranging from $27 to $45 per night and $38 to $54 for parking and mandatory taxes, and each night was close to $650. Now at that price range,

I would expect that there would be some special treatment, or at least some added value. But alas, there was the large water bottle with an $8 price tag and an outrageously priced mini-bar. The complimentary magazines, usually plentiful, were down to just one or two. Welcome amenities and welcome notes from the GM were non-existent. WiFi was variable, too. All featured some form of free WiFi, often available if you were a member of a loyalty program; however, the 'free' version was typically so slow that you felt second-class. Morning newspaper delivery? Can't even find one in the breakfast room. How about a simple flower vase in the room? You must be kidding.

2. **Imperfect housekeeping.** I've long stressed the importance of housekeeping and standards that must be upheld. Every one of the hotels I visited failed in one way or more to achieve my minimum housekeeping criteria. Some of the flaws were so flagrant that Conrad Hilton would be rolling in his grave! I don't like a knock on the door at 8:30am with the words loudly spoken, "Housekeeping!" After all, checkout is at noon and check-in for the next guest is 4:00pm; certainly, there could be some sense of timeliness. What's most surprising here is how important housekeeping is to the average online commentator. Being flawless in this regard is a vital part of the TripAdvisor paradigm of hotel reviews, and yet we are still failing to give guests what they want.

On a related note, one of the latest housekeeping ideas is to reuse towels, supposedly for eco-friendly reasons, but really to save laundry costs. At one property, even those I left on the floor were picked up, folded and placed back on the racks. Amenity bottles – half-used shampoos, for example – were not replenished. Bed sheets were often not changed daily at all six hotels. The list of errors by traditional standards could fill a page. I do not fault the housekeepers, though! Rather, I fault operational management who are probably pushing too many rooms per shift on these hourly employees.

3. **Rip-off breakfasts.** I know that room service has a cost, and most hotels, maybe all, do not make any profit from this department. But the prices have now moved to the point of umbrage. A guestroom-delivered, continental breakfast for two, including all compulsory service charges and taxes, came through in the range of $70 to $90. Sorry, but that is simply unfair. It would be borderline acceptable if the breakfast included the best pastries, juice and coffee on earth, or if it was cooked right before my eyes by Anthony Bourdain. But sadly, in this instance, the grapefruit juice was reconstituted and the bread rolls tasted store bought. The next morning, I walked to the nearest Starbucks, and, even more melancholy, I was hardly the only guest making the trek!

   Breakfasts in the restaurants were better but far from exemplary. Any way you put it, when you are coercing your guests to travel offsite, either through exorbitant pricing or reheated, stale food, you are doing something wrong, especially at the luxury level where cuisine is expected to be stellar. Think about it this way: it's often stated that a great day begins with a great breakfast. In this sense, how can a truly luxurious hotel experience be attained with a mediocre morning meal?

4. **Cutting corners on maintenance.** Now, most guests are not going to go to the extremes of examining hard goods or looking at sheets for wear and tear. But I did, and I want to report some more not-so-great news. Not one property of the six has been keeping up on room maintenance – at least for what should be expected at the luxury level. Chipped paint on doorframes and thin towels appear to be highly overlooked. Sad in a way, but I imagine everything was trimmed back to a minimum in the Great Recession, and no one thought to reopen the funding for these necessities. While I doubt this error factors in as a priority for most consumers, it is nonetheless a subtle contributor to the overall experience, and something that

may prevent an individual from falling head over heels for a specific hotel.

Even with this persnickety diatribe, all is not lost, however. Not all properties visited failed in every one of these four criteria. For example, exemplary reception and valet services prevailed. Dinner and lunch in the various restaurants ranged from excellent to outright 'wow'. General comfort – beds, air conditioning and so on – was also without fault.

As a closing remark, if these properties are representative of what guests can expect from the contemporary 'luxury' segment, we're not putting up much of a fight against the inevitable intrusion of alternate lodging providers like Airbnb. Properties at this price range should exude a feeling that makes all guests feel special, wanted and appreciated.

For the most part, this was not the case. I do not blame line staff – exemplary in service delivery to a tee, housekeeping errors aside. I do, however, point my finger at the owners, senior management, the executive team or whoever else is responsible for the rampant cost reductions. In their quest for never-ending profit increases, they have cut corners to the point of embarrassment.

Every little snip pushes the traveling public closer to property ambivalence, brand apathy and the habit of looking solely to alternate lodging providers for a bona fide luxury experience. It's a shame, though, as I thought our luxury leaders would set a higher standard to ensure healthy long-term success in the face of so many industry changes.

A Learning Lab for Kids at Four Seasons Resort Orlando at Walt Disney World® Resort

I admit, I am a Four Seasons junkie. Having worked for them for seven years during my former life at an advertising agency, you could say that I've drunk the Kool Aid. It's also worth noting that Forbes has bestowed their prestigious five-star rating on more Four Seasons properties than any other chain in the world, and every property in the brand is at least a four-star.

Every Four Seasons marks an improvement from the last. When the company opens a new resort property, it is something that one takes seriously, as it is an opportunity to observe the latest standards of excellence.

Opened in August 2014, Four Seasons Resort Orlando raises the bar even further. With 443 rooms, this makes the Orlando property one of the largest properties in the chain. For those who have been to the hometown of Disney World® and the amazing series of related theme parks, you already know how easy it is to be scared off by the mass of stroller-toting families and the conventioneers flooding the impressive International Drive Center. It is not a destination that comes to mind when considering a quiet vacation. So, I was intrigued to see how Four Seasons balances the family target demographic with the understated privacy and quiet that are both hallmarks of the brand.

Located on Disney property just a short drive away from the Disney theme parks, one enters the resort, and the Golden Oak residential area surrounding it, through a gatehouse. The drive exudes a grand sense of place as you wind past multi-million dollar homes, waterways and the golf course that abuts the hotel structure. There was the usual assortment of luxury vehicles parked about the carport and each guest receives a warm Floridian welcome. VISIT FLORIDA is right: It must be the sunshine!

Entry to the resort was slightly different from traditional. Walking in revealed an opulent staircase leading downward instead of upward because the property is on a small rise. The front desk, concierge and reception are nowhere to be seen, as they are about

50 feet to the right of the entranceway. This makes the property feel more like a splendid villa than a hotel.

The entire lobby gleams with fresh marble, dazzling mini-spotlights and natural light bouncing off the polished wall materials. Also unusual, the main restaurants are nowhere near the entranceway – only a bar and a coffee grab-and-go. There are actually four restaurants and two bars in total; however, signature restaurants are located on floors above and below the lobby level.

Since this is a resort, the grounds are also critical; it must be equally as impressive as the interior. Four Seasons Resort Orlando satisfies this requirement with five pools; the adults-only pool is well-separated from the others while the family fun area houses a lazy river, kids splash zone, waterslide and enormous lakeside infinity pool, not to mention sand volleyball, a sport court and rock climbing wall.

My tour of the guestrooms included the presidential suite which, of course, was excellent. I was more interested in the core rooms, though, to see what I could learn that was applicable to the everyday guest. First, the size of all four room categories is 500 sq. ft., with suites ranging from 825 sq. ft. to 3,300 sq. ft. for the Royal Suite. Bathrooms all feature double sinks with a separate tub and shower. Fortunately, the rooms, top end suites aside, are not inundated with added complex electronics, except for the large LED 4K and in-mirror televisions. As a great situational touch, all guestrooms include furnished balconies, and guestrooms on the resort's Park View side offer views of the nightly fireworks from Magic Kingdom Park.

Orlando is all about family, and here is where the Four Seasons Resort Orlando demonstrates breakthrough ideas:

- **Bar fridge location.** It sounds simple enough, but the in-room bar fridge is located higher so that toddlers cannot easily access the contents.
- **Mini-bar stocked on-demand.** If the guest needs the space for baby formula or milk for the kids, there is room. Mini-bars contain only bottled water and can be customized

with the guests' preferred snacks and drinks, ready upon their arrival. No added fee is charged to stock the mini-bar; snacks ordered are charged to the room bill.

- **Large balconies.** Florida is blessed with great weather most of the year. A large balcony gives parents a chance to spread out, even when the rooms are 500 sq. ft. and more.
- **A convertible sofa-bed in each room.** This is a family resort, so with the exception of weddings and groups, typically, kids will be in tow. Having the pull-out makes sense.
- **Give the kids something to do and reward them.** The property has a fantastic Passport to Adventure booklet that encourages younger travelers to explore the property, getting 'visa stamps' along the way. The reward? Free gelato.
- **Child size hangers in the closet.** Not expensive, but a very nice touch. And reinforcing the notion that the hotel deeply cares about specifically meeting families' needs.
- **Kid friendly welcome.** Just opposite the reception, there is a large touchscreen monitor with an interactive map of the property. That's standard fare, but this one is positioned at eye level for small children. Moreover, there are many kid-friendly amenities, including whimsical accessories, waiting for wee ones to discover upon check in.

I could add more, but my recommendation is to take a visit and explore the property yourself, especially if your current hotel is in a family-dominant tourism zone. And if you're planning to build a property soon that you want to appeal to children as much as it does their parents, this may be a good place to start your search for ideas.

Larry Mogelonsky

Swimming with the Big Fish at The Resort at Longboat Key Club

For most, arriving in South Florida is a warm embrace of fresh summer air that hits you the moment you descend the airport gate ramp. Peak season for Floridian resorts runs pretty much full steam beginning in December and continuing through spring break, with near full occupancies and high ADR pretty much the norm. The name resorts along the water are complicated entities, though, each featuring marquis amenities such as golf courses, tennis complexes, marinas, spas, children's camps and a diverse array of F&B outlets. Often encompassing hundreds of acres, these resorts are always impressive.

Moreover, property management structures in these laid-back, paradisiacal enclaves are increasingly horizontal, with the general manager often wearing multiple hats representing a combination of town mayor, urban planner and financial guru. It takes little time to realize that all senior managers require more than one hat to be successful. Thus, it was with great fortune that I had the opportunity to meet with Jeffrey Mayers, General Manager of The Resort at Longboat Key Club in Sarasota, Florida, an Opal Collection property, who graciously gave me several hours of his time during one of the busiest weeks of the year.

This resort is a town in its own right: 410 acres, 223 guest suites comprised of multiple long-term and short-term stay condo-style buildings (there are seven of them), 45 holes of championship golf over two newly renovated courses, 20 HarTru courts at the award-winning Tennis Gardens, eight restaurants and lounges offering casual to fine dining, an extensive spa operation, two pools plus a massive, Gulf-side, beachfront, a 291 slip marina, innovative children's camp and extensive shuttle bus services. All of this is run by a complement of approximately 500 staff (full-time equivalents).

Formerly managing the Sawgrass Marriott Golf Resort & Spa, Jeff arrived at the Sarasota resort just over two years ago. My conversation with him reflected many sports and team-oriented metaphors. What follows is a series of abridged comments gleaned from several hours of conversation. Consider how these ideas could be applied to your business.

- "In the resort business, every day is game day. Your team must get it right, every time. The guest is paying for perfection."
- "An interesting aspect of our business is the co-mingling of resort guests and club members. Understanding the diversified and unique needs of each is essential to our success."
- "Membership satisfaction is of paramount importance. Our members participate in our process and we encourage this. Imagine running your hotel with a guest advisory board. Come to think of it, what a great idea for all!"
- "We have a captive business. In other words, only our members and resort guests can dine at or use our facilities. This means that our resort guests are even more important to us; everyone has options to go and dine or golf elsewhere. Since our amenities are not public facing, we can't advertise to the local community to supplement restaurant covers or add golf rounds. We cannot take loyalty and legacy business for granted."
- "Silos kill our business. F&B, Spa, Tennis, Golf and Rooms all must work together to ensure that the guest's experience is seamlessly integrated. A bad experience in the restaurant can directly affect an ensuing round of golf or a service at The Spa. Feelings, positive or negative, tend to amplify through the familiarity of our member base."
- "If you are the GM, consider your job as that of a conductor. Your role is to motivate, encourage and coordinate all the various elements of the symphony. If one instrument is out of tune, you can hear it in the final product. And you, as conductor, have to listen very carefully."
- "All staff must embrace guest service in every element of their job all of the time. A smile from pool maintenance staff or a housekeeper going out of his way with a little additional service will do wonders. It is incumbent on all management levels to foster this type of behavior."

Larry Mogelonsky

Hotels as Community Leaders: Two Canadian Examples

Canada happens to be my home and, like the other 35 million residents, I'm proud of my country. Of course, we express this is in our own Canadian sort of way: reserved, quiet and without much boasting.

On the hotel front, there are some great things happening in Canada. And by great, I don't mean the creation of more 'soft' or 'lifestyle' hotel brands. Goodness knows we have enough of those.

There are some incredible stories of kindness and community spirit being undertaken north of the 49th parallel that underscore what makes my country great. While we've all read about hotel chains rallying their staff, and guests, to make charitable efforts – and these are quite respectable in every way – here are two independent efforts worth mentioning from the 'Great White North'.

Cranberry Village

Located in Collingwood, Ontario about two hours north of my hometown of Toronto, Cranberry Village is the brain child of Larry Law, a gifted developer with a kind spirit and commitment to help – a rarity in these days of financial pursuit above all else. As a newcomer to Canada, Larry started by acquiring a 70-room roadside motel, the Cranberry Inn. Over the next twenty or so years, he has expanded this venture by building a series of timeshare and condominium units as well as adding a golf course, a marina, a spa and several restaurants.

By any means, growing from 70 to over 400 units is exceptional for an individual of modest means. What is more remarkable about this growth is Larry's ethical commitment, not just to the community of Collingwood, but to the world at large. In addition to numerous local projects, the entrepreneur spends two weeks each year on a mission to Cambodia to work at and fund a school for underprivileged youth.

Just prior to departing on his most recent trip abroad, his latest phase of luxury timeshare properties was at a critical juncture in its construction, necessitating many vital and immediate decisions be made. And here was the owner taking off to a location where cell phone and WiFi coverage were practically non-existent!

His response, when he confided in me, was unquestionably 'Larry': "These children need me, and I am sure that only good things will come about during my short absence. My team is able, and beyond that, powers greater than me will look after things."

On a local level, Larry has strong ties to his church and supports several outreach programs. He also lends a fatherly 'open door' to employee needs. And from what I have experienced, he rarely, if ever, takes the owner's prerogative to micro-manage his team. Privately held, Cranberry does not have to report quarterly profits. As an owner, Larry tells me that he records dividends not only in dollars but also in happiness. Through doing business as a platform, he promoted compassion and care, inspiring others to achieve meaningful lives.

Fogo Island Inn

I already reported on the incredible architectural masterpiece called Fogo Island Inn. Located on Fogo Island off the northeast shore of Newfoundland, a trip here will take a day at least, with a connector flight to Gander, a one hour and fifteen-minute drive, a 45-minute ferry to Fogo Island, and a final twenty-minute ride to the Inn. This is not a spur of the moment destination. Nor are its prices!

This 29-room property has been featured in literally hundreds of articles in the consumer travel media. Fogo has transcended from being an anomaly in the world of hotel development to a 'bucket list' must-go-to-destination for just about every one-percenter in the world. With no-compromise accommodations, personal services, sky-high and non-yield managed ADR's, Fogo simply defies conventional hotel logic.

But there is far more to Fogo than one of the most iconic hotel buildings on Earth. The story of the Fogo Island Inn goes hand-in-hand with Zita Cobb, the property's visionary leader. For those who have not heard the story, here it is in a compressed version: local girl goes to university; lands in a high-tech super biz; sells her stake; returns home and commits to helping to revive the Island's economy and stimulate its culture.

In the hotel construction world, where everyone seems to pride themselves on how to buy things cheaper, Zita asks, "Can we make it here, or if not on Fogo Island, in the province? If not in the province, in our country?" In the development of the Inn, she led to the creation of industries that support the community such as local quilters and furniture craftsman. Now with the Inn complete, her groundwork has led to many regional craftsmen being able to sell their products to a much broader audience.

Zita recognized that she could not carry the burden of this development solely on her shoulders. That is why the Fogo Island Inn and the peripheral activities generated by this property are all part of the Shorefast Foundation, a registered Canadian charity committed to community development. All profits from the Inn go back to Shorefast and are reinvested in the community. Like many smaller, rural communities, Fogo Island has experienced generations where the only way for kids to be successful was to 'head for the mainland'. While Zita will never say it was her, and as demure as she can be, she'll always point to the Shorefast as her raison d'etre and not necessary Fogo Island Inn.

Larry and Zita are two individuals who quietly pursue their roles as independent innkeepers with a mission above and beyond mere profits. In doing so, their 'guest list' is more than those who simply hand over their credit cards. They are aspirational and are making a real difference each in their own ways. Do you have any other stories of community spirit you can share?

In Search of Hotel Excellence: Fairmont Le Château Frontenac

I have visited Fairmont Le Château Frontenac many times: as a youth, on business, for leisure and lately as a hotelier. Each time, more and more of the product is unveiled, and no doubt there is so much more to learn about Canada's most iconic hotel. Perched atop the walled old town of Quebec City, the copper-roofed castle is certainly one of the most photographed hotels in the world and has been recognized as a national landmark.

It is thus even more remarkable that the recently completed $75 million renovation was accomplished within the context of protecting the historical significance of most every room – rooms that include where the Quebec Act was signed to end the Second World War or the room that was the office of Quebec's premier (equivalent to state governor).

I met with Christopher Spear, the property's Director of Sales and Marketing, for a personal tour of the renovations where I was able to ask him several questions.

Fairmont Le Château Frontenac has been through numerous renovations in its 125-year history. What makes this one so special?

For me, the primary difference this time is the focus on the group segment and F&B. True, we enhanced many other aspects of the property, but the genesis of this renovation was based upon business need – our old facilities simply couldn't meet demands.

Let's split this out. Tell me about groups.

Our ballrooms were not the limiting issue, but rather the ability to manage smaller groups and the food component of our groups. This was a complex renovation. We eliminated our everyday dining facility and several retail shops, and we converted this 'terrace-level' space into a series of meeting rooms and event dining facilities. In all, this added about 15,000 square feet of space that has multiple configuration opportunities.

Did eliminating the primary restaurant create additional issues?

Removing one restaurant was part of radically rewriting the book on hotel dining, Frontenac style. On the main floor, we completely rebuilt the bar and upscale dining room. We enclosed an outdoor terrace that, while previously outstanding two months of the year, now has the same view but is no longer seasonal. This was seamlessly linked to what was formerly a bar to become our SAM bistro with about 200 seats. This is flanked by our 1608 bar with about 50 seats and next to it, Champlain, our more formal dining room with about 120 seats.

And is this enough capacity for a 611-room property?

Ample when you consider that we now have alternate dining facilities for groups and tours on the lower level. Previously, we often had a group in a defined section of the main dining room. While segregated, this nevertheless caused problems in terms of congestion and coordination.

What recommendations do you have for other hoteliers and their renovation projects?

Examine the economics of your proposal. Model the forecasted demand and your ability to both maintain and grow market share. From your projection, build facilities that meet the type of groups you are targeting. Learn from those pieces of business that you lost because you could not meet their requirements. Build in accordance with demand. Then, once your construction is underway, sell into the new product so that you open the facilities full.

Did you meet your targets?

The results have exceeded all our expectations. Not only has the marketplace responded to our initiatives, but the response from everyone that has seen the new Chateau has been overwhelmingly enthusiastic. Everyone from the local community, to planners, to past customers and customers we could not previously manage due to our size restrictions are unanimous: this is a winner!

To the Ends of the Earth

Far away from far away lies one of the most interesting resort experiences on the planet. Just off the northern shore of Canada's Newfoundland province – the closest airport is Gander, about a two-hour journey – lies pristine Fogo Island and its namesake property. With incredible contemporary architecture paying homage to the traditional fishing outport stages of the region, Fogo Island Inn promises a worthwhile adventure to all who journey to this remote part of the globe. With publicity that any hotelier would give his or her eyeteeth for, this is a 'bucket list' property for a guaranteed, never-been-here travel destination.

But your mind spins for a minute. This is the east coast of Canada, not known for luxury resorts per se, except perhaps those magnificent grande dame Fairmont properties resurrected from the old turn-of-the-century railway masterpieces of the Canadian Pacific empire. How can a property survive the harsh, intolerable winters with very short summer seasons? Under these challenging circumstances, who would make such an investment? What is the rationale?

Since its opening in the summer of 2013, this 29-room and suite property has shown remarkably strong occupancy, with ADRs that are nothing less than five-star levels – double anything in the province and in Canada east of Montreal. There is no revenue management program. Rates are fixed, with the lowest room-only rate being $875 CDN per night and full board rates starting at $1,275 CDN per night. The property is not available through OTAs or GDS – traditional travel agent commissions are offered – and currently there is not even an online booking tool, although that might change.

Apart from the jaw-dropping architecture, the property provides its guests with a host of curated outdoor activities ranging from hiking and boating to iceberg watching and orientations at the local fisheries. Better yet, with the resort's Signature Experiences, guests can let their whole days be planned for them – with excellent F&B as an accompaniment, of course.

Yes, Fogo Island Inn is the exception, not the rule, but that doesn't mean there isn't learning here for all resorts, and all hotels for that matter. And surprisingly, the real story is more about the community than the incredible property itself. To explain, I've recruited one of the resort's owners, Zita Cobb, to shed some light on the property's origins and how it functions.

Let's start with a brief overview of the Fogo Island Inn.

Fogo Island's economy suffered greatly as the cod fishery declined in the latter decades of the 20th century. In the early 2000s, eighth generation Fogo Islanders Zita (me!), Alan and my brother Anthony recognized the need for action and we founded the Shorefast Foundation, with the Fogo Island Inn as our biggest undertaking to date. The Inn is a social business, meaning that 100% of operating surpluses are reinvested in the community through the Shorefast Foundation and there are no investors seeking a specific return on their investment. The focus of the Inn, therefore, is as a charitable venture.

Tell us more about the Shorefast Foundation.

The Foundation was established in 2003 by my two brothers, Anthony and Alan, and me. After the collapse of the cod fishery, I left as a teen to study business, giving me the opportunity to travel the globe. When I returned home in 2001 after retiring, I felt compelled to act in order to help resuscitate Fogo Island's rich culture and its economy. Recognizing that traditional charity in the form of monetary handouts would not contribute to long-term cultural, social and economic resiliency for Fogo Island, my goal was to leverage an initial investment to create culturally rich and community-owned assets. The guiding principle of the Foundation is that nature and culture are the two great garments of human life, and business and technology are the two great tools that can and should serve them.

Besides the Inn, Shorefast also has two other rather large projects. One is Fogo Island Arts, which is a residency-based contemporary art venue for artists, filmmakers, writers, musicians, curators, designers and thinkers from around the world. The other big project is the Fogo Island Shop, which sells the handcrafted furniture from the Inn that is produced on Fogo Island.

Several people have commented to me that you can only do this because you are independently wealthy.

I believe that, first, there are many wealthy hotel owners, and second, that you do this because you have the community at heart. Having access to financial capital is certainly helpful for any project. But it is far from being the most important thing. Lots of people do ambitious projects when they themselves don't have access to capital – they go out and find it!

To me, the most important things are community and the relationship between capital and community – between capital and place itself. I think the most important asset my brothers and I bring to our projects on Fogo Island is a love of place and a feeling of responsibility toward the nature and culture of that place. I'd say the second most important asset we bring is a willingness to commit our lives to what we believe.

To be clear, the Fogo Island Inn is a business – it is a social business. We do worry about returns, just as every business does. The difference in our case is that the returns are not private returns, they are public returns. That doesn't make them less important, it makes them more important.

Business itself, and the way we use it, is changing. 'Traditional' business was more focused on financial returns. Contemporary business and certainly the business of the future will also be focused on ecological and social returns, which means that business, as a tool, will be increasingly used to tackle intractable problems. That's the nature of social business.

Who makes the decisions?

Shorefast has an executive director and a small team of deeply committed employees. They make certain decisions in the normal course of their work. Further reaching decisions are made by the ten-person board of directors of Shorefast. Of course, Shorefast decisions are all made with the well-being of the property in mind.

How can another property emulate your success?

Any property can become a social business. It doesn't need to be done by establishing a foundation, although that is one possible structure. Any property owner can decide to share a portion of the business or the returns from the business with the community it operates in. Any property can bring members of that community onto its board of directors. Any property can add a mandate to contribute to the ecological and social sustainability of the community it operates in. In fact, many properties are doing this already and doing it well. There is no magic in our model; what sets us apart is that we are a 100% social business.

What is the guest feedback like?

Our guests leave part of themselves in the fabric of Fogo Island when they go. And, for sure, a little piece of Fogo Island lives inside of them! Many return. It's probably best to read some of their own accounts on the various online platforms.

CONCLUSION

One of the smaller properties on Honolulu's Waikiki Beach, the Halekulani is considered by many to be the epitome of Hawaiian hospitality culture.

Photos copyright of the hotel and cannot be reproduced without its permission.

Getting Back On Track

Hotels all around the world have endured their fair share of game-changing problems in recent years, including the scrambling of the status quo that has come along with the expansions of digital booking channels, third-party review sites, smartphone usage and the shifting of consumer behavior with the rise social media. We all know these are factors affecting daily operations and there are plenty of resources to help hoteliers cope.

As such, you must constantly fine tune your business processes to evolve just as fast as the world does. Here are five areas to focus on:

1. **Embrace yet scrutinize technology.** Yes, new entrants will emerge – it's impossible for them not to given how rapidly our society moves these days. On the one hand, it is prudent to keep an open mind as to how new tech might work to your advantage as well as what new apps or networks are gaining popularity. Yet on the other hand, you cannot be a weather vane hotelier, lionizing the latest and greatest then swiftly moving on to the next best thing when it comes. Keep your tech tactics simple and streamlined, and always proceed cautiously.

2. **Motivate staff.** Enthusiasm is contagious. Guests can smell it whenever they interact with the faces of a hotel, and a passionate core will exude through every action a staffer takes. If your team is intrinsically motivated, they will be self-propelled for the best possible performance, and then all the little details that make a guest experience perfect will naturally fall into place. This starts with hiring the right people, but it also requires constant upkeep – effective training, aligning staff members with the department they are most interested in, and fostering a culture of support, camaraderie and devotion to excellence.

3. **Be a community leader.** Think of your property as the community's ambassador to the outside world, as more often than not your guestrooms will act as home base for

404

new visitors. Highlight local foods in your restaurants, local products in your gift shop and, of course, local attractions should be top of mind for everyone at the front desk. Host events for the community, build relationships with businesses in the area and develop packages so that your guests can participate in what your region does best at a discount.

4. **Advertising isn't dead.** If social media and the proliferation of viral videos over the past half-decade have proven anything, it's that the cream always rises. The same has always held true with advertising, no matter the channel. Consumer apathy is an eternal problem, but if you can develop a creative and emotionally charged promotions slate that is properly targeted at a specific audience, then you will cut through the noise whether your vector is a magazine spread, an event or a post on Facebook.

5. **The onsite experience dominates.** You can't change your location; you can't change the weather; but on property, you are god. If you can deliver an unexpectedly remarkable onsite experience, then your guests will keep you close to their hearts and disseminate your brand's qualities through word of mouth – that silent yet incredibly powerful vector to promote your hotel. This upcoming year will be one for focusing on increasing the number of return visits, and there's no better way to achieve this than through a stellar guest experience.

RevPAR vs RevPor vs RevPAG

Let's get the acronyms out of the way so there's no confusion:

- *RevPAR* = **Rev**enue **P**er **A**vailable **R**oom
- *RevPOR* = **Rev**enue **P**er **O**ccupied **R**oom
- *RevPAG* = **Rev**enue **P**er **A**vailable **G**uest

The first term, RevPAR, is the most commonly used these days, but as I've advocated before, it may not be the best overall indicator of a property's financial or business health. Hence, I vouched for using the second term, RevPOR, as it incorporated occupancy percentages to better forecast actualized revenues instead of projecting a figure based on 100% rooms booked. It's a subtle change, but one that can nonetheless have a tremendous impact when evaluating quarter-over-quarter or year-over-year performance.

Even though most diligent managers will throw RevPAR through an average or 'per capita' occupancy grinder for a more accurate calculation of earnings, it is still hard to account for seasonal disruptions. That's where RevPOR shines through; by factoring occupancy into the equation from the start, it can act as a better barometer for shifts in consumer spending habits, indicating whether or not some of your 'upselling' efforts have actually paid off.

RevPAR still has the advantage of being the 'quick snapshot', but the purpose of RevPOR is to measure the total capture per occupied room, thus allowing for quality inferences about individual spending habits over time. RevPAG goes a step further, as it takes into account the total number of guests, regardless of how many are staying in each room.

This third term is what has been employed by all-inclusive resorts under the guise of other nomenclature such as 'package revenue' as the basic provisions in tandem with 'non-package revenue' to denote all additional capture such as dining upgrades, day trips or above-board spa treatments. For these properties, comparing a summary figure like RevPAG with its package and non-package constituents can have profound effects on future income streams.

The goal for many all-inclusive resorts is to find a package price that's high enough to cover costs and turn a profit without inducing sticker shock and lowering occupancy. However, evaluating this package price without weighing it against RevPAG can leave money on the table in the form of low non-package revenue figures. Many guests feel a psychological need to spend more while on vacation, but if there's already too much included in the basic package – that is, a more expensive price tag – the ancillary, heavily marked-up services may go underutilized.

Thinking in terms of guests instead of rooms like this brings us back to the grand old days of hospitality when it was never just about putting heads in beds. The action was downstairs: in the lobby bars, in the restaurants and in other facilities. It was a guest-centric, customer-is-always-right playing field where the room was almost always secondary to the other lavish services provided, and where you were paying more for the privileged status that accompanied a guestroom booking rather than the guestroom itself.

Somewhere in the latter half of the 20th century, we deviated from this principle. We started to think in terms of rooms, and, like any self-fulfilling fallacy, that's exactly what we got. Rooms were filled, sure, but we lost our stranglehold on other operations; we must now compete with independent restaurants, private meeting facilities, unaffiliated spas and so on. If we can learn anything from the all-inclusive model, it's that RevPAG rather than RevPAR will help subtly realign our values with a more holistic approach to hospitality.

I've witnessed this progression firsthand at HITEC, where PMS platforms now have extensive integrations with other POS software providers to scrupulously track ancillary revenue performance. As well, there are now dozens of business intelligence and total revenue management solutions so that managers can make informed decisions about balancing or maximizing ADR with additional onsite capture.

While RevPAR has its merits, a holistic approach requires moving beyond to RevPOR or RevPAG. Regardless of the advanced software deployed, the decision ultimately rests with the manager and how he or she chooses to perceive the numbers. If you think in terms of guests instead of rooms, the shift in perspective may help you achieve new heights in revenue and consumer satisfaction.

Believe It or Not, Hotels Can Learn from Playboy's Big Move

Playboy threw us all a curveball when they announced that they would be ceasing to publish full nude photography in their magazines. The rationale makes sense, though; these days, free pornography is just a mouse click away and Playboy doesn't stand a chance at competing. Instead, the company is pivoting to focus on more urbane content and thought leadership to drive worldwide merchandising sales.

Free pornography has been the scourge of the internet for well over a decade, and undoubtedly the *Playboy* top brass has been wrestling with this problem ever since it started encroaching on magazine and subscription sales. The rabbit ears logo is, however, one of the most recognizable brand images on the planet, and the company is now poised to leverage its iconography as a means of transforming an ancillary revenue stream into its bread and butter.

A desperate act, but also brilliant. Twenty years ago, one of *Playboy*'s key demographics was teenage boys who would ogle the more interesting pages in the confines of their bedrooms, ever vigilant for patrolling parents. Twenty years from now, *Playboy*'s intended audience will be comprised of erudite yuppies who read the publication openly in hotel lobbies from their super-tablets while sipping macchiatos. And when you question their choice in literature based upon its lewd history, these future readers will reply, "And doctors used to prescribe heroin as cough medication. What's your point?"

Everything is obvious through the lens of hindsight. This sweeping change in strategy was likely the toughest decision the company has ever had to make.

A Universal Truth

Playboy was founded on its racy and controversial material, with boisterous interviews and piercing exposés mixed in for good measure. This was the niche that propelled it to the limelight in the 1960s and 1970s, with the suave, smoke-jacket-clad Hugh

Hefner at the forefront of the so-called 'Playboy Image' – a style and aspiration for all gentlemen to follow. Nowadays, nudity is far from the heights of taboo it was in the mid-20th century, while the 'Playboy Image' is a clear example of old-fashioned misogyny at its finest. And the octogenarian Hefner who still dates twentysomething blondes is viewed by the younger generations less as a Casanova and more as an outright pedophile. Oh, how times change.

Even with the writing on the wall, the notion of extricating pornographic images from the publication is an assault on the company's raison d'être, and it undoubtedly met heavy resistance at every juncture of the corporate ladder. The executives shepherding this transformation were purposing that their company which makes porno mags for a living stop making porno mags. Good luck pitching that to the shareholders.

But enough about *Playboy*; what's the ever-so-titillating lesson for hotels? To be as blunt as I can, and pardon my language, the takeaway is this: Sometimes the universe just doesn't give a s—t.

If it did care all the time, then we'd all still be in loincloths running from dinosaurs. As we extrapolate the Darwinist 'survival of the fittest' principle beyond the field of biology, it becomes increasingly evident that even the biggest or strongest in each environment can be hung out to dry by unforeseen and unstoppable forces. Yes, the universe has nurtured us and facilitated all human activities on our little blue dot, but it doesn't blink for a nanosecond at the bankruptcy of a billion-dollar company or the loss of thousands of jobs. The universe only worries about the long, long term. Either you adapt to your surroundings or you are replaced by a more suitable organism.

In a business sense, this is what we call 'disruptive innovation', and it has plagued the hospitality industry and every industry since, well, the invention of industry itself! At the present, we are facing the repercussions of the sharing economy in its most salient form of Airbnb along with OTA brand dilution and the primacy in spending power of the seemingly apathetic millennials. Yet, these latest three follow in a long chain of inventions or rising trends that have forced us to alter the ways in which we conduct our methods of commercial exchange.

Getting back to the *Playboy* story, suppose you were to travel back in time to 1985 and visit Hefner at his corporate head office. In all your prophetic wisdom, you proudly declare that in 30 years' time this thing called the internet, currently in its budding phase, will be everywhere, it will be dominated by free pornography, and it will annihilate the current business paradigm. You'd probably be laughed out of the room with security called as Sir Hugh lights a Monte Cristo and ushers in the next fresh-off-the-bus young model for an 'audition'.

Everything on the Table

The internet is an unstoppable force. Free pornography is one of its unforeseen consequences. As it concerns hospitality, Airbnb and the OTAs are two glaring outcomes of the World Wide Web, and no could have predicted even a decade ago that they would affect our industry as much as they do today. No matter what god you pray to, clearly they aren't picking up the phone.

Just as *Playboy* made the radical shift away from its reason of being – distribution of its pornography magazines – so too must hotel organizations exhibit similar boldness if they are to survive. This may be particularly tough to swallow for an industry that prides itself on its traditions and its timelessness. Even those seemingly fanatical ideas can no longer be immediately dismissed; they should at least be given some pause before they are sidelined.

Keep your traditions and use them as branding or marketing tools, but first acknowledge that the universe is constantly chugging forward and the past only exists through rose-colored glasses. Sometimes the world throws you a curveball and the only restorative action is to scrutinize every single aspect of your operations from a purely objective perspective. With Airbnb and the OTAs changing the ways that consumers think about travel, you cannot rely on a traditional sensibility, lest you succumb to the same fate as Hefner – outdated and irrelevant to a new generation with a fundamentally different philosophy.

Leaving everything on the table is the only way to navigate an organization through disruptive innovation. See what's working and what's not, no matter its legacy. And remember that innovation does not have to strictly apply to technology. When I say 'everything' is up for grabs, I mean everything, front of house and back of house. And if you must tear the whole house down to build a newer and sturdier one, then so be it.

For specific examples of this, you may look to the hotels which, seeing declining sales from their target market, decide to convert to extended stay residences rather than try new tactics to maintain the status quo. Instead of relying on legislation against Airbnb that is coming in at a glacial pace, you may instead choose to radically shift from a rooms-centric business model to one entirely focused on impeccable service and personalized amenities.

Challenging existing practices is a painful exercise because there will always be an ingrained fear of change. But if you think in terms of how much the universe cares about your specific plight, then it may just light a fire to help move your organization forward. Just as *Playboy* made the daring decision to abandon what was once its core revenue stream, so must you be open to all changes, as this will ensure that you evolve at the same pace as your environment.

Bring the Glamor Back

Even though it's been a while since it first hit theatres, Wes Anderson's masterpiece *The Grand Budapest Hotel* remains top of mind whenever a friend asks for a movie recommendation. It's funny, well-acted and beautifully shot, so what's not to love? But more than that, the film is a tribute to a bygone era of travel and old world hospitality when guests were eminently respected for their individual preferences and experienced managers were revered for their wisdom and commitment to their craft.

I compare an everyday walk through the lobby of a branded, four-star property with those fantastical shots of Anderson's titular hotel and my immediate thought is: we've lost something. Nowadays, we concern ourselves less with a sharp focus on developing strong person-to-person relationships and more with the multitude of number crunching tasks designed to squeeze as much profit as possible out of our ever-dwindling margins. Yes, we should worry about our margins and cash flow, but there comes a point where we will lose sight of what made us 'grand' in the first place.

That grandeur comes from many facets – a bustling spectacle of a lobby floor, opulent rooms with the utmost attention to detail, lavish amenities, exceptional food service, immaculate housekeeping and, above all, a team that cares. If every staff member loves his or her job, then all the other 'material' tasks will magically be completed faster and more effectively, whether it's ensuring that a room is spotless before a guest's arrival or filling up the bar on a week night to create a more social environment. It all boils down to hiring the right people and motivating them for consummate perfection.

Alas, it's never that simple. I've spoken with numerous managers and owners over the years, and a common quality that they all possess is a high degree of scrutiny when hiring. Most senior-level employees in hospitality understand that this is a 'people industry' and that recruiting individuals with the right gung-ho attitude is essential for pleasant guest-staff relationships and ensuring healthy company morale.

But what happens when the best and brightest of our draft picks never even consider the hotel industry as their chosen profession? Service today is very casual in its presentation. My fear is that our craft has relinquished its classical allure, and therefore will fail to attract the brainy kids necessary to secure the next generation of internal entrepreneurship.

The Brain Drain

Put yourself in the shoes of a 2017 high school or college senior. This exercise has served me well in the past when assessing what marketing messages will impact the average millennial. Today it serves a different purpose. From this youthful perspective, evaluate what might incentivize a graduate to view hospitality as a viable career path and not just as a summer job or intern 'stepping stone' placement.

What incentives did you write down? Next, take this a step further by contrasting the millennial lens on the hotel industry with that of the finance or medical streams. Specifically, attempt to answer the question: what makes hospitality better than these two career paths, or any other for that matter?

Finance takes the boat when it comes to monetary compensation as well as any flashy 'bonuses' like expensive sports cars, plush Manhattan apartments and all other images of corporate excess. Hence, anyone who values having a thick billfold will gravitate to these sorts of jobs. Medicine, on the other hand, has long been upheld as a noble endeavor with directly quantifiable results. A patient is sick; you treat them in one way, shape or form, and the patient gets better. Ergo, young adults seeking meaningful employment via helping others are more likely to apply to medical, nursing or dental school than to request a placement as your newest desk clerk.

Any way you put it, a hotel organization's pool of applicants is not the same as that for a hospital or a gaudy Wall Street hedge fund which may or may not go belly up within a year's time. It also shares very little overlap with that for engineering, biology, philosophy, political science, economics or a host of other educational streams. In fact, there appears to be a significant brain drain occurring, whereby the best and brightest of the next generation of employees are quite unlikely to end up in hospitality. Worse still, this problem is of our own making.

We haven't given today's smart and savvy youth enough of a reason to proudly join our organizations and go through the decades of necessary field experience to earn their stripes towards a high-ranking and highly lucrative management position. What concerns me here is how this will affect the rate of innovation in hotels and their corporate entities over the next few decades. Imagine that instead of setting out to be computer programmers, stockbrokers, doctors, pilots or architects, we had a horde of off-the-IQ-scale gifted twentysomethings yearning for a placement at your property.

Make It Glamorous

One of the reasons *The Grand Budapest Hotel* has stayed fresh is that it makes being a hotelier appear cool. From the snappy white glove and purple morning coat uniforms to the perpetually charismatic actions of the film's protagonist – Gustave H. as portrayed by Ralph Fiennes – the film spotlights a career in hospitality as glamorous.

"Why do you want to be a lobby boy?" asked Gustave early in the movie. "Well, who wouldn't at the Grand Budapest, Sir. It's an institution," replied Zero, the fresh-faced and wide-eyed trainee. As emphasized by this lobby boy character, beginning a stint in hospitality is not something one stumbles upon or settles into once several options have been exhausted. It is a job with responsibilities that matter and with a time-honored tradition that inductees should be thrilled to participate in. This one line of dialogue emphasizes that when you become a hotelier, you become part of something greater.

How can you make your hotel 'an institution' as Zero puts it? Glamor, prestige, acclaim – whatever word you use to describe this form of non-monetary incentive, we as an industry need more of it in order to build an empyrean reputation worthy of today's astute teens. Or, to put it another way, we have to bring back the elements of hospitality that made it great during the film's rose-colored 'grand age of hotels' in order to prevent any future brain drain from eroding the core of what our profession stands for.

Looking beyond yearly salary and other strict fiscal incentives, we must strive to attract new recruits by using emotional drivers and by promoting what is unique about our trade. Here are five ways to reinvigorate your efforts at 'selling the job' to today's youth, in no particular order:

1. **Personal wellbeing.** A career working for a hotel organization is unlikely to be tarnished by a 'burn out' phrase as one hits the prime age of 30. On the contrary, hospitality offers, for the most part, a non-hostile work environment, albeit with long and irregular hours, and a large team of affectionate faces who are there to help you rather than compete with you. This goes for operations at the hotel as well as the corporate levels. Knowing this, a new recruit has many years of contentment at the office to look forward to. And yes, for those interested in lofty remunerations, inform them that senior managers bring home a pretty penny, too.

2. **Promise of steady advancement.** If you work hard, understand the business and maintain good standings with your coworkers, it's hard not to move up the hospitality ladder. As well, given that hotel operations are as diverse as they come, there's also the prospect of horizontal shuffling. If an employee isn't happy working in sales, perhaps marketing or revenue management is more in line with his or her aspirations. Being a hotelier requires many hats, and there's never a dull day balancing all the different tasks that must be done.

3. **Dynamic work environment.** An office is an office, except when it's a hotel where you are two hundred feet from a bustling lobby floor with guests from around the world shuffling about, attendants and porters in tow, eye-catching artwork festooned on two-story walls, and corridors leading off to meeting spaces with events in progress and restaurants with top notch cuisine. Additionally, working in hospitality encourages sophistication, as you'll come in contact with various cultures and languages and get to try all the latest

spa products or chef creations. Lastly, an occupation in our industry often entails assuming the role of community leader, requiring lots of socializing with neighboring businesses.

4. **Pay it forward.** Working at a hotel can benefit new recruits in many ways, but it can also benefit those who are helped in the process – guests, other employees, casual visitors and the community at large. Like a nurse or doctor, being a hotelier means taking an interest in others' wellbeing and doing your part to improve their livelihoods, even if it's only by a smidgeon. Smiles, friendly handshakes, helping cart someone's bags to a guestroom, polite conversations, making reservations, arranging for travel plans, recommending a local attraction – all these little things do make a difference.

5. **In-house celebrities.** Hospitality is one of the few places where everyone has a moment in the sun, especially with the power of the Internet. Use social media to create in-house celebrities who might include your executive chef, a golf pro, the spa director, a PR manager or any other affable senior executive who's eager to converse directly with consumers. In this sense, you will be indirectly proffering newcomers the chance to, eventually, assume a leadership role.

Beyond this, you must look for ways to reach today's youth to express these five motivations as well as any others you know of. Think of it like channel distribution. Instead of tradeshows, you send colleagues out to job fairs. Instead of sending available rooms to the OTAs, post employment opportunities to LinkedIn or another specialized website.

If you are to take one thing away from this article – and from *The Grand Budapest Hotel* for that matter – always remember that hospitality service is an art as much as it is an occupation. The more you can instill this sense of idealism in the young minds currently or soon-to-be evaluating career options, the better chance you stand of attracting the best possible recruits.

Glossary of Terms

ADR: Average Daily Rate; a calculation of the total room revenue for a day divided by the number of rooms sold, generally excluding ancillary revenue such as F&B, parking, etc.

Comp: Room or other product given on a complementary basis, used as a noun or as a verb such as, "This guest was comped."

Comp Set: Competitive Set; all the other accommodation providers that are within the same geographic territory and targeting the same demographic as a specific hotel.

CMS: Content Management System; the 'back-end' of a modern website, allowing for revisions without directly involving a programmer.

DofM (also DOM): Director of Marketing; can also be referred to as the Director of Sales and Marketing (DofSM).

F&B: Food and Beverage; referring not only to the outlets, but also catering and room service.

FIT: Free Independent Traveler; as in leisure guests who are not part of a specific group, wholesaler or tour operator package.

GDS: Global Distribution System; a computerized system generally utilized by airlines, car rental companies and hotels, and managed by traditional travel agents.

GM: General Manager. In some properties there are variations, with a multi-tiered senior management team including a Managing Director and a Hotel Manager (other variations exist).

IT: Information Technology.

MOD: Manager on Duty; when the general manager is not in house, his or her replacement becomes the MOD.

OCC: Percentage Occupancy; the ratio of rooms in use to total rooms in house. Often, complementary (house use) rooms and out of service rooms are not considered in this calculation.

OTA: Online Travel Agency; agencies operating primarily through the Internet. Typical examples are hotels.com or expedia.com

PMS: Property Management System; the software used to internally manage and integrate rooms, revenues and ancillary services.

POS: Point of Sale; being the data accumulated through cash registers and computers located throughout the property.

Remarketing: A type of digital advertising whereby customers are targeted with ads specifically designed based on what they previously searched or what websites they browsed.

RevPAG: Revenue Per Available Guest; calculated by totalling guestroom revenue and all other profitmaking streams then dividing by the maximum capacity of guests; used mostly for resorts or all-inclusive providers.

RevPAR: Revenue Per Available Room; calculated by taking the total guestroom revenue and dividing it by the number of rooms times 365, or the number of days in the revenue period.

RevPOR: Revenue Per Occupied Room; calculated by taking the total guestroom revenue and dividing it by the number of rooms occupied; generally more useful in analysis of properties with a high proportion of ancillary revenue such as a spa, food & beverage or golf.

RM: Revenue Manager; responsible for analyzing competitive rates and advising the general manager on setting room rates to maximize yield on occupancy.

RWD: Responsive Web Design; a website that detects what device (computer, tablet or mobile) is accessing it and automatically configures the information for an optimal viewing experience.

SEM: Search Engine Marketing; this is activity undertaken to promote a property's website through paid-for marketing activities such as Google Adwords, Bing Ads, banner or display advertisements and other activities such as remarketing.

SEO: Search Engine Optimization; the process of enhancing how a property is found when using search terms within Internet search engines. Typically, this refers to the 'organic' or unpaid portion of this process, which involves elements of the website that are recognized by Google (or Bing) in rankings.

Sharing Economy: Also known as the gig economy, this umbrella term is most-often used to describes businesses that facilitate peer-to-peer exchanges of goods or services for payment, most often conducted via an online portal.

VIP: Very Important Person. A person who is 'VIP'd' typically receives a special welcome amenity, upgrades and personalized reception from a key member of staff.

Acknowledgements

In writing the fourth book in the Llama series, I would like to thank my son, Adam, who has tirelessly edited all of my work and has taken a leadership role on many of the essays – in particular, the 'In Vino Veritas' series. My daughter, Sam, contributed the cover graphics. I'd also like to thank Ruth Jones who assisted with the editing of this book and Tibor Svajko who helped with the cover design.

Next, my deepest thanks and admiration go out to all the hoteliers I interviewed over the past two years in order to make this book whole. In alphabetical order by last name, this includes Javier Beneyto, Paul Berry, Filip Boyen, Zita Cobb, Shaun d'Cruz, Rudolf van Dijk, Serge Ethuin, Tom Guay, Adele Gutman, John Hach, Sandra Heydt, Ulrich Krauer, Larry Law, Greg Liddell, Kiaran MacDonald, Franz Mascarenhas, Anne Juliette Maurice, Jeffrey Mayers, Eugene Nicotra, Tim Ostrem, Chef Baptiste Peupion, Rose Reisman, Jeremy Roncoroni, Evan Saunders, Jamaal Simington, Christopher Spear, Charles Stuart, Chef Caleb Taylor, Jodi Tower and Robby Younes.

I would also like to thank several individuals whose names do not appear as an interviewee but have nevertheless provided valuable insight. In alphabetical order by last name, this includes Dana Berry, Barbara Bohn, Chef Daniel Bruce, Heather Carnes, Pam Carroll, Colleen Isherwood, Dennis Nessler, Stephen Johnston, Michelle Renn, Henri Roelings, Anil Tenaja, Mike Taylor, Klaus Tenter, Rich Viola and Jeff Weinstein.

Lastly, I'd like to especially thank my wife of 37 years, Maureen, who has put up with me all of this time, as well as my family, friends and clients who I've had the pleasure of knowing over the years. The hotel business is one of people. I am so honored to have so many friends in this business who provide an endless stream of ideas for me to write about.

About Our Educational Program

In tandem with writing in hospitality journals and the publishing of this book, Larry Mogelonsky has also created an online educational program for hoteliers. Entitled *Llama Digital*, this interactive training tool allows managers and staff members to access articles through a web portal and then respond to questions based on the material they just read. Users can be students currently enrolled in hospitality schools or those active in the business who are looking to sharpen their expertise.

The articles in the online program are derived from this book in addition to Larry's three previous books: *Are You an Ostrich or a Llama?*, *Llamas Rule* and *Hotel Llama*. The questions are designed for a more detailed analysis of the issues in the form of written responses so that, in conjunction with learning better managerial skills, hoteliers will also improve their writing proficiency.

Furthermore, the system is built to promote a strong student-instructor dynamic whereby all questions can be graded with feedback so hoteliers can receive constructive criticism. All of this happens online, so users can interact from any place where there is internet access.

To learn more about the *Llama Digital* educational program and how it can enhance your learning in the hospitality field, go to www.lmadigital.ca.

About the Author

It's hard to imagine that a background as an engineer and packaged-goods marketer would lead to a career in hospitality.

After a formal education in engineering and business, plus a stint as a professional civil engineer, Larry's business career started with brand management at Procter & Gamble. This was followed by half a dozen years at a top ten ad agency where he was the team leader for the Four Seasons Hotels & Resorts account. Smitten with the hospitality 'bug', Larry started LMA Communications, a specialty consultancy dedicated to the hospitality industry.

Fast forward some 26 years since its inception; LMA has hotel and tourism clients across the globe, and has been recognized with over 75 awards from HSMAI (Hospitality Sales and Marketing Association International) for its creativity and strategic business acumen. The agency was also awarded TravelClick's Worldwide e-Marketer of the Year.

More recently, while retaining the chairmanship of LMA, Larry has formed Hotel Mogel Consulting, dedicated to solving critical issues for property owners and operators.

Having worked with hundreds of independent properties, it was a natural progression to reflect upon this extensive experience through the written and spoken word. Over the past four years, Larry has published 750+ articles in: *Hotels Magazine*, *Hotels Online*, *Hotel News Now*, *Hotel Executive*, *eHotelier*, *Hotel Interactive*, *HospitalityNet*, *Today's Hotelier* (Asian American Hotel Owners Association), and *Canadian Lodging News*. Every Friday, his newsletter, aptly named *The Hotel Mogel*, reaches 4,500+ hotel executives and senior managers.

In addition to periodicals, Larry has written three prior books addressing operational and marketing issues for hoteliers. Entitled *Are You an Ostrich or a Llama?*, *Llama Rules*, and *Hotel Llama*, altogether thousands of copies have been sold. All three texts are currently available through Amazon and Barnes & Noble.

Larry has been a keynote speaker at worldwide industry conferences including BTO Italia, Hawai'i Lodging & Tourism

Association, Visit Florida Governor's Conference, Cornell Hotel Research Symposium, HVS Eastern Europe and Hospitality Day Italia as well as numerous corporate events and several universities. His talks motivate audiences through his passion and vision with creative reinforcement focused on satisfying guest needs. He also serves on advisory boards for several new hotel-related technology firms.

Larry resides in Toronto with Maureen, his wife of 37 years, and their 135-pound Bouvier des Flandres named Hondo. Contact him at larry@hotelmogel.com.